WHAT NOW, LIEUTENANT?

WHAT NOW, LIEUTENANT?

An Infantryman in Vietnam

Robert O. Babcock

Deeds Publishing Company
Marietta, GA

www.deedspublishing.com

Cover design and layout by Ali Grasty and Jeff McKay.

Printed in the United States of America

Published by Deeds Publishing, Marietta, GA

First Edition, 2008
Second Edition, 2012

Books are available in quantity for promotional or premium use. For information write:

Deeds Publishing, PO Box 682212, Marietta, GA 30068 or

www.deedspublishing.com

ISBN 978-0-9776018-1-3

10 9 8 7 6 5 4 3 2 1

DEDICATION

To all those who lived through this experience with me
- whether it was in Vietnam or on the home front, and
to today's military officers, NCOs, and Soldiers who
continue to fight our nation's wars.

To Kristen, Rob, Stephanie and Mark – I hope you never
have to live through an experience such as this – but I
know you will do your duty if you are called on.

To Jan – for being there for me and being patient and
understanding during the many, many hours I have spent
at the keyboard over the past many years.

ACKNOWLEDGMENT

I would never have completed this book without the encouragement and valuable suggestions of many people. These friends have read, and sometimes reread, my work in all stages of completion. Some have read very rough first drafts, others have read pieces or all the book in more complete stages – all have made suggestions which I have incorporated to try to make it better. All encouraged me to keep writing and to get it published.

Hammond Satterfield does not realize how significant his comments were in getting me started. Hammond, an excellent writer, read my first five chapters in very rough form and gave me the spark and encouragement to write more.

Tom Brodnax, Stan Jablonski, John Tatum, Lavelle Sanford, Ken Cameron, Grace Coggins Kidwell, John Rockeman, Sandy Fiacco, Annie Fox, Bill Saling, and Patty Stewart read it when it was almost half finished. All gave me encouragement and excellent suggestions to make it more readable.

Gary Swanson, one of IBM's great sales leaders, a man who taught me how to sell and manage, and whose opinions I value highly, and David Glenn, a very good friend, gave me the shot in the arm and encouragement I needed at the three-quarter pole.

Along the way, Jan Stokes, Byrd Ball, John Hansen, Tom Basarach, Joe Kidder, Martha and Jim Battle, Joyce and Hal Mauney, Mike Welbaum,

Joe Brooks, Ron Marksity, Kathy and Moe Cougher, Ernie Redin, Bruce Bowman, Bob MacDonald, Beth Stewart, Leslie Grace, Jim Warner, Larry Wisdom, Bill Boice, Jerry Burch, John Ruggles, Jerry Hall, David Goldstein, and my kids, Kristen, Rob, and Mark gave me valuable suggestions and boosts when my enthusiasm waned.

In July 2004, at a high school reunion, I renewed friendships with some friends that I grew up with – Grace Coggins Kidwell, Kenny Ames, Jerry West, and Jerry Johnston. As we communicated and relived old times via email, they encouraged me to tell my story to them – and thus prompted me to dust this book off. My work had been sitting on the shelf for over eleven years. And thanks to LTC Steve Russell, CO Of 1-22 Infantry in Tikrit, Iraq who read a draft and encouraged me to quit procrastinating and make this book available to our current Soldiers. New lieutenants and a sergeant that I had the honor of speaking to at an Infantry Officers Basic Course Dining In at Fort Benning in late September 2005 also encouraged me to finish my book so they could read it. Thanks to all of the recent encouragers, it will be published in 2007.

Finally, my brother, Jim Babcock, was my valuable right hand in bringing this to completion. He read the book countless times, helped me make tough decisions on what to cut out, rewrite, or rearrange. He was an outstanding editor and sounding board. Jim made me think deeper into my stories, provided military detail I had forgotten, kept me to a schedule, helped me wordsmith my stories, and encouraged me every step of the way. Jim died after the first final draft was finished and will never see the published results. To all of you, especially to Jim, looking down on me from above, I truly appreciate your help and encouragement.

FOREWORD

There are as many Vietnam war stories as there are Vietnam veterans. This is the intensely personal story of my experiences training for and serving as an Infantryman with the 4th Infantry Division in Vietnam. Approximately three million Americans served in Vietnam between 1959 and 1975. It was the most divisive period in recent American history.

The Vietnam experience was as varied as the people who served. Several key factors shaped a person's experiences (the factors I served with are underlined):

1. Branch of the Service - <u>Army</u>, Navy, Marine Corps, Air Force, Coast Guard, or civilian.

2. Type of Job - All jobs were there for one purpose, to support the combat troops. Combat jobs were the <u>infantry</u>, artillery, armor, and combat engineers. All others provided invaluable support to those troops.

3. Rank - Private, Specialist, Sergeant, <u>Lieutenant</u>, Captain, Major, Colonel, General

4. Region of country - Vietnam had several diverse regions. In the north were mountains with cities and rice fields along the coast. The <u>central</u>

highlands consisted of jungles, mountains, and coastal plains. Further south, was the heavily populated area around Saigon, rice fields, and thick jungles. In the far south was the marshy delta of the Mekong River. Some troops spent their tours with the Navy off the coast of Vietnam or flying with the Air Force from air bases in Thailand or Guam. Major differences existed within each of these geographies - duty in a city or major base area was much different from duty in the jungles or rice paddies.

5. Time period served - Advisor phase (1959-1964), <u>Buildup phase</u> (1965-1967), Tet and Major Troop Involvement phase (1968-1969), Withdrawal phase (1970-1972), Vietnamization advisory phase (1973-1975)

6. Public opinion - varied from <u>ignorance and apathy</u> in the early stages through <u>mild support</u>, disillusionment, opposition, public protests and rioting, then to relief and indifference as the war finally ended.

This is only one of three million stories waiting to be told.

Contents

VIETNAM STATUE
DEDICATION, 1984

January, 1983. Sleet and snow pelted Atlanta, Georgia, bringing the city to a screeching halt. The IBM meeting I was running for 150 salesmen from throughout the Midwest was temporarily suspended. A festive atmosphere permeated the group as we congregated into one apartment and partied while we weathered the storm.

Many changes had come to my life since I left Vietnam. My wife, Phyllis, and I had gotten on with our life, had two children, Kristen and Rob, gotten divorced, and were both remarried. I had been working for IBM for fifteen years.

Though never totally out of my mind, Vietnam was still not a popular topic of conversation in American society. Most of my friends and fellow workers had either missed serving in the war or were too young to have participated.

I am not sure why the subject of Vietnam came up in our conversation that night. But when it did, two of us started relating our stories. The circle of people around us became quiet as they listened with intense interest.

It was as if they were curious about Vietnam, did not know how to ask about it, but were very interested when they found someone who would talk of their experiences without being prompted. I found it was not an unusual phenomenon, especially in bars after a few drinks.

As we talked, I found the other vet, Hal Reynolds, was also a veteran of my division, the 4th Infantry Division. He had served a year after me, first as a rifle platoon leader and later as an armor lieutenant. He had the distinction of having been in the one tank battle between American and Russian tanks during the war, having been wounded when his tank was hit. With several beers under our belts, Hal and I took turns telling tales of our wartime exploits.

As the evening wore on and the conversation shifted to other topics, Hal and I sat down and continued our discussion. He had stayed more in tune with Vietnam than I. He informed me of the 4th Infantry Division Association and the Vietnam Veterans of America, organizations of which I have since become a life member. And, he had attended the dedication of the Vietnam Memorial Wall in Washington, DC in 1982.

After I returned to my home in Kansas City and Hal to Oklahoma City, we stayed in touch via periodic phone calls. During one of those calls in the summer of 1984, he asked, "Babcock, do you want to go to Washington, DC with me on Veterans Day? They're dedicating a Statue of three fighting men at the Vietnam Memorial Wall." Without hesitation, I committed to be there.

When I told my wife, Jan, about my plans, I was surprised when she said she wanted to go, too. She had never shown much interest in Vietnam, had not experienced it with me, and had never asked much about it.

It was with much anticipation, and some trepidation, that I boarded the plane in Kansas City that November day. I did not know what to expect as we arrived in Washington, DC on Friday afternoon before the Sunday dedication ceremony. We were staying in the hotel where the 4th Infantry Division Association was making their headquarters for the weekend.

My hopes were very high that I would meet some of the men I had served with. Since returning from Vietnam, I had only been in touch with two men, my battalion commander and my company commander, but had not talked to either of them in several years. Hal was not scheduled to arrive until later that evening so Jan and I were on our own as we went to the hospitality suite to see who was there.

As I scanned the room, none of the faces looked even vaguely familiar to me. Many of the men, standing in small clusters around the room, seemed to have similar uncertainties as mine as to what they would experience. After giving up on seeing a familiar face, I decided to wade in and start talking. As I approached each individual or group of men, I always asked the same question, "What unit were you in and when were you there?"

Most of the men had served later in the war than I but I did find one man from Headquarters Company of our battalion who had gone over on the troop ship with us from Fort Lewis, WA. Although we did not know each other, we knew some of the same people and remembered many of the same experiences.

I was talking to a man, Swede Ekstrom, who introduced himself as a helicopter crew chief and had served during the same time period as I. We had an interesting conversation even though I felt he was rather boisterous. Another man joined us and pointed out a cluster of men at the other end of the room. In that group was a thin fellow who he identified as a recipient of the Medal of Honor, First Sergeant David H. McNerney.

Having always been awed by the Medal of Honor and anyone who was brave enough to earn it, we immediately moved down the room to meet him, shake his hand, and listen to what he had to say. (Many, if not most, Medals of Honor are awarded posthumously).

With only a few questions, I learned he had earned the nation's highest honor in the spring of 1967 while operating with the 1st Battalion, 8th Infantry Regiment. His action took place in the same area where our battalion had been operating. He was an unassuming man. As we continued to ask him questions, he pulled a small, laminated copy of the Medal of Honor citation from his pocket. Squinting to read the small print, Swede and I eagerly read the following:

> Rank and organization: First Sergeant, U.S. Army, Company A, 1st Battalion, 8th Infantry Regiment, 4th Infantry Division. Place and Date: Polei Doc, Republic of Vietnam, 22 March 1967. Entered Service at: Fort Bliss, Texas. Born: 2 June 1931, Lowell, Massachusetts.

Citation:

1st Sergeant McNerney distinguished himself when his unit was attacked by a North Vietnamese battalion near Polei Doc. Running through the hail of enemy fire to the area of heaviest contact, he was assisting in the development of a defensive perimeter when he encountered several enemy at close range. He killed the enemy but was painfully injured when blown from his feet by a grenade. In spite of this injury, he assaulted and destroyed an enemy machinegun position that had pinned down five of his comrades beyond the defensive line. Upon learning that his commander and the artillery forward observer had been killed, he assumed command of the company. He adjusted artillery fire to within twenty meters of the position in a daring measure to repulse enemy assaults. When the smoke grenades used to mark the position were gone, he moved into a nearby clearing to designate the location to friendly aircraft. In spite of enemy fire he remained exposed until he was certain the position was spotted and then climbed into a tree and tied an identification panel to its highest branches. Then he moved among his men readjusting their position, encouraging the defenders and checking the wounded. As the hostile assaults slackened, he began clearing a helicopter landing site to evacuate the wounded. When explosives were needed to remove large trees, he crawled outside the relative safety of his perimeter to collect demolition material from abandoned rucksacks. Moving through a fusillade of fire, he returned with the explosives that were vital to the clearing of the landing zone. Disregarding the pain of his injury and refusing medical evacuations, 1st Sergeant McNerney remained with his unit until the next day when the new commander arrived. First Sergeant McNerney's outstanding heroism and leadership were inspirational to his comrades. His actions were in keeping with the highest tradition of the U.S. Army and reflect great credit upon himself and the Armed Forces of his country.

Wow! I was impressed and awe struck standing next to this genuine hero. However, the next few minutes' conversation showed that some of his biggest feats of bravery were not included in the citation.

Swede, my new friend, the helicopter crew chief, started talking to him about the evacuation of the wounded. In his boisterous way, he seemed to want to claim some of the credit and act like he had been part of the action. I was put off by this guy until the conversation continued. It turned out he had, in fact, been the crew chief on a helicopter that came in to take out the wounded!

The key that proved Swede was not just bragging was when he talked about the news reporters that were on his chopper. David McNerney's eyes lit up brightly as he and the crew chief jointly told the remainder of the story. It took as much courage, albeit of a different kind, as what he had done earlier under enemy fire.

The chopper had been flying news reporters to a fire base when they heard the call for a "dust-off" chopper. Since they were close, the pilot diverted and headed for the landing zone First Sergeant McNerney had prepared. As the chopper landed, McNerney and his men started bringing the wounded out to load on the chopper. Seeing that the helicopter was partially loaded with reporters, McNerney ordered them off to make room for his wounded.

When the reporters refused to get off, he, along with Swede, scrambled aboard and physically removed them to make room for more wounded. The helicopter left with the wounded while the reporters scurried for the relative safety of the company's defensive position. As more "dust-off" choppers came in to evacuate the wounded, McNerney steadfastly refused to let the reporters back on until all his wounded men had been evacuated. Swede and his chopper made several trips with wounded before making a final trip to pick up the reporters.

According to Swede's story, the newsmen were shaking in their boots by the time they were finally lifted off the ground and headed for safety.

My awe was magnified by this story. You are not too surprised to find a veteran sergeant who shows courage in face of the enemy. However, many brave men would not have the courage to stand up to the press and all the possible repercussions if something had happened to them. But First Sergeant McNerney was concerned primarily with the welfare of his wounded men and getting them back to medical care. This was just the first of many memorable events that Jan and I experienced that weekend in our nation's capitol.

Hal Reynolds soon arrived and another group of veterans came up to talk to First Sergeant McNerney. Jan, Hal, and I decided to start visiting other hotels that were hosting Division hospitality suites. We visited the 101st Airborne, the 1st Cavalry (Airmobile), the 1st Infantry Division (the "Big Red One"), the 25th Infantry Division ("Tropic Lightning"), and the Marines. The same thing was happening at each of the reunions. Men from all walks of life, dressed in everything from jungle fatigues to business suits, were standing around reliving that most memorable time of their lives. Everywhere we went, we could feel the emotion of the moment.

While visiting the Marine party in the JW Marriott Hotel, we heard the Red Cross "Doughnut Dollies" had a hospitality suite upstairs. We made our way up the crowded elevators to that party. Like the others, it was wall to wall humanity. The difference here was the presence of the women who had served with us as volunteers with the Red Cross. They understood what we had been through, and had also been ignored when they got home.

One scene from this party still stands out in my mind. A Marine, who obviously had had too much to drink, was overtaken by the emotions of the moment. He cornered Jan and started rambling about all he had been through. Though not easily intimidated, Jan did not know how to deal with this guy. I tried to step between them and ease him away from her but he was intent on letting his pent up emotions flow. He was not endangering her and it was obvious he needed to tell his story and vent his emotions.

After a few minutes, a man in a Navy officer's uniform stepped over to intervene. He gently took the Marine by the shoulder and ushered him to a quiet corner of the room. He kept his arm around his shoulder while listening to the Marine talk. We would see this same Navy officer the next day.

By now it was 2:00 AM. Several men were talking about making the several block trip to the shadow of the Lincoln memorial where the Vietnam Memorial stands. Since we had a car, we volunteered to drive. Later, reflecting back on the events, it was a strange happening. Here we were, with my wife, in a strange, crime infested city, inviting several men we had never met to get into the car with us in the middle of the night. However, at the time, danger never once crossed my mind. These were not potential assailants; they were brothers in arms, men who had lived the same experiences I had.

We were surprised to find a large number of visitors at the Wall even at this early hour in the morning. However, unlike it had been when we had visited on Friday afternoon, there was not a cross section of men, women, and children. With the exception of a few wives, like Jan, the vast majority of the visitors were men of a similar age as me, paying homage to their comrades in arms who had paid the ultimate price in defense of our country. Each man there was looking for a name or names that brought back a flood of memories and pain.

One of the men who had ridden with us kept running his hand over a portion of the Wall. He obviously was deeply moved so I asked him if he wanted to talk about it. The story he told sent chills down my spine. Twenty-two of his comrades had been killed in an ambush. He was the only survivor. He had played dead while the NVA searched the bodies and killed the wounded. I found out he, too, was a member of the 4th Infantry Division and the same battalion First Sergeant McNerney had served with. Little did I imagine that, several years later, I would meet this man again.

We walked the short distance from the Wall to the Statue of the Three Soldiers that was to be dedicated that weekend. We were struck by the authenticity of the figures and the emotion they evoked in us as they stood there in silence, gazing toward the Wall which held the names of 58,160 fallen comrades. As we studied the figures in detail, we all found one minor flaw - there were no vent holes in their jungle boots to let the swamp water out. A machine gunner picked out another flaw I had not noticed.

The machine gun bullets strapped across the shoulder of one man were pointed up rather than down. "You don't carry ammo like that; it would get hung up in the underbrush. You always point the bullets down so they won't catch vines." Not being a machine gunner, I had missed that subtlety.

By the time we got back to our hotel room, my emotions were spinning from all we had experienced in the past few hours. And I still had two more days to experience them before we headed for home.

The sun was well up in the sky by the time we crawled out of bed on Saturday morning. We wasted little time in getting dressed, eating breakfast, and heading back toward the activities.

The afternoon's activities were centered on the Mall, in front of the Smithsonian Air and Space Museum. A crowd had gathered by the time we came out of the museum to join them in front of the temporary stage. The Capitol building shone in the afternoon sun behind the stage. The Washington and Lincoln monuments were in perfect alignment as I looked down the Mall away from the stage. The Vietnam Memorial Wall and its Statue were not visible from that point but their presence was felt.

After some warm up singers finished, Chris Noel, the voice I remembered so well from Armed Forces Radio came on stage. Although eighteen years had passed since I had ogled her picture in "Stars & Stripes", she had taken good care of herself and was still a beautiful lady. And, her sultry way of opening and closing her radio show with a "Hi, love" and "Bye, love" had not diminished over the years.

Watching Chris perform was a highlight, but the next events on the show still send chills up my spine. As Chris wrapped up her singing, she introduced several men who had earned the Medal of Honor, including David McNerney, and brought them onto the stage. They each received a rousing ovation as they were introduced. The third man brought on stage was the Navy officer we had seen the night before - a Navy Seal Medal of Honor recipient.

To wrap up the show, Chris introduced Lee Greenwood to sing his relatively new (at least to me) song, "God Bless the USA." What happened next still shines in my mind as if it had happened yesterday. As Lee sang what now has become such familiar lyrics, " ...and I'll gladly stand up, next to you, and defend her 'til I die . . .", two of the Medal of Honor recipients picked up the American flag and waved it proudly from the stage. One was gripping the flag with the hook replacing his missing right hand; the other was gripping it with the hook replacing his missing left hand. There wasn't a dry eye on the Mall as Lee sang the song over and over again. The two heroes did not waver as they continued to wave the flag they had almost given their lives to defend.

The rest of Saturday found us between the Wall and making the rounds of the Division hospitality suites again. After such an emotional Friday night and Saturday afternoon, our fatigue caught up with us and we retired early so we would be rested for the dedication on Sunday.

Overnight a cool, rainy front moved through Washington. We awoke to a gray, misty, cold morning on Sunday. But the rain did not keep me indoors. By mid-morning we had made our way to the Wall to be in position for the afternoon Statue dedication ceremony. Nothing was going to keep me from being at the Wall; the reason so many of us had congregated there that weekend.

The entire area around the Vietnam Memorial Wall was a sea of humanity as we waited for the helicopter to make the short flight from the White House with President Reagan. I do not remember what he said that afternoon nor do I totally remember how I felt. I do remember the emotions I saw on veterans faces as they caressed the Wall, saw old buddies for the first time in years, and struck up conversations with total strangers. The feeling of camaraderie and belonging was everywhere we turned. The common greeting among the vets was an emotional, "Welcome Home, Brother!"

We met Hal's radio operator that afternoon. He had saved Hal's life by pulling him from their burning tank when it was hit. It was the first time they had seen each other since the day of the tank battle and was quite an emotional experience. His wife, my wife, and I stood aside and let them enjoy the reunion. The five of us stayed together throughout the dedication ceremony. (Two years later, the radio operator was tried and convicted for murdering his wife who stood there with us that afternoon. Who knows whether his Vietnam experiences contributed to his violence).

That weekend changed me. From being a passive Vietnam vet who fought the urge to share my experiences, I welcomed the chance to share my views on the Vietnam experience with others. I wanted Americans to understand we Vietnam vets were not bad guys, that we were good Americans doing what our country had asked us to do, and had done it very well (thank you very much).

I was not standing on soap boxes yet, but I was starting to get involved. It also started the spark to smolder in me to write the following account of my Vietnam experiences.

A year later, on the tenth anniversary of the fall of Saigon, the national conscience seemed to change. It was then that the American public started paying attention to us, listening to what we had to say, and recognizing us with long overdue welcome home parades.

Two years later, I wrote the first story in this book. Five years later, Jan gave me a twelve inch tall replica of the Three Fighting Men Statue which sits in a place of honor in our home. Seldom does a day go by that I don't look at the Statue and think of the experiences of the men and women who fought the Vietnam War.

WRITING MY STORY

The most memorable year of my life was spent in Vietnam during the last half of 1966 and the first half of 1967. Serving first as a rifle platoon leader and later as company executive officer, my entire Army career was spent with Bravo Company, 1st Battalion, 22nd Infantry Regiment of the 4th Infantry Division.

Writing about my Vietnam experience had been smoldering inside me since my visit to the Vietnam Memorial Wall on Veterans Day, 1984. I finally decided on November 20, 1986 to start writing.

It was the 20th anniversary of one of the saddest memories of my year in Vietnam - the day a "friendly" mortar round from the U.S. 25th Infantry Division landed on our blocking position in the jungle. That night I recorded the events of November 20, 1966 and continued for the next seven years to add to the book.

I started writing with the intention of having a record my sons and daughters, Kristen, Rob, Stephanie, and Mark could read someday when they ask the question, "What did you do in Vietnam, Dad?" My father-in-law, a World War II Marine, died without ever relating his war experiences to his children.

After having a few friends read several of the early chapters, I found that more than just my children have questions about what went on in

Vietnam. With this encouragement, I started writing with renewed interest and enthusiasm, trying to capture the story of my experiences as an Infantry officer in America's most unpopular war.

I totally believed in what we were doing. In 1966, we believed it was better to fight communism in Vietnam than in California. History shows our efforts were not in vain, even though the war is recorded as our first ever loss. Communism has fallen apart, democracy is still the government of choice in the world, and no battles have been fought in California.

As years passed, I began to wonder why so many of us were sent to fight a war our government was not determined to win. The more I study the war, the more I am absolutely convinced our high ranking political and military leaders betrayed our fighting men and our country by not either making an all out effort to win the war, by never getting into it in the first place, or, at the very least, not tying the hands of the people who were trying to fight in Vietnam. War is like being pregnant, you can't do it part way. Vietnam era Secretary of Defense Robert McNamara's book documents explicitly the incompetence of our senior governmental leaders in the conduct of the war.

However, what the government failed to do in trying to win the war should take nothing away from the individuals who were required by that same government to serve there. Regardless of the outcome, we as soldiers served our country well and have as much to be proud of and no more to be ashamed of than any veteran. We followed the orders of our superiors and accomplished the missions given us. The Vietnam veteran is as much a part of our national history as any veteran of any war.

Ernie Pyle, the famous World War II correspondent wrote, "Battles differ from one another only in their physical environment - the emotions of fear and exhaustion and exaltation and hatred are about the same in all of them." There is a common bond shared by veterans of all wars. There is no question in my mind, I am proud to have served as an Infantryman in response to my country's call.

My stories take several forms. Some of them come from letters I wrote to Phyllis, my wife at the time, and my parents. Most come from memories I had never written down, and some reflect on things that have happened since I returned from Vietnam.

The book can be read in the conventional way, front to back, to capture the entire story of my experiences or it can be read as a series of short stories. Some of the stories are linked together by extracts of the letters I wrote home.

The book is as factual as I can remember. I have tried to cover as much ground as I can to capture events, feelings, combat actions, funny stories, mistakes, and other things I am sure have shaped my life more than I will ever realize.

The experience of writing this book, the long lost friendships I have renewed, the new friendships I have made, and my better understanding of how significant the Vietnam experience is to me, has made all the time spent writing and rewriting this very worthwhile.

After leaving the book in virtually completed form on the shelf for fourteen years, several good friends have finally convinced me it is time to quit putting it off and to go ahead and get it published.

This is for you, Kristen, Rob, Stephanie, and Mark, and also for anyone else who wants a first hand account of one man's experiences in Vietnam. I hope this answers your question, "What did you do in the Vietnam War, Dad?"

And, maybe it will prompt you to ask someone else you know to tell you about his (or her) experiences in Vietnam.

Crest of 22nd Infantry Regiment

GLOSSARY

AIRBORNE - a soldier who has been through Army paratrooper training and is qualified as a military parachutist.

AIRMOBILE - the First Cavalry Division (Airmobile) was a new concept in the Vietnam war. Numerous helicopters were assigned to the division and units were moved rapidly around the battle field via helicopter assaults. Other units moved by helicopter but did not have nearly as many helicopters as did the First Cavalry Division (Airmobile).

AIT - advanced individual training, typically an eight week training period following basic training where a soldier learns his individual military occupational specialty.

ALPHA - phonetic designation for the letter 'A'

AK-47 - the assault rifle used by the North Vietnamese and Viet Cong.

AO - area of operations for a military unit.

APC - armored personnel carrier.

ARVN - the Army of the Republic of South Vietnam.

AZIMUTH - a compass heading to follow.

BATTALION - the primary fighting unit in Vietnam. It had approximately 650 men organized into three (and later four) rifle companies and a headquarters company and was commanded by a lieutenant colonel.

BASE CAMP - semi-permanent headquarters for a brigade or division size unit.

BATTERY - an artillery unit equivalent to a company.

BLOCKING POSITION - a military unit positioned between an enemy force and their route of advance or retreat.

BODY BAG - a zippered plastic green bag used for retrieval and movement of bodies from the battlefield.

BRAVO - phonetic designation for the letter 'B'.

BRIGADE - a military organization made up of three infantry battalions and an artillery battalion, plus support troops. Approximately 2500 men were in a brigade, commanded by a colonel. The Brigade took the place of a Regiment as it was known in World War II and Korea. My brigade consisted of the 1st Battalion, 22nd Infantry Regiment; 1st Battalion, 12th Infantry Regiment; 2nd Battalion, 8th Infantry Regiment; and the 4th Battalion, 42nd Artillery Regiment (Regimental designations were kept to preserve military lineage and unit histories).

BUNKER - a fortified fighting position, typically dug into the ground with overhead protection of logs and dirt to withstand artillery and air strikes.

CA - combat assault.

COMBAT ASSAULT - an attack by helicopter against an enemy force. Troops were inserted into a landing zone to get maximum manpower into a battle zone quickly.

C4 - plastic explosive.

C-RATION - canned food which was the primary food source for troops in the field. In addition to cans of food, it had a sundry pack containing coffee, cigarettes, toilet paper, and a spoon. There were twelve different C-ration meals in a case.

CHAPLAIN - a religious minister in the military.

CHARLIE - phonetic designation for the letter 'C'. Also a name for the VC.

CHIEU HOI - an open arms program of the South Vietnamese government. Enemy troops could surrender under the chieu hoi program, get paid for any weapons they turned in, and be treated better than other prisoners.

CHINOOK - a CH-47 helicopter used for supply and troop transport, it had two large rotors and could carry approximately 40 men or heavy equipment loads.

CHOPPER - helicopter.

CIB - combat infantryman's badge, an award earned by infantrymen who have been in combat against an armed enemy. First awarded in World War II and continued through the present time.

CLAYMORE - antipersonnel mine used in defensive positions and in ambushes, portable, easily set up and detonated by a hand held charger handle.

CO - commanding officer.

COMPANY - the primary infantry fighting force. It consisted of approximately 180 men divided into three rifle platoons, a weapons platoon, and a company headquarters. Commanded by a captain.

CONTACT - running into the enemy and exchanging fire with him.

CP - command post.

DEF CON'S - defensive concentrations - artillery or mortar fire aimed at pre selected targets around an infantry unit's defensive perimeter.

DEROS - date eligible for return from overseas.

"DEE DEE" - Vietnamese for "get out of here".

DIVISION - a military unit consisting of approximately 10,000 men (much bigger now). It is divided into three infantry brigades and has all the support troops needed to make it self sufficient - medical, transportation, supply, etc. It is commanded by a major general (two stars).

DUST OFF - medical evacuation helicopters, also called medevac.

ELEPHANT GRASS - tall, sharp edged grass found in the highlands of Vietnam. It was difficult to see through and move through.

FATIGUES - combat uniform worn by all branches of the service in Vietnam. Jungle fatigues were light weight, dried quickly when wet, and had many large pockets.

FIRE BASE - a place where an artillery unit was set up to provide fire support for an infantry operation.

FIREFIGHT - an exchange of gunfire with the enemy.

FIRST SERGEANT - the ranking sergeant in an infantry company. He served as the right hand man to the company commander.

FLARE - an illumination device lowered by parachute. It could be fired from artillery or mortars, dropped from airplanes, or fired by hand.

FOURTH INFANTRY DIVISION - an American Infantry Division formed in World War I which fought in the campaigns across France. In World War II, the "Ivy" Division stormed Utah Beach on D-Day and fought their way again across Europe. In Vietnam, the Division fought the North Vietnamese Army in the central highlands from August 1966 until their return to the States late in 1970. In the Global War on Terror, they fought in Iraq in 2003-2004 and are credited with the capture of Saddam Hussein. They also fought in Iraq in 2005-2006. As this goes to press, they are poised to return to Iraq, for the third time, late in 2007.

FTX - field training exercise

GOOKS - the enemy in Vietnam, either VC or NVA. This is one of the slang terms used by the GI's to describe our enemy.

GUNSHIP - an attack helicopter armed with machines guns and rockets, used in close support of infantry operations.

H & I FIRE - harassing and interdictory artillery or mortar fire fired at suspected enemy locations. Air Force planes also dropped H&I fires in the form of bombs or "dragon ships" firing Gatlin guns.

HOOTCH - a temporary place of shelter, simply constructed of whatever materials were readily at hand. It usually had a poncho as a roof. All infantrymen became very adept at building hootches.

HOT - an area under fire.

HUEY - the UH-1 series of helicopters which were the workhorse of the Vietnam war.

II CORPS - pronounced Two Corps, the Central highlands military region in South Vietnam. It was commanded by a lieutenant general (three stars).

KIA - killed in action.

KILLING ZONE - the area in an ambush where all firepower is directed to bring maximum casualties on the enemy.

LANDING ZONE - an area large enough for a helicopter to maneuver without danger of tail or main rotors coming in contact with surrounding trees, buildings, etc.

LAW - light antitank weapon, shoulder fired rocket for use against enemy bunkers or tanks, disposable.

"LEG" - any soldier who is not AIRBORNE qualified. To an AIRBORNE soldier, a "leg" is the lowest form of humanity.

LP - listening post, consisting usually of two or three men posted a hundred yards or more in front of a unit in a defensive position to provide early warning of approaching enemy forces.

LST - landing ship, troop.

LZ - landing zone for helicopters.

M-16 - the standard rifle used by American forces in Vietnam. It fires a 5.56mm round and weighs approximately 7.5 pounds. It can fire semi-automatic or automatic. It is still used by American military forces today.

M-60 MACHINE GUN - standard machine gun used by American forces in Vietnam. It fires a 7.62mm NATO round from a belt. It has just recently been phased out of use in the active Army.

M-79 - single barreled grenade launcher which looks like a fat sawed off shotgun. It fires a 40mm grenade or a shotgun round. It has been replaced in the American Army today by a weapon which incorporates the functions of the M-79 and the M-16, the M-203.

MONTAGNARDS - primitive tribes people who live in the hills and mountains of Vietnam's central highlands.

MIA - missing in action.

NCO - non-commissioned officer, any sergeant.

NVA - North Vietnamese Army. These troops came from North Vietnam via the Ho Chi Minh trail through Laos and Cambodia into South Vietnam.

OASIS - a forward supply area located southwest of Pleiku, first established during the battle of the Ia Drang battle in 1965.

"OSCAR" - radio call sign for our company. Real names were never used; code names were used for all units. A numeric suffix designated individual units or individuals within the company.

OUT - radio code indicating, "I am through transmitting and do not expect a response from you."

OVER - radio code indicating, "I am through transmitting and expect you to respond to me."

PATROL - small unit seeking out the enemy, either reconnaissance or combat.

PLATOON - the primary maneuver unit in a rifle company. It has an authorized strength of 43 men, but usually operated with between 25 and 35 men. A platoon has three rifle squads, a weapons squad, and a platoon headquarters. It is led by a lieutenant, the platoon leader.

PLF - parachute landing fall. The methodical method used by paratroopers to safely land by parachute.

POINT - the man or unit who leads the way on a combat mission.

PONCHO LINER - a nylon insert for the standard issue rain poncho. It is used as a blanket.

PRC-25 - the standard radio used by an infantry unit.

R&R - rest and recuperation, a six day vacation away from the combat zone. All soldiers were authorized one R&R during their tour in Vietnam.

REGIMENT - a unit designation dating back to the beginning of the American Army. Though Regiments have now been replaced with Brigades, the Regimental designation is retained in each battalion to preserve the lineage and history of America's fighting units.

ROGER - radio code meaning "I understand".

RTO - radio telephone operator, the man who carries the radio for a leader.

SHORT TIMER - or "short", a soldier nearing the end of his twelve month tour in Vietnam.

SQUAD - the basic maneuver unit in a rifle platoon. It consists of ten men, further divided into two fire teams. It is led by a squad leader, usually a sergeant, but occasionally by a specialist when there are not enough sergeants in the unit.

TRACER - a round of ammunition treated to glow when it is fired so it can be seen. American tracers were red; NVA and VC tracers were green.

22ND INFANTRY REGIMENT - a proud Regiment that dates back to the War of 1812. At the Battle of Chippewa, the Regiment defeated the British and earned the motto, "Regulars, By God". The gray uniforms worn by the cadets at the United States Military Academy at West Point are designed after the uniforms worn by the "Regulars" in the Battle of Chippewa. They fought with distinction through the Indian Wars, the Spanish American War, the Boxer Rebellion in the Philippines, in World War II (they landed on Utah Beach on D-Day), and in Vietnam. In 1993, elements of the 22nd Infantry Regiment saw action in Somalia, and in 1994 and 1995 they served in Haiti. In 1997 and 2002, elements were in Bosnia and Kuwait. In 2003 and 2004, elements of the 22nd Infantry Regiment served in Afghanistan and Iraq in the War on Terror and returned to Iraq in 2005-2006 and again in 2007-2008. (Anyone who reads this and would like to join the 22nd Infantry Regiment Society should write us at P.O. Box 682222, Marietta, GA 30068 or check our web page at www.22ndinfantry.org. For specific information on 1-22 Infantry, and many Vietnam pictures, go to www.1-22infantry.org).

VC - Viet Cong.

VIET CONG - communist forces who lived and fought in South Vietnam. They typically worked in small guerilla units, unlike the NVA who fought in larger size units.

WIA - wounded in action.

WILCO - radio code meaning, "I understand and will comply".

SECTION ONE

Training Before Vietnam

August 1965 - July 1966

No Longer a "Leg"

October 1965. The line of soldiers stood at rigid attention as they faced the bleachers filled with their classmates. Beads of sweat trickled down the back of their necks from their freshly shaved heads.

The mid-morning Georgia sun made ovens of their heavy, steel helmets. Their fatigues and boots, freshly starched and spit shined when their day began four hours earlier, showed the wear of the two mile run they had just completed.

Each had scrambled rapidly from the bleachers and sprinted to his place in line when he had been called down by the colonel. He had asked for a soldier from Brooklyn, one from Los Angeles, one from Minnesota, one from Puerto Rico, one from Chicago, and for one from Alabama.

He had called out the tallest, the shortest, the oldest, the youngest, the fattest, the skinniest. He called down a Jew, an African-American, an Italian, a Catholic, a Pole, and an American Indian. Many hands shot up when he asked for the best lover to come forward. And finally, he asked for a soldier to come down from his native state of Oklahoma. At six foot, two inches tall and two hundred pounds, I scrambled from my seat and became one of the largest men standing at rigid attention in front of the class. Like the others, sweat ran down from my short brown hair and glistened on my neck and glasses.

"Do you know what these soldiers have in common, except for being ugly?" he asked the class. "They are all volunteers. Each man in this line, and each of you in the bleachers, has volunteered to be here. You have volunteered to spend three weeks going through the most grueling physical and mental training you will ever experience."

"And, when you have mastered everything we are going to teach you, you will willingly jump out of a perfectly good airplane while it is flying 1,250 feet above the ground. And you won't do it just once; you will do it five times."

"Why do you want to do this? You have volunteered because you want to earn the silver wings that will designate you as one of the elite. You no longer want to be a dirty, filthy, slimy "Leg", you want to be AIRBORNE!"

The colonel continued after pausing for effect, "You can have all the money you would ever want, and you could lose it. You could have the best job in the world, and you could lose it. You could have the most beautiful wife in the world, and she could leave you."

"But, once you have successfully completed this course, you will have something no one can ever take away from you. You will have accomplished something that few ever dare to try - you will be one of those special few who can call themselves 'AIRBORNE'."

"Long after you have left the Army, you will be able to tell your kids and grandkids you are 'AIRBORNE' and they will look at you with a little more pride. You have volunteered because you want to set yourself apart as the special person you want to be - AIRBORNE!"

"What do you want to be?" the colonel shouted. "Airborne!" came back from the bleachers. "I can't hear you!!" the colonel screamed. "AIRBORNE!!!" rocked the bleachers as the 650 classmates felt the spirit of the new adventure they were about to begin.

Three days earlier, I had graduated from the Infantry Officers Basic Class at Fort Benning, Georgia. For eight grueling weeks, we had worked long, hard hours to learn the basics of being an Infantry leader. As we progressed through the course, it was common talk among my classmates that many of them were looking forward to Airborne school.

I sat on the fringes of the conversation, convinced no sane human being would ever be crazy enough to jump from a perfectly good airplane. I had volunteered for Ranger school. Walking through swamps and eating snakes was something I could see myself doing but no way was I going to jump out of an airplane.

But, the herd instinct finally hit me. As I listened to my buddies talk about Airborne school and as we marched by the Airborne jump towers each day, I started questioning myself. "You're as good as they are. Don't be a coward. If they can do it, so can you. Come on, Wimp, sign up - see what you are made of." And soon, I found myself signing the paperwork volunteering for Airborne school. All that stood between me and Airborne school was approval by my unit.

My unit, the Fourth Infantry Division, quickly approved my request for Airborne school but denied my Ranger school request. They would allow me to be gone another three weeks but wouldn't agree to the extra eight weeks of Ranger school. Soon I would find out why they wanted me reporting to my unit rather than getting additional training.

Now, I was proudly standing in front of the bleachers, adrenalin pumping, ready to leave the world of dirty, slimy "Legs", I was going to be AIRBORNE!

AIRBORNE!!! (I still think of it as a resounding scream in my head) school fit its reputation of being the most grueling, toughest physical thing I had ever done. Nothing, either before or since, has put the physical demands on me we had during those three weeks.

Training started promptly at 6:00 each morning. Each day began with a thorough inspection for a fresh AIRBORNE haircut (which is effectively a shaved head), starched fatigues, highly spit-shined boots, and polished brass belt buckle. The slightest imperfection found us dropping for push ups in the early morning Georgia dew.

After the inspection, we were led through the Army's version of aerobics - the Daily Dozen. By the time we completed that, all the shine was gone from our boots and all the starch gone from our fatigues - the grass, sand, sweat, and dew took care of that.

Next came our first formation run of the day - never less than two miles and usually in the range of three or more miles - staying in tight formation, and chanting all the time, "I want to be an AIRBORNE Ranger, I want to live a life of danger . . ." And it still wasn't 8:00 AM.

Whenever you made even the slightest mistake, or did not react to their satisfaction, the AIRBORNE sergeants screamed at you to, "Drop, give me twenty!" That meant you owed them twenty push ups, right now! The lieutenants were treated differently. We got, "Drop, SIR, give me twenty." They loved to harass second lieutenants.

AIRBORNE training started with Ground week. We learned how to make a five point parachute landing fall (PLF), how to exit from the mock door of an airplane, how to guide our parachute while suspended in the Swing Landing Trainer. And, Ground week was where we were introduced to the 34 foot tower.

In a sturdy tower, thirty-four feet above the ground was the simulated door of an airplane. The height was carefully selected. You were high enough to know you would be seriously hurt or killed if you fell, but you weren't so high as to lose the perception of the ground coming up at you.

It was on this tower you started learning to deal with the fear of height. A cable stretched from the tower to a berm (an elongated mound of dirt) 200 feet to the front. The procedure never varied. We climbed the steps of the tower, fastened our parachute harness to the cable, stood in the door, and waited for the instructor to talk to us. When he was ready, we shouted out our name and number (which was painted on the front of our helmet) and leaped out to what some men considered to be certain death or injury.

We tried to remember all we had learned about exiting from an airplane - spring up and out from the door, tuck your chin into your chest, keep your legs tight together, your elbows tucked tightly into your sides, and your hands on your reserve chute, ready to pull the reserve handle if your main chute malfunctioned.

At the same time, we practiced screaming out loud, "one thousand, two thousand, three thousand, four thousand". In a real jump, we were to pull our emergency chute if our main chute had not deployed by the time we reached, "four thousand".

From the tower, we felt the jerk of our harness catching on the cable by the time we reached "three thousand." After riding the cable to the berm, several classmates stood ready to catch you and helped you unfasten yourself.

Without hesitation, you sprinted back to stand at attention by the sergeant who had graded your jump. The most minor infraction got you a, "Drop, Sir, give me twenty!" A more serious mistake could cost you as much as fifty.

Ground week was followed by Tower week. In addition to continuing to practice what we had learned in Ground week, we learned to make mass exits from the 34 foot tower, a skill we had to master before we could jump as a group from a moving airplane.

Tower week got its name from the 250 foot towers where we got our first real experience in a parachute. If you have ever been to a Six Flags amusement park, you know what the towers look like. The difference was we did not have a seat to sit in and our ride stopped at the top. The only way down was via parachute, and it wasn't attached to anything once it was bumped loose.

We were lifted to the top of the tower with our chute deployed, released the safety strap, and were bumped loose to float back to earth. Sergeants on the ground with loudspeakers coached us into doing the correct PLF when we landed.

After a few times to get over the early fright, the 250 foot tower proved to be almost fun. Looking across Fort Benning at the leaves approaching the peak of their fall colors was a beautiful sight as we rode to the top. However, when we reached the top and were bumped loose to start floating down, we forgot there were any leaves in the world - all our concentration was on making a good PLF and not hurting ourselves or catching the wrath of the sergeants.

November 1, 1965, the first day of Jump week, found 600 troopers up before daylight after spending a restless night tossing and turning. The sergeants had taught us everything they could before sending us out to try the real thing. Now it was time to put our training into actual practice and see what we were made of!

After a demonstration on chute safety, we clambered onto the back of cattle trucks and were taken to Lawson Army Airfield. Lawson Field has a long history; it has been the take off spot for Airborne troopers since the program first started during the early stages of World War II.

As we unloaded from the trucks, we gazed uncomfortably at the Air Force C-130 Hercules airplanes (affectionately known as "Herky Birds") sitting on the runway apron. In a short while, we would be jumping from those perfectly good airplanes.

After stopping at the equipment room to pick up our parachute, we moved to a staging area where we carefully put it on. Never had we been so careful to make sure we did everything right. It is amazing how much more attention to details you pay when your life is hanging in the balance.

As our jump time slowly approached, we filed into the briefing room, a large metal hangar type building. Looking around the room, we saw the walls were covered with AIRBORNE memorabilia - pictures of the first classes, insignia of all the AIRBORNE units, and miscellaneous other pictures and citations.

You felt a real sense of history sitting in that room. Troops who had jumped into Normandy on D-Day in World War II had been briefed in this room while doing their training. Rows of wooden benches, worn from years of use, held us as we sat in eerie silence, partially to escape the wrath of the sergeants, but mostly because we were all deep in thought, wondering what would happen to us before the day was over. Our pulses raced with anticipation as we gazed in reverence around the room.

Terrified is not the proper word to use, they had convinced us we would be successful because we were the best trained soldiers in the world. But, apprehensive very well described my feelings as I sat in the briefing room waiting to hear the weather report and last minute instructions.

Sixty-six Airborne troopers loaded onto one C-130. Each planeload was divided into four "sticks" of sixteen or seventeen troopers. It took two passes over the drop zone to get everyone off the plane - one stick went out each side of the plane on each of the two passes.

Since our class had over 600 students and we only had four C-130's, over half of us had to wait our turn. I was on the second load, assigned to the third stick. It seemed an eternity sitting on the concrete apron, deep in thought, trying to remember everything I had been taught, waiting the thirty minutes for the planes to return.

Finally, the planes taxied up to us. We climbed on board for our chance to join the elite group of soldiers who call themselves, "AIRBORNE!"

Canvas seats ran the length of the airplane, one row on each side and two rows in the center. The side doors from which we would jump were both open. After takeoff, the noise of the wind added to the noise from the four engines of the airplane. The heat in the plane was intense as we climbed to our jump altitude of 1,250 feet. We leveled off as we passed over Fryar Field and the first two sticks disappeared, one man quickly behind the other, through the doors.

One small detail was not covered in ground training. Just before he made his jump, one of the troopers on the first stick vomited down the length of the plane as he headed for the door. The smell added another dimension to the heat and noise as we circled around for our turn to jump.

"Stand up!" "Hook up!" "Sound off for equipment check!" screamed the jumpmaster as we went through the ritual known by all AIRBORNE soldiers. "One, OK!" "Two, OK!" "Three, OK!" all the way up to the door where the stick leader shouted, "All OK!" We had all confirmed the equipment of the man in front of us was in good condition, his static line was securely fastened to the plane, and nothing was tangled to keep the chute from opening.

"Stand in the Door!" Tension continued to mount until the lights over the jump doorway turned from red to green and the stick leader vaulted out the doorway as the jumpmaster slapped him on the butt and screamed, "GO!!"

Everything became a blur as each of us shuffled up quickly to fill the place of the man in front as one trooper after the other disappeared through the doorway.

Quickly, I reached the door and slapped my hands on the outside of the plane, with one foot sticking over the edge. I stood motionless in the door for only an instant. In one fluid motion, the jumpmaster swatted me on the rear and screamed, "GO!!"

As I sprang from the doorway into the openness of space, my mind raced as I tried to remember everything I had been taught. The blast from the propellers of the C-130 drove me backward, proving why it was important to keep a tightly tucked position so I wouldn't twist wildly in the air.

My chin was tucked tightly to my chest, my legs were tight together, and my elbows were tight against my sides. One hand was on the handle of my safety chute as I started my count, "One thousand, two thousand, three thou----". I felt the welcome tug of my opening chute before I got to "four thousand". A huge smile crossed my face as I looked up and saw the most beautiful sight I had ever seen, the fully deployed green canopy of my parachute. The heat and noise and smell had been replaced by silence. My eyes focused on the C-130 moving away from me, spilling out other troopers experiencing their first jump.

I floated down for some unknown time, happy to be alive, before I became aware of the voices blaring up from the loudspeakers below me. "Check your canopy!" they repeated over and over. I did not know about anyone else, but that was the first thing I had done when I felt the tug on my harness as the chute opened. I did not need to be reminded - that beautiful green canopy was the only thing separating me from a horrifying plunge to earth.

It was an exhilarating feeling to know I had actually done what I had questioned myself about having the guts to do - I had jumped from a perfectly good airplane. And, Phyllis was on the ground watching me do it.

As I came closer to the ground, I tried to remember what I had been taught about landing. A good PLF consisted of landing on the balls of your feet, twisting around to catch the sides of your calf, your thigh, your butt, and your "push-up" muscle or the part of your back leading to your shoulder.

Your head was not part of the five points of contact on a good PLF. I landed on my first, fourth, and sixth points of contact - my feet, my butt, and my head. Fortunately, my helmet protected my head. Unfortunately, I had my billfold in my hip pocket and nearly drove it through my "fourth" point of contact when I hit it. But, I was so happy to be on the ground, to be alive, and was so proud of myself; all I could do was grin from ear to ear. I jumped up, gathered my chute, and hustled off the landing zone.

The Airborne sergeants didn't let up on their harassment as they screamed at us to, "Double time!" back to the place where we turned in our chutes.

But I didn't care - I had done it, I was on the way to being AIRBORNE! The Elite! If I never jumped again, I had proven to myself I could overcome my fear of the unknown and trust in my training and my own skills in a life or death situation.

I'm sure all the wives got very tired listening to us that night as we sat in our Camellia Apartment living room and relived over and over our experiences of our first jump.

The second day, we made two jumps. On the second jump, someone hit my chute as we were coming down. It did not cause a problem but I started thinking, "What could go wrong if someone 'stole my air'?" If their chute came up under mine, it could cause mine to collapse. By the time we made our third jump, I was scared to death. I made a very weak exit from the door, got my static lines twisted and had to bicycle kick to untwist them (I did remember my training after all). I screamed at everyone who got within twenty yards of me on the way down to, "Slip away!" My PLF was a joke but I landed without a scratch and was just happy to have made it without getting killed.

The weather continued to hold and we made our final jumps on the third day - November 3. That was an eventful date in my life - it was my brother Joe's birthday, it was the day my wife and I had gotten engaged two years earlier, and the day my Aunt Lucille had gotten married. This was to add another memorable event to that date.

My last jump was a dream as it started. I had overcome the fear I felt on my third jump. It was a mass jump, with all of us jumping from ten planes in one continuous wave. My exit from the plane was good and I enjoyed the view of the brightly colored leaves dotting the Georgia/Alabama countryside as I slowly drifted down.

My drift was to the right front as I approached the ground, the easiest way to make a PLF. There was not much wind and things were going just great until I started my PLF. For some unknown reason, my mind told me to do a left rear PLF, not a right front one!

I started my body rotation to the left and rear while my momentum was carrying me to the right and front. When my feet touched the ground with this conflicting motion, the weakest link popped - the small bone in my right leg, just above the ankle.

I heard the break and my foot immediately started to tingle as I fell. My chute started dragging me along the ground. I jumped up, ran around it, and lay on it to collapse it - the primary thing I had been trained to do when being dragged. I lay there on my chute knowing I had broken my leg and called, "Medic!"

I heard a scream from one of the AIRBORNE sergeants, "Get up and look up!" About that time, another trooper landed not five feet from me! I quickly jumped to my feet and spent the next few minutes hobbling around, watching the sky, and making sure no one landed on me.

Finally, everyone was on the ground. I flagged down an aid jeep and joined two other troopers already on it. It had been a bad jump - thirty-two of us had broken our legs. The wind had come up and caused some of the problems, mine was just plain stupidity. To this day I do not know why I was thinking left rear instead of right front as I descended.

Broken leg or not, when you make your jumps, you qualify as "AIRBORNE". The silver wings I earned that day are my proudest military possession except for the Combat Infantryman's Badge I earned the following year in Vietnam.

I had proven to myself I could do something I had no desire to do except to prove to ME I could do it. As they told us the first day in orientation, no one can ever take away from you the fact you are "AIRBORNE" - not a dirty, filthy "leg".

A final few points. It took me forever to convince Phyllis to come to Martin Army Hospital to pick me up after my leg had been put in a cast. I had thoroughly convinced her there was no way I could get hurt. She felt sure I was joking when I called.

My next dilemma was - how to tell my Mother about my broken leg? Even though I was grown, married, and in the Army, I knew she wouldn't have approved of my going through jump school. When I had called my Dad and told him what I had volunteered for, he agreed we should not tell Mother until after it was over.

Unknown to me, Larry Mathis, a friend from college days and fellow AIRBORNE school classmate, called his folks in Pittsburg and told them about my accident. They were friends of my Aunt and Uncle and called them to see if I was okay. Another quick phone call and my Mother knew her little boy had gotten hurt jumping out of an airplane. I can only imagine the grief my Dad went through while trying to get in touch with me at Fort Benning and at the same time explaining to Mother why he had not attempted to stop me from doing such a stupid thing.

In the meantime, Phyllis and I were driving home, en route to Fort Lewis, Washington and our next assignment. I was very worried. What was I was going to tell Mother?

As we drove into the driveway at home, Mother came bolting out of the kitchen and met us before I could get out of the car. "Don't you ever do such a foolish thing as that again! . . ." she started.

It's nice to know you're loved by your Mother.

Twenty years later, I took my twelve year old son, Rob, to Fort Benning to watch a new class start AIRBORNE school and to watch a class make their first jump.

Nothing much had changed except there were now women among the troopers, they were jumping from C-141 jets as well as the C-130 "Herky

Birds", and the sergeants screaming at the troops had different names over their shirt pockets. The pictures and wooden benches in the briefing building were still there and the feeling of history was even stronger because now I was a part of it.

Official AIRBORNE picture
Bob Babcock
October 1965

Training at Fort Lewis, Washington

"What in the hell happened to you, Sir?" First Sergeant MacDonald growled as I hobbled into the Bravo Company orderly room. His tone of voice added to the gloom of that rainy, late November morning.

Two days earlier, Phyllis and I had arrived at our new duty station, Fort Lewis, Washington. Those first two days had been spent checking into post housing and doing the seemingly endless processing that comes with any new post assignment. Now I was ready for duty with my new unit, Bravo Company, 1st Battalion, 22nd Infantry Regiment of the 4th Infantry Division.

"I broke my leg in AIRBORNE School, First Sergeant," was my reply. He shook his head with a look of disgust on his face and motioned to a chair. "Have a seat, Sir. The Old Man will be with you in a minute," he said as he disappeared into the Company Commander's office. Soon he reappeared and said, "Lieutenant Fiacco will see you now." I got up, hobbled in to the CO's office, and gave my best salute as I stood at attention in front of the "Old Man's" desk.

Lieutenant Fiacco was a slender, sandy haired, athletic looking first lieutenant. He left me standing at attention as he eyed me up and down. I stood as tall and as rigidly as my six foot two inch frame would hold me. With a very stern look on his face he asked, "What in the hell happened to your leg, Babcock?" Once again I responded with how my leg had been broken. He replied, "I don't need a lieutenant with a broken leg, what good are you to me?"

In my best military voice, still braced firmly at attention I responded, "Sir, I can walk on my walking cast, I will put a plastic bag over it to keep it dry, and will do everything I can to do my job over the next month as my leg heals. I will not let you down, Sir." Still staring sternly at me, he responded, "Have a seat, Lieutenant."

I sat on the front edge of my chair as he started my orientation to the company. "The company is terribly under strength. In fact, we only have 40 of our authorized 180 men assigned. With all the things that have to be done around here, we are lucky to be able to muster enough men from the entire battalion to do any decent training."

Lieutenant Fiacco continued, "There is a strong rumor going around we are scheduled to get a large group of replacements right after the first of the year. That should really keep us busy."

"Babcock, you are going to be the platoon leader of the third rifle platoon. Your authorized strength is 43 men but there are only eight now. Sergeant Roath has been running the platoon for the past six months."

He continued, "Sergeant Roath is good, you can learn a lot from him. He is a combat veteran and was a prisoner of war in the Korean War. He will stay in the platoon and be your platoon sergeant. One word of caution, he does not like second lieutenants. I want you to learn from him and not get in there and screw things up. Any questions?"

After I had asked all the questions I knew to ask, he called First Sergeant MacDonald back in. "Get Sergeant Roath down here so he can take Lieutenant Babcock upstairs to his platoon area." Sergeant Roath soon appeared in the CO's office. He was blond with the ruddy complexion of a man who spent a lot of time in the elements. He stood about the same height as Lieutenant Fiacco - 5'9" was my guess.

My uneasiness was multiplied as I looked at his "Indian Head" Second Infantry Division patch on his right sleeve and his Combat Infantryman's Badge (CIB) above his left fatigue shirt breast pocket. (A unit patch is worn on the right sleeve only when you have served in combat with that unit. CIB's were a rarity in those days since it had been over twelve years since the end of our last war).

He had an obvious look of scorn on his face as he sized me up and focused on the cast on my right leg. For the third time in less than an hour I got the same opening comment, "What in the hell happened to you, Sir?"

We walked in silence from Lieutenant Fiacco's office and up the stairs toward our platoon area. He finally broke the silence with, "Lieutenant, if you get any of my men killed in combat, I'll kill you."

And "that" was the beginning of my first day with Bravo Company, First Battalion, Twenty Second Infantry Regiment of the Fourth Infantry Division. My name and "hell" had been mentioned three times in the same sentence and I had an offer to be killed. Having heard enough stories about how new, green second lieutenants are treated when they join their first unit, I was not devastated by their treatment but I sure was uncomfortable and apprehensive about what lay ahead.

By the end of January 1966, my leg had healed and was back at full strength. The rumor Lieutenant Fiacco had heard was true and my platoon was filled, overnight, with 48 men, most of them fresh out of basic training and ready for Advanced Individual Training (AIT). Our entire brigade was filled with troops to "train and retain". Even though it was unofficial, we all felt certain we would be in Vietnam before the summer was over.

AIT consisted of weapons training with the M60 machine gun, .45 caliber pistol, 81mm mortar, M79 grenade launcher, M90 rocket launcher, hand grenades, and other specialized weapons. We also did extensive training on small unit tactics at the fire team and squad levels.

Many other subjects, such as map and compass reading, radio procedures, first aid, land navigation, escape and evasion, artillery fire adjustment, and other skills infantrymen needed to survive and perform their mission in combat rounded out the eight weeks of AIT.

Most of the teaching load fell on the four platoon leaders. We tried to share the load as best we could. Even at that, during one week, I was the primary instructor for eighty hours of live fire day and night squad attack exercises. At the end of the week, I was physically and mentally exhausted. The intense lecture load was tough but that was nothing compared to the responsibility of teaching troops how to work together under combat conditions, with live ammunition, without shooting each other. And I was still a rookie myself.

After successfully completing the eight weeks of AIT, capped off by a graduation ceremony with all the military pomp and circumstance, we took a deep breath over the weekend, and went into our platoon and company training phase. It was during that two month period we really learned to work together as a unit. Feeling certain we would be going into combat together, the leaders made special efforts to learn everything we could about the individual men - their strengths and weaknesses, their quirks, and other important idiosyncrasies.

Every day we learned something new and valuable. During hand grenade training, we learned one man could not master the skill of throwing one. Despite repeated attempts at teaching him with dummy grenades, we had to dive for cover behind the protection of the concrete bunkers every time he threw a live grenade and it landed only a few feet in front of his position. We made sure he did not carry hand grenades when we got to Vietnam.

Two men in my platoon showed unique skills at path-finding. Ernie Redin and Mark Petrino had grown up playing in the woods of their native Connecticut. They possessed keen skills of observation, alertness, and selecting the best path through the forest. They became the two men I alternated as point man in critical times. Point man was a dangerous and extremely important job - a skilled point man was priceless. He kept the unit from walking into an ambush as well as leading them to their objective. Because of the skills Ernie and Mark demonstrated, I am certain they saved more lives in Vietnam than we will ever know.

A quirk I learned was Ernie would follow a compass azimuth heading as straight as an arrow. Mark would always drift five degrees to the right. Knowing that, I could compensate for the drift when I gave Mark a heading to follow. It was learning quirks such as this that was invaluable. Too many men went into combat without knowing the capabilities of the men they were depending on to do the job. By training together as a unit, we gained an advantage far too few men in Vietnam had. I have always been thankful we had the advantage of five months training together before we saw actual combat.

It was also during this period we selected our leaders. Besides Sergeant Roath, I had only three non-commissioned officers (NCOs) in my platoon. My mission and organization required twelve NCOs to serve as fire team leaders, machine gun crew chiefs, and squad leaders, in addition to Sergeant Roath. Since most of our troops had been drafted, we had a good cross section of America in the company.

Three men quickly distinguished themselves as leaders. Doug Muller was an aeronautical engineer college graduate from New York. Aubrey Thomas was a native of St. Thomas in the U. S. Virgin Islands and had served a short time in the British Army. Willie Cheatham had grown up on the streets of Detroit. All three had been drafted. Aubrey and Willie were black, Doug was white - all had natural leadership skills. Doug and Aubrey became squad leaders and Willie became my most reliable fire team leader.

Some leaders are born, others have to be trained. We were successful in training some outstanding small unit leaders during those long, rainy days at Fort Lewis. Each day we gave our men the opportunity to show their leadership skills. Soon we had an outstanding group of young leaders, not just in my platoon but across the entire company. Again, we had the advantage of building a team before we came under enemy fire.

As training progressed, formal platoon training tests were conducted. A keen sense of competition permeated the battalion as we all honed our skills to show we could function as a unit. After a day and night of constant challenges, my platoon finished with the second best score in the battalion - second only by a few points to the score of Dick Collins and his platoon. We did not feel too bad being beaten by Lieutenant Collins since he was a West Point graduate and in another company. We had earned our place as the best platoon in our company and one of the best in the battalion and brigade.

Bravo Company developed a unique "esprit de corps" during our Fort Lewis training days. Lieutenant Fiacco insisted the platoon leaders lead by example. We would not ask our troops to do anything we were not willing to do ourselves and help them learn from the experience.

Lieutenant Fiacco practiced what he preached and spent most of his time in the field with the troops, as did First Sergeant MacDonald. The officers, NCOs and troops were quickly learning we were a unique company and took great pride in ourselves. The other companies did not have the leadership spark Lieutenant Fiacco and First Sergeant MacDonald inspired in all of us.

Physical conditioning was another element of training Lieutenant Fiacco led by example. Before we completed our training day, he led us in daily five mile runs around the back roads of the training areas. This was in marked contrast to the other companies who sat back and poked fun at us as we ran by. Our men complained, but we knew Bravo Company was better prepared than most for what lay ahead of us.

Towards the end of company training, we got the official word. We were shipping overseas to USARPAC - United States Army, Pacific. Vietnam was not mentioned in the orders but we all knew beyond a shadow of a doubt what our destination was to be.

The first of June was the beginning of our final training before we left the States - a fourteen day Brigade Field Training Exercise (FTX). After two days of intensive preparation, we were up long before daylight on the first day of the FTX.

Our brigade was to attack a mythical Southeast Asian objective, pacify the natives, and wait for further orders. Our battalion was to lead the attack, Bravo Company led the battalion, and my third platoon had the lead for our company and thus led the brigade into the FTX.

We had a spring in our step as we entered this "final exam" stage of our training. Soon after we left the line of departure, we came upon a river. A sign reading 'Bridge Blown Out' attached to a roadblock kept us from crossing the bridge. Several umpires stood by to insure we followed the rules of the FTX.

Not to be slowed down, we quickly found a spot to ford. Our teeth chattered as the freezing cold water from the spring thaw raced by us on its way from the Cascade mountains to nearby Puget Sound. We had barely reached the opposite bank after wading through the chest deep water when the "aggressors" opened fire. We spread out and returned fire, forgetting how cold we were. The radio quickly crackled to life as Lieutenant Fiacco called, "Do you want an air strike?" Without hesitation, I replied, "Affirmative!" as I tried to assess the situation in the confusion of the gunfire.

He told me, "Mark your position with smoke." In less than a minute after I threw out a yellow smoke grenade, two F-4 Phantom jets came screaming out of the sky toward us. The noise was deafening as they came to the bottom of their bomb run and turned their noses back skyward and hit their afterburners to make a quick getaway.

I had frequently called for an air strike during our training. Everything was always simulated and no real airplanes ever appeared. You can imagine the shocked look on all of our faces when real airplanes responded to our call. That really brought it home to me, we were about to finish training and go on to the real thing. (The "real thing", we found out, was much more spectacular and awesome than this.) Fortunately, the planes did not drop real bombs or they would have gotten us. We learned from that experience to respect the power of an air strike and to hug the earth and use whatever terrain features were available for protection when we called one in.

The FTX was a success but it strongly pointed out to us the confusion and chaos that can reign when so many men are involved in an operation. We saw which leaders responded well under pressure, which ones did stupid things, and the true meaning of SNAFU - Situation Normal, All Fouled Up. We were all sobered with the knowledge our next operation would be for real and mistakes would be paid for in American lives - potentially our own.

Our five months of training at Fort Lewis were very eventful. I was transformed from a green, broken legged "shave tail" to a qualified, confident infantry leader. During that time I also gained the confidence and respect of Sergeant Roath. He was always true to his tradition of looking down his nose at second lieutenants, never failing to point out he was a "senior" NCO and I was a "junior" officer, only slightly more intelligent than dirt. But, he showed me in subtle ways he thought I was doing okay.

Part of my platoon – during training days at Fort Lewis
My platoon sergeant, SSG Frank Roath, is out front

FAREWELL PARTIES
AT FORT LEWIS

The Army is big on pomp, ceremony, and tradition. Having a major unit leave the States for Vietnam was the only thing needed to start a string of formal farewell parties for the officers and their wives.

Our last three weekends at Fort Lewis were highlighted by formal, mandatory dinner parties. Mandatory meant just that, be there with your lady or be ready to explain your absence first thing on Monday morning while standing at attention in front of the battalion commander's desk. Death, your own, was about the only acceptable excuse for absence.

The first party was a battalion officer's party, hosted by our battalion commander, Lieutenant Colonel Leonard Morley and his wife, Chartley. The second was a brigade officer's party hosted by our brigade commander, Colonel Judson Miller and his wife. Finally, General Arthur Collins, commander of the 4th Infantry Division, and his wife hosted a Brigade Task Force officer's party on our final weekend at Fort Lewis.

Dress for the officers was simple. Dress blue uniform with bow tie was the uniform of the day for all three parties. Dress for the wives was a different story - they must show up in a formal dress but they could not (or would not) be seen in the same dress three weeks in a row.

On a second lieutenant's pay of $292 per month, this turned out to be a rather expensive situation. Fortunately, Phyllis was an excellent seamstress, having majored in home economics in college. As I trained through the week, she worked feverishly at her sewing machine. Each Saturday night, my blond, good looking wife showed up in a new dress that reflected her sewing expertise while respecting my meager lieutenant's pay.

All the parties were much the same. They started, with military precision, promptly on time, with a receiving line. Each officer and lady was presented by the adjutant to the host and hostess and then continued down the line shaking hands with all the field grade officers and their wives. I am sure the receiving line tradition is as old as the Army itself.

After the receiving line ritual, the lieutenants and our wives clustered in one corner of the room, the company commanders and battalion staff officers clustered in another corner of the room, and the field grade officers and their wives moved around the room mingling with all the groups. These groupings stayed pretty much intact through drinks, dinner, and the dancing that wrapped up the evening.

Phyllis understood Army protocol and etiquette very well. In college, she had been active in her sorority, had been in several beauty contests, and had been honorary regimental commander of the Pershing Rifles. She made sure we spent the right amount of time talking to all the influential officers and their wives. I readily followed her lead to insure we made the right impression. (It was several years later before I realized similar protocol was just as prevalent in the business world.)

By the beginning of the third party, we were all tiring of standing around acting like we were having a good time. We had spent most of the preceding weeks in the field and were fortunate if we had had four hours sleep a night. We wanted to be home catching up on our rest, not continuing to put up with Army pomp and protocol.

The officers and wives of Bravo Company were a close knit group and always stuck together at these functions. Breaking with protocol, Sandy Fiacco and his fiancé, Sandy, mingled with us rather than with the other company commanders. Bill Saling, from Headquarters Company, and his wife also joined us each week. It was this select group which added the excitement to the Brigade Task Force officers' party. With a grin on his face, Colonel Morley came up to us and said, "Come out in the hall with me, Sandy, I have a mission for you."

There were three battalions plus the associated support units at the party. Each of the infantry battalions had their own tradition and motto. We were the "Regulars, By God!", the First Battalion of the Twelfth Infantry was the "Red Warriors", and the Second Battalion of the Eighth Infantry was the "Black Panthers".

The Commander of the "Black Panthers" had brought their mascot to the party - a three foot long ceramic replica of a black panther. The battalion adjutant stood careful guard over it as it was displayed with pride on the Panther CO's table. "Sandy, I want that panther," was the simple order given by Colonel Morley.

Working to stifle a smile, Sandy assembled the officers and wives out in the hall to give us each our responsibility. Our exhaustion and marginal desire to be at the party quickly disappeared. We tingled with excitement as we all committed ourselves to making sure the mission was completed successfully. Lou Dinetz, our rotund first platoon leader, was dispatched to the kitchen to prepare for his key role in the capture.

We moved back into the banquet hall and began to mingle into the crowd. As we passed the table where the black panther was sitting, the adjutant eyed us suspiciously as if he knew we were up to something.

No one noticed the waiter, dressed in white shirt, bow tie, and apron wrapped around his dress blue uniform trousers busily cleaning off tables as he approached the prized panther. Finally, when the time was right, Bravo Company's officers, wives, and fiancé struck!

Still unnoticed by the adjutant, Lou Dinetz, the "waiter", reached across the table and grabbed the panther. In a single motion he turned, handed it to me and I passed it on to Walt Ferguson. As Lou and I stood in front of the adjutant, Walt tucked it under his arm and sprinted for the exit door. Before the startled adjutant could react, the wives all congregated around him to block his pursuit.

An officer in the United States Army would never run over a lady so he was helpless! Sandy, Bill Saling, and Russ Zink, our executive officer, formed a blockade across the exit door to stop the pursuit of anyone who might try to rescue their mascot.

Walt flew out the door of the officer's club. Ron Marksity, our weapons platoon leader, sat poised at the front curb in his shiny green 1965 Corvette, engine running and ready for action. Walt unceremoniously plopped the panther on the front seat and scrambled back as Ron squealed away into the night.

At reveille formation on Monday morning, Colonel Morley marched an elite sixteen man honor guard from Bravo Company across the parade field to the spot where the "Black Panthers" were holding their morning formation. He saluted the battalion commander smartly and proudly presented the panther back to him in front of all his troops. One minor alteration had been made - a pink bra and panties had been painted on it, and the yolk of an egg ran down its head.

LEAVING HOME

June 30, 1966. The reality of what lay ahead of me started to soak in as we completed crating our equipment to be loaded on the ship. The only thing left between us and Vietnam was a short leave to move Phyllis back to Oklahoma. In three weeks, we would be aboard a ship headed across the Pacific Ocean, en route to Vietnam and unknown dangers.

Phyllis and I had made up our minds to take our time and have some fun on our long drive home. Rather than retrace the direct route we had taken to Fort Lewis almost eight months earlier, we pointed our burgundy 1965 Mustang south. We were headed for fun and excitement in San Francisco and Las Vegas! For all we knew, we might never have another opportunity together.

San Francisco was a favorite city of ours. We had both been there but never together. We hit the highlights - cable cars, Fisherman's Wharf, Chinatown, and the other tourist stops. But a highlight of San Francisco was a real eye opener for a couple of small town Okies - the night we went to North Beach to see the latest craze hitting the country - topless night clubs. We sat in wide eyed amazement as we watched Carol Doda's performance at her famous Condor Club. They didn't have shows like that in a Bible belt town like Heavener, Oklahoma! (I'm not sure Phyllis enjoyed the show quite as much as I did).

After San Francisco, our next stop was Las Vegas. Our reservations were at one of the nicest places in Vegas at the time, the Sands Hotel. This was to be our last few days alone for at least a year, if not forever, so we were not worrying about the paltry pay I received. Showing an early spark of my later career in sales, I did a sell job on the desk clerk. Letting him know where I was headed, we soon found ourselves checked into the bridal suite - all for $14 a night, a great price even in 1966. The room was complete with its own private swimming pool.

My good luck held as we hit the casinos. One slot machine seemed to have compassion for what lay ahead of us. It was uncanny how every time we walked past this one machine, I put in a quarter and won a jackpot. All of our expenses were paid from the winnings off that one slot machine. The cloud of Vietnam never totally left us but we had a wonderful three days in Vegas before we turned our Mustang east and finished the trip to Oklahoma.

By the time we made it home, I had only ten days of leave left. The reality of where I was going continued to slap me in the face as I savored the few days we had with our families.

The memories of my last few days at home are hazy. One afternoon does stand out. Three high school buddies and I spent an afternoon drinking beer and reliving old times. All four of us were on leave from the military.

Jerry West had just returned from spending a year as an infantryman with the original Marine contingent in Vietnam. He was the first one I knew personally who had been there and I was anxious to find out from him "how it really was." But there was a noticeable change in Jerry from when I had last seen him two years earlier. He was no longer the happy go lucky kid he had been when we were growing up. He was very hesitant in talking about Vietnam. I did not know whether he did not want to spook me or whether there were just some bad experiences he did not want to talk about. (To this day, I still have not talked to Jerry West about his Vietnam experiences - some day soon I plan to do that).

Fred Sonaggera was also home on leave from the Army, en route to Officers Candidate School at Fort Benning. That was the last time I ever saw Fred, he was killed in Vietnam in April of 1968. My other high school buddy,

Jerry Johnston, had chosen the Army Reserve route to serve his country. We all four talked on a different level than we had just a few short years earlier - we were growing up and dealing with the realities of adulthood and our responsibilities to our country.

Besides Phyllis and our parents, it was toughest on me to leave my Granddad. We spent as much time as we could, as we had done all my life, sitting on his porch swing, swatting flies, and watching the world go by. He was very proud of me for answering my country's call to service. He had not served in the military and was very proud of those of us who did. The pocket knife he gave me while we sat on the porch swing became a prized possession I used frequently in Vietnam. (It made me sick when I lost it a few years ago.)

A few days before I was scheduled to fly back to Fort Lewis to board the troop ship, the nation's airlines went on strike. President Johnson announced on radio and TV, "Soldiers, sailors, and airmen who miss their port calls will not be considered AWOL. Each serviceman should get to his duty station as soon as possible after the strike has ended."

Being the "gung ho" and conscientious soldier I was, I was not going to let a small thing like an airline strike keep me from doing my job. Lavelle Tatum, a long time family friend, came to my rescue. "Bob, John Edward (her son and my best friend) knows a big shot at Tinker Air Force Base in Oklahoma City. I'll bet he can help you get a flight." In less than an hour after my initial phone call to John, he called back to tell me a military hop had been arranged.

The next day, Phyllis, my parents, and her parents left home to put me on the flight. John Tatum met us at Tinker AFB. It was tough to leave Phyllis and our parents; it really compounded it to have John standing there. He and I had been inseparable as kids growing up.

We had played Army together until we got old enough to replace that with an interest in football and girls. Four years of football at the University of Oklahoma, coupled with his history of asthma, had kept him from passing an Army physical. He later told me that seeing me get on the plane was one of the toughest things he had ever done. He had looked out for me, fought my fights for me, and would have given anything if he could have gone with me, or in my place.

When I boarded the Oklahoma Air National Guard C-97 and looked out the window at Phyllis, my parents, her parents, and John, my heart was in my throat. My eyes filled with tears. I will never forget that empty feeling when the plane taxied away and I lost sight of them. Would I ever see them again? It was a long flight to Fort Lewis.

The day I left home to head for Vietnam – July 1966

SECTION TWO

Starting My Tour

July 21, 1966 - August 27, 1966

Boat Trip to Vietnam

When you spend sixteen days on a troop ship, you have a lot of time to write down your thoughts. Rather than try to rewrite my experiences, I have included here excerpts from the letters I wrote to Phyllis. If you find this is more detail than you want, skip or skim this chapter and go on to the next section.

1st Day - 21 July 1966

Well, we are on our way. It seems hard to believe but I guess it's true. Today dawned clear at Fort Lewis on our last morning in the United States for a year. I got up and was at work at 6:30. The company was already busy cleaning the barracks for the last time. The troops were not really too interested in cleaning the building since they knew someone else would be using it, not them.

It was really interesting to see all the stuff that was thrown into the Dempsey Dumpster. There were thousands of dollars worth of perfectly good civilian clothes, shoes, suitcases, socks, coat hangars, books, army equipment, ping pong paddles, etc. thrown away. There just was not enough room to take everything the company had accumulated... By 8:30 the inspections were over and we were ready to get on the busses to go to the boat but, of course, they had not come yet. So, we sat on our duffel bags and, in typical Army fashion, waited. The busses finally showed up about 11:30.

On our bus were all the officers and key NCOs. Most of them were fairly quiet except for Sergeant Goodermuth who was jabbering, as usual. Everyone was looking out the windows drinking in the sights of the Great Northwest for the last time — at least for a year. It was really hitting everyone, including me, that we were actually leaving.

When we got to the boat, we unloaded to the music of the 6th Army Band. It was much as I had envisioned it would be when you go off to war. The band was playing march music, the troops were lined up on the dock shuffling along awaiting their turn to board the ship, and the wives, parents, children, and sweethearts were lined along the fence trying to get a last glimpse of a special soldier. Two or three of our NCOs even had time to go to the fence to talk to their wives before we boarded.

Stan Cameron, my man who has turned conscientious objector, kept saying he would not get on the ship. I put an armed guard on him to make sure he did not try anything foolish. He is still a level-headed kid and did not give us any static when it came his turn to board. I stayed off the ship until he was completely up the gangplank so I could stop him if he had tried anything.

Once all the troops were on board, they let the visitors come out on the dock alongside the ship. I was really glad you were not there. It was hard on me to keep back the tears as it was and it would have been doubly hard if you had been standing out there, so near yet so far away.

Mrs. Morley and Jean Saling were there with a banner which read, "And they're off, the Regulars, By God". There were many wet eyes on the dock and on the ship when we pulled out this afternoon at 3:00.

Mount Rainier was showing up in all its brilliance as we moved out of Tacoma, Washington. Today was the first time we have been able to see it since we got back. It was as if the mountain had decided to come out from behind its cloud covering to bid us farewell.

As we passed Seattle, the Space Needle and city skyline joined Mount Rainier, all outlined against the blue sky. (Never mentioned in the letter, but I remember the vivid thought that this might be the last sight I ever saw of the United States, and a beautiful sight it was.)

2ND DAY - 22 JULY 66

Greetings from somewhere in the Pacific! I woke up this morning after a good, long night's sleep on my third tier bunk, looked out the window and saw - fog. When the fog finally burned away just before noon, nothing but water could be seen in all directions. The water is a real pretty dark blue, much prettier than the green color of the ocean around the shore.

We had a fire drill and abandon ship drill this afternoon. We had to put on our life jackets, secure the portholes, and go to our lifeboat stations. It was very organized, much better than I expected.

We got some hot poop about our schedule today. As things look now, we will stop in Okinawa for about five hours on 2 August. We will not get a chance to get off the ship, but they will put off our mail there. We should land in Vietnam on 5 August at Qui Nhon, just above Nha Trang.

Our base camp will be just a few miles west of Pleiku as far as I can tell from talking to people who seem to know. Pleiku is in the central highlands. It does not get as hot as it does along the coast. General Collins told us yesterday the terrain is fairly open, not completely jungles as I was afraid it would be. It still sounds like the rest of the division will be 50 miles south of us when they come over in September.

Morale among the troops is high aboard ship. I had a platoon meeting this afternoon and no one had big complaints, just minor stuff like having to stand in line all day to get into the PX when it is open. Everyone is joking and having a good time. It is really good to have that good an attitude when you are on your way to war. Vietnam seems like a long way off. I am sure it will seem more real when we get closer...

I will quit for tonight. There is a card game going on in here, just as there has been ever since we got on board. So far I have not gotten into any of the games because I can not see any sense in losing my money, and that is what would happen if I tried to play with these experts.

3RD DAY - 23 JULY 66

This afternoon I had a little excitement. About 1:30, First Sergeant MacDonald came to our room and told me he wanted Nikulin thrown in the brig. It seems that Nikulin has gone back to his old practice of disobeying orders the NCOs give him. I had to run all over the ship trying to find someone who knew what paperwork had to be submitted to get the job done.

After I got the paperwork filled out, I had to have Major High sign it, the ship's doctor had to give him a physical, and the ship's captain had to approve it. It took about two and a half hours to get this accomplished and get Nikulin turned over to the MP's. It would have been much easier to throw him overboard and forget about him.

I have never said much about the ship so I will try to fill you in on what the USNS Nelson M. Walker is like. It is a nice looking ship, 610 feet long. There are seven decks. Our speed averages about 20 miles per hour (17 knots) which takes us 500 miles or so per day.

Everyone has the run of the ship except for the crew quarters, engine room, and control areas. There are two ship's stores. One sells candy, cookies, crackers, etc. and the other sells cigarettes, shaving needs, film, cameras, watches, and other nice to have items.

Our troops are on the deck below us in one big room. Their quarters are definitely cramped. Their bunks are four high with less than 18 inches between bunks. A ship's newspaper will come out every day starting today. It is supposed to keep us up to date on current world news, sports news, and our location and conditions. Every night, they have a bingo game with cash and merchandise prizes. Sometime before the voyage is over, there is supposed to be a talent show.

4TH DAY - 24 JULY 66

Lieutenant Fiacco inspected the troops for personal appearance this morning and then he, Ron, and I went to Protestant chapel. The service, held in the recreation room, was really nice. A tape recorder served as the choir and organ. It was a regular church service, the only difference was that the room was swaying.

After church, we borrowed a guitar from one of my men and had a good time singing in our room. Sandy played the guitar and we all sang. He even made up a song about Bravo Company and our new home in Pleiku...

After noon chow I went down to the brig to see Nikulin. He is really a funny guy. He is not mad at me or anyone else. He seems to be perfectly happy in the brig. I talked to him for ten minutes and can not figure him out. I guess he is just an individualist and marches to a different drummer...

5TH DAY - 25 JULY 66

Well, it started last night. We ran into rough seas early yesterday evening and the ship started pitching and rolling quite a bit. It kept getting worse throughout the evening and has been pretty rough last night and all day today. A lot of the troops down in the hold got sick, or at least were not feeling too well. We were sitting here in the cabin talking about getting seasick. We got a headache just from thinking about it. Everyone on the ship feels about like me, not sick but ready to throw up at the slightest mention of sickness.

This morning we had a company formation on the rear deck and marched everyone by the water fountain to take their first malaria pill...

6TH DAY - 26 JULY 66

The sea is still moderately rough but I am getting used to the motion and feel better this evening than I have since the first or second night out.

We had PT this morning on the rear deck and the afternoon was dominated by a platoon bull session. This gave the troops an opportunity to ask me the questions they had on their minds and I got a chance to quell some of the wild rumors that get started on a ship.

I am duty officer tonight. It will probably be a long night, partly because I do not get to sleep and partly because we cross the International Date Line. At midnight when we cross the line, it will become Thursday the 28th instead of Wednesday the 27th as it should be. I do not try to understand how this works; I just know it is one day which counts on our year that we do not have to go through.

7TH DAY - 28 JULY 66

My notes seem to get shorter each day because nothing new is happening and I hate to be repetitious...

My night as duty officer went pretty quiet. I had to break up two poker games but that was it.

We had two courts martial this morning which kept me from catching up on my sleep. This afternoon we had another fire and abandon ship drill. To completely round off the afternoon, our battalion air liaison officer gave us a class on calling in air strikes.

Oh yes, one more funny little thing I have forgotten to mention. The 1st Battalion, 12th Infantry Regiment (the other battalion on the ship with us) has made it an order that all officers and men will have their hair cut in a Mohawk before the boat lands. Their nickname is the "Red Warriors" so they are trying to look the part. It is unique but I do not think Colonel Miller or General Westmoreland will let them keep it that way when they get to Nam (and they did not).

8TH DAY - 29 JULY 66

Greetings from the balmy Pacific! It is easy to tell now we are heading south. The weather is getting much warmer and more humid. Spirits remain high. After supper I went up on deck and spent an hour and a half talking to several of my men. Everyone I have talked to, without exception, has a good frame of mind about Vietnam. I am really fortunate to have such a great bunch of guys in my platoon...

9TH DAY - 30 JULY 66

Good morning! It is a beautiful day out here on the Pacific. I am sitting up on the officers' sun deck in a lounge chair, soaking in the sun. We are still expecting to hit Okinawa on 2 August. There is a slight possibility the officers will get to go ashore...

10th Day - 31 July 66

Since last night was Saturday night, we really splurged and did the town, or at least as much as you can under the circumstances. Sandy, Walt, and I went below to the mess hall and played bingo. My Las Vegas luck did not hold out and I did not win a thing, but I enjoyed playing anyway.

After playing bingo, we went to the movie and saw "The Train" with Burt Lancaster. After the movie, we went up on the second deck and watched the moon until about 1:30 this morning. It was really beautiful. The sky was clear except for a few clouds floating around. The moon was reflecting off the smooth water. It made me wish you were there...

11th Day - 1 August 66

This afternoon we had an officer's class on the Pleiku area. According to intelligence reports, it should not be too bad around there. The average temperature is in the 80's. The average humidity is 82%, extremely high. The hottest temperature is in May when it has gotten up to 97 and the coldest is in January when it has gotten down to 42, but the average for January is in the 70's. The rainy season runs from May to September and the dry season goes from November to March. October and April are transitional periods.

12th Day - 2 August 66

Land Ho! This morning when I got up, land was in sight. We were passing by some islands in the Mariannas chain. It was really good to see land after not seeing it for twelve days.

We will get into Okinawa around 5:00 this afternoon. Everyone is in high spirits and is eagerly anticipating it. They have changed their minds and are letting E-6's (Staff Sergeant) and above off the ship. If they have an area where it can be fenced off, they will let the troops off, not to go to town but just to get on dry land and stretch their legs...

13th Day - 3 August 66

We are now just 1200 miles from Vietnam. As it looks now, we probably will not get there until Saturday, 6 August.

We sighted land about 4:30 yesterday afternoon. After sailing along the length of the island from north to south, we landed at Naha. As we sailed along the coast, I could envision the scene twenty-one years ago when US troops made the big invasion in World War II. If you remember, I wrote a research paper in high school on that battle and have always had an intense interest in the Battle of Okinawa. I was like a kid in a candy store trying to drink in everything I could see.

It gave me a funny feeling to stand there and think of all the men who fought and died on the island. The Japanese kamikaze pilots made their suicide dives on American ships in the very same waters we were passing through.

Also, you could see the cliffs where the Japanese fanatics jumped and committed suicide rather than be captured by the Americans. All in all, I was tremendously impressed at getting to see the place I had read so much about.

My night in Okinawa was quite an experience. After docking at Naha, an MP captain gave us a short briefing on what we should and should not do. We were heading for the bright lights of town before 8:00.

The bar district, the only place open at night (and the only place we were interested in, even if other places had been opened), is about four blocks square. The entire area is lined with bars, brothels, night clubs, hotels, and a few shops. Our first stop was an air conditioned bar where we started getting the feel of the place. The barmaids gave us dirty looks for sitting alone. After one beer, we left and headed out to try other bars.

At the next bar, the girls met us at the door and led us to a table for eight. We sat down, ordered another beer, and they said something to the waiter in Japanese. When the waiter came back, he had our beer and drinks for the girls, which we had to pay for at a dollar each. It did not take long to get wise to that so we moved on to another place.

This time when the girls came to sit down by us, we told the waiter we were buying only for ourselves. The girls quickly got the idea, got up and left us alone. This went on every place we went. Every time a GI walked in the door, a girl grabbed him and stayed as long as he would buy her drinks.

After about an hour of bar hopping, I separated from the others and went hunting for something to buy you. Women stood on every street corner hawking their wares. Again my sheltered, small town upbringing was shocked when condoms were the first things they all tried to sell. After convincing them that was not what I was interested in, I bought you a couple of things I think you will like.

Meanwhile, back at the ship, the enlisted men were very restless. Seven men from Alpha Company blew up their air mattresses, tied their clothes in a waterproof bag, jumped over the side of the ship, and paddled to shore. The first five got off okay but ran into their platoon leader in a bar. He did not do anything but told them they had better get back to the ship ASAP. The other two were spotted in the water and the MP's were waiting on them when they got to land.

Back at the bar district, a single rock and roll band moved from bar to bar. After following them and listening through two performances, Lieutenant Fiacco jumped on stage, took the microphone and brought the house down with his singing. The Okinawans thought he was great and the GI's kept encouraging him with wild applause and cheers.

(An interesting little sidelight - Chief Warrant Officer Lunsford, Sandy's future father-in-law, was in the audience. Not many troopers have to worry about their father-in-law when they are on their last night of shore leave prior to going to war. Sandy did not let Chief Lunsford crimp his style any, though)...

So much for my evening on Okinawa. I think everyone who went ashore had a good time. None of the GI's got into trouble that I know of. The rumor is going around that one of the ship's crew got into a fight, was stabbed and killed. At least he isn't on the ship now.

(Not in my letter home, but an interesting side story... MAJ High required that at least one officer from each company stay on board the ship at all times. We worked out a duty roster among the lieutenants. Ron was the ranking lieutenant so he took the first hour and a half duty and I was the second ranking so I got the last hour and a half. Walt relieved Ron, Lou relieved Walt, and I was to relieve Lou. But as the evening progressed and I was having more fun and new experiences, I made the overt decision to skip my turn on duty – the one and only time I ever was AWOL. I knew that Lou wouldn't leave until properly relieved so I was covered. He was upset when I got back but got over it without causing me any problem. And, Sandy was with me and knew what I had done).

14TH DAY - 4 AUGUST 66

We are now scheduled to arrive at Qui Nhon early Saturday morning. As now planned, the first troops will go ashore about 8:00 on Saturday morning. Our battalion will follow the 1st Battalion, 12th Infantry ashore. General Westmoreland is supposed to be there to meet us, and of course Colonel Morley and Colonel Miller will welcome us ashore.

This evening we had a Protestant Communion service on the sun deck. Sandy, Bill Saling, and I went together. The service really meant a lot to me. There were all ranks present, from captain to private, Negro and white, all turning to God during our time of spiritual need.

This communion service and the two church services I have attended on board ship has refreshed in my mind the importance of God to me in every part of my life. I feel badly about skipping church so much in the past year. My sudden church attendance may seem hypocritical, like when we went to church at Fort Benning the Sunday before jump week. But, I guess when you feel a need for religion, it is good to get it regardless of how you have been in the past.

My love for you, all the love and support you can send me in your letters, and the belief that the Lord will help me take care of myself and my men is what is going to get me through this coming year with flying colors.

As you can probably tell, Vietnam does not seem as far away as it did a few days ago. I can honestly say I am not afraid. I feel like my people and I are well prepared to overcome anything that may come our way. I suppose I am just getting fidgety like a caged lion.

15TH DAY - 5 AUGUST 66

The ship has been bustling with activity all day long as the troops prepare to land. All our American money had to be exchanged for military pay currency (MPC). Most of the people have had to repack their rucksacks and duffel bags after living out of them for two weeks.

The people are cleaning and checking their weapons with more interest than they have ever shown before. The 1st of the 12th "Red Warriors" have been cutting hair all day to insure that everyone has a Mohawk haircut, which is now required of everyone in the battalion.

I got Nikulin out of the brig this afternoon. Sergeant Burruel spent the afternoon getting him and his equipment squared away. I think he has learned his lesson and is not going to give us any more trouble.

I also talked to Cameron for 45 minutes. He still maintains he is a conscientious objector and will not pick up a weapon. I tried to get it through his thick head the VC do not care who he is, they will shoot him if they get a chance, but he will not listen to me.

It is hard to tell if he really believes like he says he does or if he is just plain yellow and is trying to hide behind his religion. I guess we will find out when the first round is fired. People who have been in war say many conscientious objectors change their beliefs real fast when someone starts shooting at them.

I went topside after supper to watch another ocean sunset before our voyage ends tomorrow. I stayed there until after 10:00, just watching the ocean go by and visiting with some of my troops as they strolled on deck. Occasionally, scattered around the horizon, lights from the ships of the Seventh Fleet could be seen like twinkling stars. Periodically, lightning flashed in the southwest. Some of the troops were convinced it was artillery fire on Vietnam, but we are still 150 miles from there and a long way from seeing any of that.

Two hours ago, while I was on deck, one of C Company's platoon leaders was playing with a loaded .45 pistol in his cabin and it went off. The bullet went through the bulkhead, across the gangway, and lodged in the other bulkhead. No one was hurt but, needless to say, Major High was furious.

The platoon leader is getting an Article 15 out of the deal, which is really bad on an officer's record.

I do not know how often I will get to write when we get on shore but you can count on it every day if it is at all possible…

16TH DAY - 6 AUGUST 66

The 1st Battalion of the 12th Infantry is already on Vietnamese soil and we are following behind them in a couple of hours. Colonel Morley came aboard this morning and we are definitely going to Pleiku. We will be located eight to ten miles south of there. We are flying there this afternoon and will be on the defensive perimeter of the base camp tonight.

Charlie Company is staying at Qui Nhon tonight to make a landing in the morning for General Westmoreland and the television cameras. It looks like they have been doing a lot of brown nosing to someone.

My next letter will be from our base camp.

21 July 1966 – The day we left for Vietnam

FIRST WEEK IN COUNTRY

6 AUGUST 66

The LST (Landing Ship, Troop) moved up along side the USNS Nelson M. Walker, waiting to take another load of troops ashore. As I loaded the LST, my mind wandered to the other times American troops had boarded LST's to land on hostile shores.

This time, we did not have to climb down nets to get into the boat, and we did not have to worry about fighting our way ashore. All we had to do was walk out a side door of the Walker, carrying our rucksacks and duffel bags, and stand tightly packed on the LST while we waited for it to finish loading troops.

I much preferred our way of landing to that of our World War II Fourth Infantry Division counterparts. It was D-Day, June 6, 1944, exactly twenty-two years and two months earlier. They had stormed ashore on Utah Beach through a hail of German gunfire, not knowing whether or not they would survive the day. I was very uncomfortable though. They still had not given us any ammunition for our rifles. They could tell me the area was secure if they wanted to, but I did not like being unarmed.

The heat was stifling as we half dragged, half carried our duffel bags off the LST onto the sandy beach at Qui Nhon harbor. By the time you add a duffel bag to the packed rucksack on our back and the combat equipment we were wearing, each man was carrying more than a hundred pounds of equipment. (I never knew if it was right or not but someone told us the temperature was 130 on the beach when we landed - you could not get me to argue with that).

We moved from the beach to the busses waiting to take us to the airfield where we would fly on to Pleiku. My first Vietnam impression, after the heat, was the wire mesh covering all the windows on the bus. We knew it was there to keep the Viet Cong from throwing grenades in. The seriousness of what we were embarking on added to the weight of our equipment as we boarded the busses.

A sense of uneasiness, coupled with an intense desire to be aware of all that was around us, accompanied us on the short bus ride through the town of Qui Nhon, past the Vietnamese people on the streets, to the airfield. Did one of these people have a grenade to throw into or under the bus? Were there mortars poised in the hills overlooking Qui Nhon ready to blast this newly arrived unit? They still had not issued us any ammo.

At the airfield, a crusty, weather beaten Air Force sergeant told us to line up, go by the tent they had set up to issue ammunition, and pick up four boxes (80 rounds) of M-16 ammo each. He didn't carry a weapon and seemed amused at the uneasiness of this new bunch of green American troops.

It is a well known fact that American soldiers hate to stand in line. That was not the case here. As soon as we got our 80 rounds of ammo, most of us went to the end of the line and waited to get more. Before they broke the line up, I had 160 rounds of M16 ammo stuck in my ammo pouches. Most of my people had 240 or 320 rounds and were all still standing in line for more. (I never did understand why they tried to ration ammo to us that day. Never again did I have less than 400 rounds of ammo. Most of my people carried in excess of 700 rounds at all times.)

We stood around the airfield scanning the surrounding hills, wondering what would come next. Soon we got the order to load onto C-130 Hercules airplanes for the trip to the central highlands and our base camp at Pleiku.

I remembered we had loaded 66 fully equipped paratroopers in "Herky Birds" during AIRBORNE school. My logic said that since we had a lot more equipment than we had in jump school, we would probably put about 50 men on each plane. Wrong again. The entire company of 180 men jammed onto the C-130! I stood on the rear ramp as they lifted it prior to taxiing to the end of the runway. It became obvious that safety regulations in combat are different than in the States.

We were too crammed in to even sit on our duffel bags, we all stood, now knowing what sardines must feel like. As I looked over the sweat drenched faces around me, there were feeble attempts at humor but most men just looked straight ahead, wondering what was next. As the plane rumbled off the runway and gained altitude, we welcomed the coolness.

The flight to Pleiku lasted only half an hour. Lieutenant Fiacco rode in the cockpit with the pilots. Excitement oozed from him as he jumped down from the cockpit.

He had watched as one of our Air Force fighter planes blasted the ground with napalm in support of troops engaged with the VC. This story only heightened our concern that this was the real thing and we could probably expect to be fighting before the day was over.

Engineer dump trucks awaited us at the airstrip. We loaded onto the trucks for the trip to our new base camp, ten miles south of Pleiku. Just as we had been trained, we sat in the truck, back to back, facing out, weapons loaded and at the ready, poised for anything that might come our way.

We were again confused about what this place was all about. Driving through the streets of Pleiku, we saw American soldiers walking the streets without a rifle or any of their combat gear. As far as we knew at that time, everyone and everything in Vietnam was potentially bad and we had to always be ready. All these soldiers seemed to be interested in was shouting jeers at this convoy of green "cherries" and going into the next bar. We had not yet learned that Pleiku was a fairly secure town and we did not have much to worry about there.

But, we did not let our guard down as we left Pleiku heading south to what was to become the new base camp and home of the 4th Infantry Division.

It was after 6:00 PM as we pulled into what was to become a sprawling base camp. Now, only a few tents spotted the cleared area which stretched between the thick jungle obscuring the eastern horizon and two tall mountains to the west.

Montagnard (pronounced Mont an yard) villages dotted the ridges to the east and north past the jungle. The two mountains to the west, officially known as Dragon Mountain (but referred to by the troops as "Titty Mountain" because of its obvious resemblance to what we had left at home) were the dominant terrain features in the area. Radio antennas were mounted on top of the mountains. Our attention was quickly drawn to the wreckage of a C123 airplane and a helicopter strewn across the side of one mountain. We later learned that flying in the fog of the monsoons had claimed these two aircraft the year before.

Major High, our battalion executive officer, assembled the officers and walked us to the portion of the perimeter we were responsible for defending. He told us, "The First Cavalry Division spotted a battalion of North Vietnamese troops day before yesterday just beyond that hill you can see to the southeast." He pointed at a hill approximately three miles away. "Now go ahead and get set up."

Our "pucker" factor raised another notch as we looked at each other, certain we were going to get our baptism of fire at any moment. Sandy Fiacco assigned each of the three rifle platoons a portion of the company perimeter and worked with us to insure we placed our machine guns where they had the best fields of fire across the front.

Keeping everyone alert and remembering all our training was not a problem as we got ready to do for real what we had been trained for the past seven months. And so started my tour in Vietnam.

That first night was described in a letter written to Phyllis:

By the time we had our briefing and picked up our troops, their equipment, extra ammunition, and C-rations, it was beginning to get dark. The fading daylight barely illuminated our defensive position as my platoon moved uneasily in for the night.

Our fields of fire consisted of a path the width of a bulldozer blade that had been cut in front of our positions. On the other side of the bulldozed path was dense jungle. We dug hasty prone shelters, loaded our weapons, fixed bayonets, and got ready for anything to happen. Well, it did!!!

It rained, and it rained, and it rained, and it rained some more. I learned my first lesson in Vietnam - never try to sleep in a foxhole when it is raining. A foxhole collects water and you will get very wet. All I had to keep dry was my poncho and it did a terrible job.

Every time I moved, a stream of water rushed under the poncho and soaked me. I ended up trying to lay on my gas mask and equipment to keep out of the water. My poncho kept some of the rain off but I was wet and miserable all night long. It is hard to know what wet is until you spend a night in a monsoon...

I was very proud of my troops because they controlled their jitters and no one fired a shot all night. (This was not the case from other positions around the perimeter. Shots were being fired and flares were shot up in the air all night long as troops shot at shadows.) It is an eerie feeling to lay there in the rain and try to figure out where every sound is coming from.

I really surprised myself because I was not scared. I was very alert, but not scared. A loaded rifle with a bayonet on the end of it makes a pretty good sleeping companion under these circumstances. (This was the last time we fixed bayonets at night for the remainder of the tour, but it seemed like a real good idea that first night.)

As they say, it is always darkest before the dawn and that is really true in Vietnam. That is also the time you have to be the most alert to attack, and we were that. When it finally got daylight, I was tickled to death to get up and move around. I was wet, cold, and miserable but everyone was in the same situation. We laughed at each other and maintained real high spirits. We all looked like drowned rats, fresh from a mud bath. We did not have any enemy contact at all...

My next letter, written three days later, continues to describe that first week:

We are in our fourth day in Vietnam and I am finally finding time to write a little longer letter. We have been busy and quite a lot has happened since we have been here...

We worked all day Sunday, the 7th, digging foxholes and building hootches to keep us safe and dry. I vowed the first night I would not spend another night as wet and miserable as I was then, and so far I have not.

We built a nice little hootch between two trees using bamboo, ponchos, ammo cases, commo wire, and anything else we could get our hands on. We talked one of the engineers into using his bulldozer to dig a bunker for the four people in my hootch, so we have a nice little defensive position right outside our front doorway.

The area is changing by the hour. The engineers are busy clearing the jungle with bulldozers. There are approximately 200 Montagnard tribesmen cutting bamboo and helping clear the area. These people are really primitive. They wear nothing but a loin cloth and a ragged old shirt. Most of the people do not wear shoes and if they do, they are usually boots or something a GI has given them.

We have killed a couple of bamboo viper snakes. Bamboo vipers are very poisonous and are the same color as the bamboo they live in. We really stay alert watching for them. A Montagnard can kill a snake instantly with his machete. We are not quite as adept as they are - we tend to shoot them and not get close enough to use a machete. We also have to be careful we do not shoot one of our troops in the process.

The situation is not at all like I thought it would be. Our supplies have not made it here yet so we are living out of our rucksacks. It rains every night, and off and on during the day, so it is impossible to keep clean.

Morale is high among the troops, even though we are all muddy and filthy. Conditions will improve daily and we should be in squad size tents by the end of the week. Every day more supplies come in from Qui Nhon. We have had nothing to eat but C-rations since we have been here but they expect to have a hot meal for us by tomorrow or the next day.

The natives are really something else. They are small people and are generally filthy and ragged. As I said, they wear nothing but a loin cloth and shirt. They start to work around the perimeter soon after daylight and work until 6:00 at night. All day long the kids come around and try to beg cigarettes and C-rations from the troops. I try to run them off but they come right back.

Some of the kids are real cute despite being dirty and ragged. You can not help but feel sorry for them but I will not let myself or my people have anything to do with them. I want to discourage them coming around our positions. As soon as we get the area cleared of vegetation, we will not have to worry about them. There will be concertina wire and a mine field all around the perimeter and they will not be able to get in.

The entire area is full of huge mahogany and teak trees that would be worth a mint in the States. They are being bulldozed over and blown down like pine trees would be cut down at home. The Montagnards are doing a very interesting thing with them.

One of them will lay down beside a big teak tree that is three feet in diameter. One of the other guys will mark the tree above the head and below the feet of the guy lying down, and then several of them will start chopping the tree with their machetes until they have cut the section out. At the end of the day, several of them start rolling the log toward their village, quite a hard job. We found out they are taking them back to their village and will carve their casket out of the tree for use when needed. Occasionally, a helpful bulldozer driver will scoop up the log and take it to the village for them.

A Vietnamese madam drove up to the perimeter in a three wheeled French made Lambretta Sunday afternoon and tried to convince me to let my men partake of the prostitutes she had brought out with her. She did not know English and I do not know Vietnamese but I have learned one phrase, "dee-dee" which is supposed to mean, "get out of here!" When I used it on her it turned her smile into a frown but she still did not leave. Some of my men were not helping the problem any.

When I finally pointed my rifle at her, she got the hint and moved on to another part of the perimeter to see if she had better luck with someone else's troops who did not have such a "bad assed" platoon leader. My troops were good natured about it but some of them didn't approve of my actions. Who knows what other kind of unexpected challenges I will get next.

Yesterday was a very bad day. It was cloudy most of the day, rained intermittently, and was just generally miserable. At mid morning, there was an accident in Charlie Company. A guy was cleaning his pistol and it went off and killed the guy in the tent with him. It was strictly a case of negligence on the part of the man who fired the weapon but the repercussions were terrible.

Colonel Miller wanted to make an example of the case so he relieved the company commander, a West Point officer, of his command. He also relieved the platoon leader, and took a stripe away from the platoon sergeant and squad leader. He charged them all with neglect of duty. The guy who shot him is going to get court martialed for manslaughter.

Captain Kerans is now the new company commander. It was a terrible thing. It was not the fault of any of the leaders but they suffered the consequences since they are responsible for everything that happens or fails to happen in their command. One good thing about it though, it deeply embedded in everyone's mind that you have to be extra careful when everyone is carrying live ammo.

Well, that incident added more gloom to what was already a miserable day for me. I hope we are never separated again on our anniversary, or at any other time as far as that goes. I really miss you, and it was doubly bad yesterday. To celebrate our second wedding anniversary, I had two swigs of rum that Russ Zink gave me for breakfast. I even put on clean fatigues and shaved. That was the extent of my celebrating. I also had Sergeant Benge take my picture so you can see what your husband looked like the day of our second anniversary.

Today my spirits are considerably better. We are still working hard and conditions are slowly improving. It does not take long for an American GI to make a place as much like home as possible. Our equipment should all be here by the end of the week and we should be in good shape...

My next three letters rounded out the happenings for the first week in country:

10 AUG 66

Another day in a combat zone is gone and I am one day closer to coming home. Last night was quiet on the perimeter except for the usual downpour of rain. It started about 1:00 this morning and has been raining off and on all day.

I am beginning to get to the point where I just ignore the rain and mud. I have been muddy for so long I would not know what it was like to be clean. So far, the mud and bugs have been the most disagreeable things. We still have not fired a shot or been shot at.

This is really a funny war, or at least up to now it has been. As I had expected, they are constantly on our backs to keep our steel helmet and web gear on. This really gets to be a drag after awhile. They also are always harassing us to keep our areas policed of all paper, cans, etc. The Montagnard natives are running around and through our perimeter all the time during the day. Right now it just does not seem like we are in a war zone. It is more like one big, hilarious field problem.

Everything that happens seems to be different than I expected. Instead of being afraid of the VC, I am more concerned with keeping the kids out of my area. If I look mean enough and say, "Dee-dee", loud enough, they usually get the idea and leave my area, at least until I turn my back and start doing something else.

These kids are always begging C-rations, cigarettes, boots, shirts or anything else they can talk us out of. If we give one kid anything, he will be back with all his friends trying to get something else.

We are still eating nothing but C-rations. They opened a PX yesterday afternoon. I went down and bought two cases of beer and two cases of cokes (really RC Cola, Cokes seldom made it to us, the rear echelon people got the Cokes and Pepsi) to give the people in my platoon.

The beer and cokes were warm but it was a welcome change from nothing but water. We limit each man to two cans of beer a day while we are on the perimeter...

Lou Dinetz went on an ambush patrol with a unit of the 25th Infantry Division last night. When he came back to base camp, he had the first real war story of the 4th Infantry Division in Vietnam.

As they lay in ambush, a patrol of NVA came by and they blasted them. They killed several of the NVA and one of our guys on the patrol was wounded. Lou said it was quite a scary experience as they moved back to their rallying point with the wounded man and waited for daylight to get extracted. I'm glad it was Lou in that first action and not me - we will all have our time before long.

14 Aug 66

Operation Phyllis was a success! My platoon went on our first patrol yesterday and named it after you. This was the first operation of any kind by our company - they picked the best to be first.

Our mission was to go on a reconnaissance patrol of about three miles to see if we could find any sign of enemy activity. Our route was semi-circular around a lake east of the company perimeter. We left base camp at noon, walking, and returned around 4:30.

I was first briefed on the patrol night before last, so we had plenty of time to prepare. Yesterday morning I got in a helicopter and flew over the area so I would know what type of terrain to expect.

The route was mostly open except for a few rice paddies along a creek and a couple of wooded areas. We waded the creek and rice paddies and got wet but it was a welcome relief to get some of the mud washed off my boots and pants legs.

Two Army photographers went along, taking pictures. One of them got my complete name and hometown so there might be a picture of me released to some newspapers. I think most of them are to be used in the Army historical record of the war. It was interesting to all of my people and me to know our pictures were being taken so we tried to look rough and rugged...

It still rains every night and day and the conditions are generally miserable. We haven't gotten the hot chow they have been promising us for four days and we continue to eat C-rations, and nothing else, for eight days. The entire area around the perimeter is a quagmire. We are beginning to get used to living in mud so we just slosh along and ignore it.

Base camp is really getting to be a pain in the ass. Battalion and Brigade are constantly coming up with crap to harass the troops needlessly. They gripe because the people and weapons are not kept clean but that is impossible. You get dirty five minutes after you clean up. Water is also hard to get at times.

Yesterday the company got a Vietnamese interpreter as an attachment. His name is Sergeant Quang, pronounced Kwan. He is from Saigon and has been attached to my platoon to get indoctrinated in the American Army way of life. He can speak English, French, and Vietnamese...

On 15 August, I wrote the following letter to my parents:

We are starting our second week in a combat zone and still not a shot has been fired. We are still manning the defensive perimeter all the time, fighting the rain and mud instead of the VC. Every day we work more on our defensive positions and perimeter and make our area more secure. Yesterday the engineers spent the day cutting down trees in front of our positions and clearing the brush with bulldozers.

Daddy, I was thinking about you because they were wasting some beautiful wood. All of the trees were mahogany and teak. Some were four or five feet in diameter and very tall. They would have been worth a lot of money in lumber in the States but over here they were just piled up to be burned or buried.

We have to have clear areas in front of our defensive positions and they were in the way and had to go. This is just an example of what a waste can come from war. There just is not time to spend saving the good trees...

I am trying to find a substitute for milk and I think I have come up with a pretty good one. There is a cocoa beverage powder which comes in C-rations that I mix with dry cream substitute and sugar from C-rations and water. It makes a pretty good drink. I will send you the ingredients so you can try it for yourself. Of course you have to drink it out of a dirty, jagged edged C-ration can to enhance the taste.

I am really getting used to roughing it. After so long in it, I have learned to just ignore the mud and rain. We now have one of my platoon tents up so two nights out of three I get to sleep on a cot in a tent. The other night I have duty on the perimeter and sleep on an air mattress in my hootch.

When it rains, I strip my clothes off, take a shower, and hope it does not quit raining before I get the soap rinsed off.

Right now I am lying on my cot and writing by candlelight. We still have not had a hot meal and are eating C-rations three meals a day. I am getting used to it. We have been issued two pairs of jungle boots and allegedly will get four sets of jungle fatigues tomorrow. (I do not recall ever having more than two sets of jungle fatigues).

Our old leather boots are rotting since there is no way to keep them dry. I understand the jungle fatigues will dry out a lot faster than our regular fatigues - anything will be an improvement.

Really, the conditions are far from ideal but I am safe and am tough and flexible enough to adjust to them. One month is nearly gone and there are only eleven more to go. The morale of the troops is high, which is really important. As long as they keep their sense of humor, things will be okay.

The rest of August was much the same as the first week as we continued to improve our base camp and get acclimated to Vietnam. Two more men in our brigade were killed as a result of accidents. We had expected to lose some men to the enemy but I did not expect the accidents that seemed to happen almost every day. Our company maintained its good luck and we were not involved in the accidents.

On the 27th of August, we flew to Tuy Hoa, along the coast, for our first battalion size mission - providing security for the rice harvest along Highway 1.

We used virtually anything we could get our hands on to keep the monsoon rain from drenching us in our bunkers – often to no avail

SECTION THREE

Tuy Hoa - Securing the Rice Harvest

August 27, 1966 - November 1, 1966

TUY HOA & HIGHWAY SECURITY - 8/27/66 TO 11/2/66

Short stories and excerpts from letters I wrote home are the best way I can think of to capture the day to day feelings and events of my tour in Vietnam. Fortunately, Phyllis and my parents kept all the letters I wrote. Over the years, I have read the letters several times. Each time I read them it brings back a smile, or a tear, from a memory I had forgotten. In addition to the letter excerpts, I have included a number of short stories that were not covered in my letters.

For the reader who wants to get a good feel for my day to day life throughout the year, it should prove to be interesting. I made a commitment to Phyllis before I left for Vietnam to tell it to her straight and to try not to hide what I was going through or feeling.

For the most part, I did what I said I would do. There are some things I did not write because it just did not seem appropriate at the time or I was too busy to go into the details when I wrote. Many of the things I did not write in my letters are captured in short story form in this book.

Unless otherwise noted, all the excerpts are from the letters I wrote to Phyllis.

29 AUG 66

...We left Pleiku and came to Tuy Hoa (pronounced Tooe Wah) after noon on Saturday, 27 August. This place is fabulous. Instead of mud like we slogged through every day at Pleiku, the entire area is a big sandy beach. Everyone gets to go swimming in the South China Sea when we are in the base area. The troopers from the 101st Airborne Division are treating us great. Just like on D-Day in World War II, the 22nd Infantry is again linked up with the 101st.

The first night, we went down to the 2nd Battalion of the 327th Airborne Infantry. They sold us all the cold beer and soda we wanted for our troops. It was only the second time we have had anything cold to drink since we got here.

Yesterday, my platoon had the battalion's first real mission of the war. We went out west of Tuy Hoa on Highway 7B and provided a forward security element for a company of engineers. (See story "What Now, Lieutenant?")...

"What now, Lieutenant?"

We had been in Vietnam less than a month and had just flown to Tuy Hoa from our base camp at Pleiku. Our battalion was "op-con" or under the operational control of the 101st Airborne Division's First Brigade.

We were all excited to be working with the famous 101st "Screaming Eagles". Their fame stemmed from World War II when they jumped behind the lines on D-Day in 1944, and with their stand at Bastogne during the Battle of the Bulge. The 101st Airborne had been in Vietnam over a year and had been involved in some heavy fighting.

The second day in Tuy Hoa, word came down that a platoon was needed to secure an engineer unit clearing mines from a road west of Tuy Hoa. The road had last been cleared by the French before their defeat in 1954. Since we were the best company in the battalion, we were selected for this first "real" mission since our arrival in country. I was both pleased and apprehensive when Lieutenant Fiacco told me my platoon had the mission.

We were to be picked up by "deuce and a half" (two and a half ton) trucks early the next morning and taken out to join the engineers on the road. I found out the engineer unit we were supporting had been with Captain Bill Carpenter, the famous "Lonesome End" from West Point's football team, when he had called an air strike in on his own position when he had been overrun less than three months earlier. I vividly remembered having read about Captain Carpenter's experiences while we were at Fort Lewis.

We were up bright and early, checking our equipment and weapons thoroughly, making sure we had plenty of ammo, testing our radios to be sure they worked right, and just generally feeling nervous, very green, and inexperienced.

The big green trucks picked us up on schedule. Soon we were speeding west through Tuy Hoa, watching the people closely. Regardless of what people told us about the towns being relatively safe, we did not trust anyone. Sticking to our training, we kept our weapons at the ready, ready to pounce from the truck and respond to any hostile action.

A few miles outside Tuy Hoa, we saw a unit of American troops laying at ease along the side of the road. A lump came in my throat as I realized this was it. We had to get off the trucks and do what we were sent over here to do.

As I climbed down from the truck, I scanned the troops looking for someone with captain's bars. When I could not find him, I asked one of the men where the captain was and he said, "That's me".

I really felt like a green rookie after looking at him. He had no rank insignia, his uniform was well worn, in marked contrast to my still new jungle fatigues. Knowing he had been almost overrun with Captain Carpenter put me more in awe - for the first time I was on a genuine combat mission with real combat veterans.

"Glad to have you, Lieutenant Babcock," he said. "I want you to patrol out in front of us and make sure we don't run into any ambushes. Stay at least a quarter mile in front, work both sides of the road, but stay off the road. It is heavily mined. Any questions?"

My concept of combat engineers was they went first and cleared the road and we would follow along and be available as a quick reaction force if they ran into anything. I quickly remembered the Infantry's job is out in front, not behind anyone else.

"No sir, no questions. Are you ready for us to move out now?" "The sooner you can get out there the sooner we can get on with our work," he replied. I overcame my instinct to salute as I turned and headed back for my platoon.

Walking back to my platoon, which Sergeant Roath had formed into a loose perimeter along the road, I took off my helmet, took the gold lieutenant's bar off my camouflage cover, and tossed it into the muddy water filled ditch alongside the road. I sure did not want to bring attention to my rank if that experienced captain was not going to show his.

My troops listened closely as I briefed them on our mission. We saddled up and moved past the engineers and along either side of the road, careful not to set foot on it. Stepping on a land mine was not in our plans that day.

The morning sun beat down on us unmercifully as we moved along uneventfully. Soon we approached a valley cutting off the right side of the road and forming a box canyon at the foot of steep mountains about 400 yards from the road. (Throughout this book, I will use 'yards' instead of 'meters'. We always referred to distances in meters but most American readers better understand yards - the distances are roughly equal).

The engineer captain called me on the radio, "Oscar 61, check out that valley to your right flank. Someone shot at a helicopter from in there yesterday." With that information, I was not too excited about the next phase of our mission. "Wilco," (Army lingo for "understand and will comply") was my reply as I stopped our movement and prepared to move into the valley.

Since caution is the better part of valor, I remembered my training and decided to prep the area with an artillery barrage. Frequently, I had simulated calling in artillery fire but this was my first time to call real fire on a real target.

Charlie Battery, 4th Battalion, 42nd Artillery responded quickly as I called in and adjusted several 105mm artillery shells. As the shells crashed into the box canyon, I felt comfortable I had the artillery aimed at the right target if we needed it. (Many times after this, the same artillery battery responded like the true professionals they were when we called for fire support).

While I adjusted the artillery fire, Sergeant Roath set up a machine gun crew and a rifle squad along the road, ready to support us with fire. With a knot in my stomach, I moved into the valley with my other two squads, one on either side of the valley. We made sure we stayed close to the foot of the mountains and not out in the open where we would be easy targets.

Our finely honed senses soaked in everything as we worked our way up the valley to the end of the box canyon, ready to fire on the first thing that moved. An Army tactics instructor would have been proud of us - each man crouched low, keeping the proper distance from the man to his front, and constantly searching for signs of movement. No sign of activity was seen as we came to the end of the canyon.

With the same caution, we searched every potential hiding place in the canyon and on the surrounding mountains as we returned to the road. Still nothing. Breathing a sigh of relief, I radioed back our negative report and started moving down alongside the road again, wondering what our next challenge would be.

As we moved, loud explosions pierced the quiet as the engineers periodically found mines and blew them up. The day continued to get hotter and the sun continued to beat down. Despite the heat, we were too keyed up to let our guard down. My next opportunity came from our left flank, about 100 yards off the road.

"Sir, come over here - I've found some mortar shells," came from one of my men. When I moved over to check it out, I saw several 82mm mortar shells concealed by brush in a shallow hole. (The Communists had started using 82mm mortar shells during the Korean War, a single millimeter larger than the American 81mm shells. When captured, our 81mm shells would fit into their 82mm mortar tubes but their 82mm shells would not fit into our 81mm tubes and could not be used against them.)

I radioed our find back to the engineer captain. He responded, "Good job, blow them up and move on."

Since we did not have any plastic explosive (C4), I had to use the only thing available to me - a hand grenade. I moved the platoon into a perimeter, behind cover, out of range of the grenade.

Taking a grenade off my belt, I straightened the safety pin so it would come out easily, and tied a fifty foot piece of string to the pin.

Having been indoctrinated on the dangers of booby traps, I was very careful not to move any of the shells as I searched for a hole to slip the grenade into. I found a small hole and slipped the grenade down among the mortar shells.

Sergeant Roath and Sergeant Benge, my third squad leader, stayed close and found a little ridge of dirt, about fifty yards away, to hide behind. Pleased with how in control I was, I sent them to cover, walked to the end of the string, yanked it, and ran like hell. Covering the distance in no time, I dived over the ridge and slammed myself onto the ground. I hunkered down, trying to "make myself one with Mother Earth" and waited for the massive explosion. We waited and nothing happened.

I started to notice the sweat, and the heat seemed more intense.

All eyes were on me as my platoon peered out from their positions, wondering what had gone wrong. The piece of string was still clutched in my hand. I pulled it in and, sure enough, the safety pin was firmly attached. We either had a dud grenade or something else had gone wrong.

Sergeant Roath looked at me, grinned, and said, "What you gonna do now, Lieutenant?" More sweat started to roll down my face as I contemplated my next move.

I knew I had only one choice, go see what was wrong. With my entire platoon watching me, I cautiously crawled back to the cache. Expecting an explosion at any minute, I slowly closed in on the mortar shells.

As I rose up on a knee to see what the problem was, I could see the safety lever on the grenade. It had partially flipped away but had hit one of the mortar shells and stopped, not allowing the firing pin to hit the fuse. Here I was with a live grenade, safety lever barely in place, and a pile of enemy mortar shells I had to assume were booby trapped. To say I was concerned is an understatement.

But, I knew I was the only one who could do anything. To back away now was to show my platoon their platoon leader was a coward. Sweat continued to roll down my face and back as I eased up closer to the mortar shells.

Carefully, I slipped my hand down through the hole I had dropped the grenade through and firmly grasped the safety lever against the body of the grenade. As I started to pull my hand back out the hole, it would not come out. My hand, with the grenade in it, was too large for the hole. Now I was really in a predicament!

I had a live grenade in my hand with no safety pin. If I let it go again, chances were good the safety lever would fly off and let it explode in five seconds - and I was pretty sure I could not make the fifty yards to cover from my crouched down position in that length of time (world class sprinters are barely that fast and I did not think my adrenalin would make me into one in five seconds).

If I moved the mortar shells to get my hand and the grenade out, I would have set off any booby trap that might have been set.

I lay there for what seemed like an eternity with more sweat rolling down the back of my neck. My mind whirled as I looked around the perimeter at my men, each watching me intently. Sergeant Roath eased up toward me and with another grin said, "What you gonna do now, Lieutenant?" "Get back, Sergeant Roath, no sense in both of us being in this mess," was my reply.

Finally, I decided to take a chance on the booby trap and jerk my hand, and the grenade, out of the hole. When I did, several of the shells moved - but, fortunately, nothing exploded.

My next decision was an easy one. Getting up, I walked over to a rice paddy, and threw the hand grenade as far as I could. It exploded with a roar, shooting a spray of water high into the air.

I radioed the engineer captain, "I will mark the location of the shells. You can blow them with C4 when you get to this point. I am moving out. Out."

We continued our mission along the road. About a half hour later, a tremendous explosion shook the area as the engineers set off the captured mortar shells. Suddenly, I felt very tired. I wanted to sit down and rest, but could not.

We continued to patrol. We had expected to be finished and back at base camp before dark but such was not the case. As darkness engulfed the area, the engineer captain finally decided to quit for the day. The trucks, which had been following the engineers all day, pulled up to take us back to Tuy Hoa. We now had to ride back down the road we had just spent the day walking.

Expecting to be ambushed at any time, we were ready to fire at anything as we sped through the small villages with our lights out. The Vietnamese families, squatting in their huts, eating rice, were oblivious to our concerns. Fortunately, none of them came out of their houses or we might have blown them away.

It was nearly ten o'clock when we finally made it back to base camp. Sergeant Angulo, our mess sergeant, had saved hot chow which the troops quickly devoured. Lieutenant Fiacco met us at the gate and took me to Colonel Morley to debrief our day's actions. I could tell both of them had been worried about our not returning until so late.

When I finally got back to my tent and went to bed, I slept well. It had been a hard and exciting day. My first real combat patrol was under my belt and, more importantly, I had earned my keep in the eyes of my platoon.

29 Aug 66

(Cont'd). . . The engineer unit we were working with reported to brigade headquarters we did a good job. They passed that word on to Colonel Morley. It is really a good feeling to come in from your first mission and have the battalion commander compliment you. They had held hot chow and cold soda for us. We felt like conquering heroes.

Mail has been flooding in on me the last couple of days. Keep the Kool-Aid coming because it really enhances the taste of this water. We fill our canteens out of irrigation canal water and put iodine pills in to purify it.

2 Sept 66

Our first battalion size operation is in its fourth day. We moved south of Tuy Hoa on my 23rd birthday (Tuesday, 30 Aug) and are now set up along Highway #1. My platoon has about a mile and a half area of responsibility. I have it broken down into four outposts scattered along the road at strategic points. My main responsibility is a bridge which has been partially destroyed but is still passable. I have a squad at the bridge and my command post is in sight of it.

Yesterday my platoon went out on another patrol. We were checking out a valley which comes into our area from the base of a hill where an old Buddhist shrine and an abandoned village were located. There were reports a VC company had been sighted up there last week, but we did not find them. We walked from 8:00am until after noon in water from knee to waist deep with elephant grass over our heads. There was not a dry place to take a break all morning...

I moved Cameron, the conscientious objector, into my radio operator job. He still will not carry a rifle and it was causing a morale problem in his squad. I think he will work out okay in this job, he is still a good soldier.

4 SEP 66

Today has been a pretty good day... After chow, I went to church. It is funny, or I should say ironic, to go to church with a loaded M-16 in your hand... The battalion had their first contact and casualties yesterday. A platoon from Charlie Company was hit and had one killed and two slightly wounded. There are a lot of caves in the area where they were ambushed. They called in air strikes to finally get them out of their jam.

Yesterday I took a patrol out into the mountains but did not find anything. We waded water, climbed over rocks, thrashed through jungle, and sweated but that was about all. We probably will not go out again until Tuesday or Wednesday...

Tell me about your kids at school. As a homeroom project, you could adopt my platoon for a year.

6 SEP 66

I had a little accident yesterday morning. (See story on "My Burned Face")...

MY BURNED FACE

"Oscar 61, this is Oscar 6. Be ready to move out in thirty minutes to go help Romeo (Charlie Company). Out." was the message that crackled over the radio.

Charlie Company had been ambushed a couple of days earlier, earning the dubious distinction of losing our battalion's first killed and wounded in action. They were going back to the same spot to see if they could get the VC that had ambushed them. Our mission was to move into a blocking position and kill or capture anyone who retreated as they swept the area.

Thirty minutes is not much time to get ready to move out, especially when your platoon is spread out in outposts along a mile and a half of Highway 1.

We scrambled into action to get ready to move out. Sergeant Roath jumped into the jeep and sped down the road to alert and pick up the rest of the platoon. Stanley Cameron, my radio operator, started packing the gear he would need and checked his radio, making sure we had a fresh battery.

It took me no time to get my gear ready to go. Rather than sit and wait for everyone else, I decided to make myself useful and help with the routine duties Cameron or Sergeant Roath usually did. One of the things that had to be done was to close the latrine.

An abandoned, shallow, dry well served as the latrine for our outpost.

With military sanitation standards firmly ingrained, we would not have dreamed of leaving a latrine without burning the contents to prevent the spread of disease.

Burning a latrine was a very simple thing, something I had watched my men do almost daily since we arrived in Vietnam. Diesel fuel was poured into the latrine, a match was thrown into it, and all the waste burned.

Even though that was not typically an officer's job, I decided to help out by handling that chore. I did not have any diesel fuel but we did have a five gallon can of gasoline, which would accomplish the same purpose.

After pouring a gallon of gasoline down the well, I stepped back and threw in a match. Nothing happened, so I assumed I had not gotten enough gasoline into the latrine. As I picked up the gasoline can and started to pour more, a blast of fire leaped from the well and ignited the stream of gasoline.

The searing heat and smell of burning hair immediately overcame me as my face, neck, and hair were scorched. As I jumped back, the gasoline can fell from my hands. Luckily, it fell away from the well and did not explode.

I do not know whether the pain from the burns or the fear of permanent scars scared me the most. Cameron ran over to see what had happened. "How bad is it?" were the first words out of my mouth. "It does not look too bad, Sir, just like a bad sunburn. And your hair is singed pretty badly," was Cameron's reply. My glasses probably saved my eyes from injury.

I was in somewhat of a predicament. We had a mission to perform but my face was really hurting. I was not about to admit to Lieutenant Fiacco (or anyone else) I had been so stupid. But, I could not hide the fact I was burned.

I was still scared about the potential scars that might result and wanted to get back to the aid station. On the other hand, this was our first mission where contact with the VC looked like a certainty and I needed to be there with my men.

I asked Jackson, our aid man, to look at my burns. He did not have enough experience to know how serious they were but he did have some greasy ointment he smeared on my face.

Sergeant Roath came back down the road with the rest of the troops. In typical fashion, he asked, "What in the hell happened to you, Sir?" He was a good friend by now but I was not about to tell him what I had done. As usual, he liked to take every opportunity to point out how dumb second lieutenants are - my actions had pretty much proved his point. He looked at me with a grin and shook his head when I didn't reply.

"Are you ready to go?" he asked. In keeping with the good Army tradition that the mission always comes first, my response was, "Sure, let's move out."

We headed across the marsh that paralleled Highway 1. Before long we were waist deep in water with tall marsh grass all around us. The grass kept any breeze away and the exertion of walking through the water had us sweating profusely in no time.

The salty sweat just added to the aggravation of the burns. The pain had subsided to a dull throb as we trudged along, ever alert to the imminent danger from the VC.

Before the day was over, we had patrolled five miles through marsh, rice paddies, open ground, and mountain foothills. Charlie Company did not find any VC as they swept the area where they had been hit. We did not find any as we swept in from the other side.

After nothing was located there, Colonel Morley diverted us to another objective to sweep. With no results, we called it a day and returned to our outposts.

My burned face was the lesser of two disturbing aches. The other was the absolute fatigue caused by the day's mission. All I wanted was to get back to my outpost and settle in for the night.

Unfortunately, soon after we got back, we were alerted to pack up and move back to the base camp. Our new mission was to relieve a company from the 101st Airborne and take up perimeter guard responsibility. Overcoming our fatigue, we moved back to Tuy Hoa and worked into the night improving the defensive positions we had taken over.

Early the next morning, I was at the battalion aid station to let Doc Maurer look at my burns. He said, "Babcock, you are a lucky guy. A few of these spots are second and third degree burns but I don't think you have to worry about any scars when everything heals. But how did you do this?"

After swearing him to secrecy, I told him what had happened. When he quit laughing, I thanked him and returned to my unit.

My face was spotted with water blisters for several days as the healing process started. Perimeter duty had the advantage of putting us back on the beach of the South China Sea. Every day I swam in the salt water to help the healing. Things kept getting better, and then I started to peel.

Imagine a face which had been exposed constantly to the sun for two months and how brown it was. Contrast that to the pink skin of a baby as the old skin came off and the new skin became exposed. I looked like I had leprosy - spotted and looked terrible! Fortunately, I seldom had a chance to look into a mirror so I was not too self conscious about my looks. But it was obvious how I looked whenever someone saw me and did a double take.

One day, Colonel Morley saw me and said, "My lord, Babcock, what happened to you?" I was over the embarrassment of my stupidity so I told him the story.

His response capped off the whole incident very nicely, "Bob, don't you know second lieutenants aren't qualified to burn shit. From now on, leave that job to someone who is qualified." And I did.

Patrol to help C/1-22 IN - after I burned my face – and before it peeled. Stan Cameron,
my radio operator is in the background. (My helmet was normally worn but my forehead
burned too much to wear it all the time on this day).

My burned face – after it peeled.

6 SEPT 66

(Cont'd) ...I will learn one of these days not to screw around with gasoline. At least I will not have to shave for a few days...

7 SEPT 66

The Vietnamese elections are coming up on 11 September. They are afraid there will be riots in the towns so they are putting them off limits to U.S. troops except for official business, effective tomorrow. Maybe I will get to town one of these days...

I just took a shower for the first time in what seems like a month. It is difficult to realize how great it feels to clean up until you have spent a month trying to keep clean out of a steel helmet filled with swamp water...

9 SEPT 66

The Bravo Company gypsies are ready to move again. We got the word from "Rawhide" (Colonel Morley's new radio call sign) that our company will fly to Ninh Hoa tomorrow morning to take up a security mission for a Korean unit...

We had our first night operation last night. The support people from Headquarters Company relieved us on the perimeter and our company moved out at 1:30 in the morning for a village about a mile and a half south. The VC have been coming in at night, harassing the villagers.

We were to sweep through the village and push the VC into a blocking position Charlie Company had set up south of the village. By daylight, we were half way through the village and had not found any VC so we thoroughly searched the houses in the last half of the village.

After seeing how these people live, it sure makes you appreciate being an American and having everything we do. The furnishings consisted of a crude bed or hammock, a cabinet or two, and a table. The beds did not have mattresses of any kind, just a blanket on some boards.

The entire area stunk from animal and human waste. The people were filthy. We did not find anything of value except for three VC suspects.

11 SEPT 66

Well, we finally had a little excitement last night and this morning... (See stories on "Relief of Bridge Outpost" and "Bringing Out the Downed Pilot").

RELIEF OF BRIDGE OUTPOST

"Oscar 61, this is Oscar 59 Bravo, over," came the 9:00 PM call from the three man outpost. They were located outside a village several miles south of us. "This is 61 Echo, send your message," was Stanley Cameron's (my radio operator) reply.

"We have possible contact. The Vietnamese PF (Popular Forces) platoon just came running out to our position shouting 'beaucoup VC, beaucoup VC!' They keep jabbering and I can not understand them but they seem really scared," was the message from the outpost leader.

I responded, "This is 61, do you see anything in the village?" "Negative," was the reply, "what do you want me to do?" "Hold your position, stay alert, and I will get right back with you," was my response.

With that, I sprinted up to Major High's tent. I did not know much French but I did know "beaucoup" meant "many". Lieutenant Fiacco was on a mission with the second platoon and I was in command of the company. Rawhide, the battalion commander, was back at base camp in Pleiku and Major High was in command of the battalion. I quickly recapped for him the radio call.

"What do you think you should do now, Lieutenant?" was his calm question. (Damn, I was learning to hate that question). "I think I should take a force out there to reinforce them."

Major High agreed, "Take about twenty people with you so you can reinforce them and still have enough security to come back here tonight. It's seven miles out to their position and I want you to be sure to have enough troops to fight off an ambush."

From Major High's radio I called the outpost, "Hold on, I am bringing help." You could hear a sound of relief in the response, "Roger, everything is quiet here now, but hurry."

Once again I had a dilemma. Where was I going to get twenty troops to reinforce the outpost? The second platoon was with Lieutenant Fiacco at Ninh Hoa, the weapons platoon was still down in Mosquito Valley, and my third platoon and the first platoon were on perimeter security duty. I did not have twenty infantrymen available for the mission.

My platoon sergeant, Sergeant Roath, and two of my squad leaders, Sergeant Benge and Sergeant Burruel, were taking a well earned night off from perimeter security duty.

They were in the middle of a poker game in the supply tent with First Sergeant MacDonald, Sergeant Angulo (the mess sergeant), and another sergeant. All six of them had a good start on being rip roaring drunk when I walked into the tent.

I explained the situation and asked for ideas on how to pull off the mission. Sergeant Angulo immediately volunteered himself and all his cooks. He took off to roust them out of bed (they had to be up at 4:00 AM to cook breakfast and always went to bed early.) First Sergeant MacDonald volunteered himself and all the rest of the company support personnel.
In less than fifteen minutes, we had assembled the most unlikely crew you would ever expect to go on a combat mission.

Sergeant Angulo and his four cooks were chomping at the bit to go, "kick some ass." First Sergeant MacDonald had produced the radio communications section of four men, two company clerks, the supply clerk, two men from first platoon who had been on sick call, and himself.

With my three NCOs, my radio operator and me, we had a force of cooks, clerks, and drunks consisting of twenty one men.

The other sergeant (whose name will go unmentioned here) was standing in the shadow of his tent, trying to avoid the trip. When First Sergeant MacDonald saw him in the shadows, he exploded. "Sergeant, get your ass on the truck, you yellow bellied bastard!" as he physically jerked him from the shadows and pushed him to the back of the truck. The sergeant trembled with fear as he meekly climbed into the back of the three-quarter ton truck.

When all the men had loaded on the trucks, we took off and headed for the ammo dump. Sergeant Roath was driver and I was shotgun on the lead truck, Sergeant Benge was driver and First Sergeant MacDonald was shotgun on the trailing truck. At the ammo dump we picked up two cases of hand grenades, extra M16 and machine gun ammo. As we headed out the front gate to go help the outpost, we felt like the cavalry heading out to save the wagon train. And, Sergeant Angulo kept talking about how he was going to "kick some ass".

It was the night following the Vietnamese national elections. All available intelligence reports had predicted for days the VC would be very active trying to disrupt the elections. That added to our concern as we started the seven mile trip through small Vietnamese villages.

Since the road ran between flat rice paddies, I decided we would be safer if we ran without lights so the VC could not see us coming. Sergeant Roath turned off his lights but did not slow down a bit.

He and Sergeant Benge were both still feeling the effects of their evening of drinking. After a few minutes of hurtling down the road in the dark at forty miles an hour, something did not feel right to me. I told Sergeant Roath, "Turn your lights back on. Let's see what's out here."

He turned them on none too soon! As his lights lit up the darkness, we found ourselves two feet from, and headed for, a deep canal that ran parallel with the road. Sergeant Roath unhesitatingly swerved back to the middle of the road. Sergeant Benge stuck right on his tail. I quickly decided it would be safer to leave the lights on the rest of the way and take our chances with the VC.

As the trucks rolled to a stop in front of the outpost, Sergeant Angulo was the first man to leap off the truck. In his eagerness for action, he forgot about the case of hand grenades laying on the rear of the truck. He tripped and fell to the road like a sack of flour, landing hard on his right shoulder. After spouting off a string of profanities that would have embarrassed a sailor, he quickly jumped up and started forming the troops into a defensive perimeter.

As we surveyed the situation, we found something of a surprise. Lying on the ground around our five man outpost was the Vietnamese platoon, sound asleep. They felt more secure with our five men guarding them than they did with their thirty men. It didn't do anything to raise our opinion of the South Vietnamese militia (and so it was for the remainder of our tour).

We woke the Vietnamese platoon leader and got a better picture of what was happening. They had not seen any VC in the village but they expected them to come in at any time. We asked him where they normally came from and he pointed toward a tree line on the other side of the village.

First Sergeant MacDonald was listening to the situation and turned to me and asked, "What do you want to do now, Lieutenant?" (There was that same question again.)

Since we had developed a mutual respect and friendship over the ten months we had worked together at Fort Lewis and in Vietnam, I turned the question back to him, "Good question, First Sergeant, what do you think?"

Since he had survived several major battles in the Korean war and had a lot more soldiering experience than I, I was not too proud to let him give me his thoughts on what to do. "I think we should set up an ambush and get the little bastards." I quickly agreed with him.

As I stepped to the radio to call Major High, First Sergeant MacDonald noticed the other sergeant was still cowering in the back of the truck. "You spineless, no good coward, get out of that truck!"

I had to grab the First Sergeant to keep him from climbing into the truck and throwing the sergeant out on the road. I am convinced Mac would have beaten him to a pulp if I had not restrained him. We did not have time for that; we had an ambush to set up.

I called Major High on the radio, "This is Oscar 61, we have an opportunity to get us some bad guys. Request permission to stay out the rest of the night, over." "Negative," came the unexpected reply. "I have another mission for you at first daylight. Leave some help there and come on back." Overcoming our disappointment, we started getting ready for the trip back over the same seven miles of hostile highway we had just traveled.

After conferring with First Sergeant MacDonald, we decided to leave five men and most of the extra hand grenades and ammunition to reinforce the outpost. I thought if anything did happen, which appeared unlikely now, our ten men could take care of themselves and maybe even get some help from the militia platoon. Getting volunteers to stay was not a problem.

Specialist George Wilhelm, our ranking company clerk, and his buddy from Brooklyn, Specialist Danny Schemp, one of our commo sergeants, would not hear of not staying. Two of Sergeant Angulo's cooks eagerly volunteered to stay and Specialist Lisui, our mild mannered clerk/typist from Samoa even volunteered.

Sergeant Angulo wanted to stay and be in command of the outpost but his shoulder was hurting badly. He protested vigorously when I would not let him stay, he still wanted to "kick some gook's ass". First Sergeant MacDonald wanted to leave the other sergeant, but I did not want to leave that problem with the outpost.

As we loaded into the trucks for the dash back to base camp, we had our M16's loaded and ready with our fingers on the triggers. Sergeants Roath and Benge had sobered up nicely and were ready to show off their driving credentials as they started the trip back.

I had learned my lesson about driving fast with your lights off. With lights glaring and the gas pedals on the floor, we sped down the road, expecting an ambush from every clump of trees or village we passed. We made it back to base camp unmolested, in half the time it took us to get to the outpost. It is amazing how fast you can drive when you are sober and scared.

As we pulled into the battalion area, I immediately headed for Major High's tent to see what our mission was that would cause him to not let us set up an ambush. The relief of the bridge outpost was only a warm-up for what lay ahead. In four hours, with daylight just breaking, we were on a mission which made us quickly forget what we had just done.

A typical patrol in Tuy Hoa – lots of water to wade through

BRINGING OUT THE DOWNED PILOT

It was after 1:00 AM as I got my briefing from Major High on our morning's mission. I was still keyed up from our harrowing experience of providing relief to our bridge outpost.

"Yesterday afternoon, between 4:00 and 5:30, one of our battalion forward air controllers was flying a reconnaissance mission when his plane went down. The wreckage was found just before dark."

"A man was lowered down to it and found the pilot, dead in the cockpit, and the plane still burning. We do not know what caused the plane to go down, but we suspect it was shot down by a .50 caliber machine gun."

"Your mission is to be there at daylight and bring out the body. We have only three helicopters available so you are limited to 24 men, including yourself...," Major High continued giving me the details on the terrain and other items I would need to know to accomplish the mission.

Needless to say, I did not look forward to this next challenge. I was drained from the mission we had just completed, I did not like the prospect of running into a .50 caliber machine gun, and, most of all, I did not look forward to pulling a burned dead man out of an airplane. My mind could picture the grotesque sight that would greet me when I got to the airplane. As usual, I did not get to vote, so the mission was mine to accomplish.

It was an easy job for me to select the three squads that would go, Sergeant Benge and his third squad, Sergeant Burruel and the two machine gun sections from his weapons squad, and Specialist Muller and his second squad. Sergeant Roath, Stanley Cameron, my radio operator, and I would take up three of the slots.

I sent a runner to the perimeter to bring back Muller to join those of us who were not on perimeter duty. It turned out the night off for Sergeants Roath, Benge, and Burruel had been anything but relaxing. At least they were all sober after the mission to the bridge outpost.

Major High had instructed me to bring my men off the perimeter at 4:30 AM and be ready to get on the helicopters by 5:30. After briefing my squad leaders, I decided I would try to get a little sleep. With two hours before we had to start getting ready, I was convinced some sleep would do me a world of good.

As soon as I closed my eyes, I could see an image of the pilot in the burned out cockpit. I tossed and turned and tried to think of something else but my mind always came back to what lay ahead of me. After half an hour, I gave up on sleep, got up, and cleaned my rifle to occupy my time and my mind. I had never had a job to do that I dreaded so much. Maybe it was because I knew the pilot (we had talked frequently during the boat trip to Vietnam) or maybe my mind was just painting too vivid a horror picture.

It was still dark as we loaded onto the helicopters. Our destination was ten miles straight south. The plan was to land on the beach and work our way inland. Not knowing where the .50 caliber machine gun was, the helicopters would not fly over the crash site to let us see what we were going after. We had to rely on our map, compass, and high level observation from a helicopter on station above us after we were safely on the ground.

Just before the helicopters took off, one of the battalion intelligence sergeants ran up to my chopper and handed me a Polaroid camera. "Take pictures of the plane and the path it cut as it crashed. We want to try to determine what caused the crash and which direction it was coming from as it crashed." I really was not thinking of myself as a photographer that day, I was thinking only of getting in there, getting the pilot, and getting the hell out.

We flew at low level over the South China Sea. The pilots ascended briefly to get their bearings before they hovered in for a landing on the beach, just a few yards from where the waves were hitting the sand. It took us no time to leap from the helicopters and disappear into the brush, a forty yard sprint away. It was just getting daylight as we cautiously started working our way inland. The terrain was rolling sand dunes covered with thick thorn bushes.

One machine gun team set up on the top of a dune to cover the point squad as they hacked a path through the bushes that tore at our fatigues. When the point got out of sight of the covering machine gun, we set up the other machine gun team on a sand dune and leap-frogged the first team to be ready to take over again.

After about an hour of slow but steady movement, we had covered 500 yards and could see the crash site. As we had planned, the three squads formed a defensive perimeter around the site. Sergeant Roath, Sergeant Benge, and I had the job of pulling the body out of the plane.

As we had discussed the mission a few hours earlier, Sergeant Roath was insistent he should do the dirty work since he had seen so many similar sights during the Korean War. I could not disagree with his logic and gladly let him come along. Sergeant Benge volunteered since he thought it would take more than two of us to get the pilot out.

My heart was pounding as we approached the plane. Had the VC set up their .50 caliber machine gun in a position to fire on the wreckage? The crash site was well within range of a machine gun set up in the surrounding hills. Had they been in during the night and booby trapped the airplane? What would we find in the cockpit of the plane? A few small wisps of smoke were still coming from the wreckage as we peered into the cockpit, expecting the worst.

Nothing even remotely resembling a human was left. The fire had burned intensely and nothing was left of the pilot's body but the trunk. The only recognizable things on the body were his dog tags and a Saint Christopher's medal. The thought that crossed my mind was, "It's a damned dirty shame anyone had to die like that." I just hoped he had been killed by gunfire and had not burned to death.

Once we knew what we had to deal with, we quickly went to work so we could get out of there. As instructed, I took a roll of Polaroid pictures. The close-up pictures of the bullet holes in the tail of the plane left no doubt it had been shot down by a .50 caliber machine gun.

We removed the body, zipped it into a body bag, and moved away from the wreckage. We knew now there was a .50 caliber machine gun around there somewhere and we did not want it to find us. Using the same caution, we moved back to the beach. By the time we reached it, we were ready to slump down for a rest.

As I lay on the sand, listening to the waves pound the beach, it seemed more like a serene vacation spot than a place that had claimed the life of an American pilot only a few hours before.

Our rest was short as the sound of the helicopters could be heard in the distance as they came to extract us. They radioed for us to pop smoke to mark our location. After identifying our red smoke, they hovered in, kicking sand into our faces as we rushed to board. Soon the choppers were again airborne, leaving the crash site behind, another grim scar on the Vietnamese landscape.

As we were gaining altitude, a radio call from a gunship circling overhead caught our attention. "Single VC spotted on the beach three hundred yards south of pickup site." We tensed as we waited for the helicopters to turn to take us back to get him. As I alerted my men over our company radio net, we were told we were heading back to base camp, the artillery would take care of him.

Charlie Battery, 4-42 Artillery responded quickly. As we listened on the radio and watched from our choppers, they dropped fifty rounds of artillery fire on the man. We never knew whether or not they got him, or whether he was a VC or just an innocent fisherman. After what we had been through the night before and that morning, we did not have much compassion for any of the Vietnamese people.

By 9:00, we were back on the ground at our base camp. An aid truck met us and took the pilot's body to graves registration. Sergeant Angulo had saved hot breakfast for us and the intelligence section wanted to ask me a thousand questions about what we had seen and to explain everything in the Polaroid pictures. Guess who won?

The intelligence people had to wait on the questions. I was hungry and anxious to hear Sergeant Angulo and the other rear echelon guys tell their tales about their mission to the bridge outpost.

Helicopter with part of my platoon as we flew to pick up the downed pilot – taken from my helicopter.

On the beach, waiting for our helicopter pickup up after we pulled out the downed pilot.

12 SEPT 66

Today is going to be spent doing nothing all day long if I can get by with it. I feel like I deserve the day off after having to recover that body yesterday.

This sure does not seem like a war torn country today. Everything is peaceful and quiet. There is a cool breeze blowing across the beach and, all in all, it is just generally a nice day...

13 SEPT 66

...I have spent most of the morning in my tent taking care of my girl friend. I have to give her a lot of attention because I do not want her to get temperamental at a critical time. Of course the girl friend I am referring to is my M-16 rifle. I gave it a good cleaning this morning to get all the sand out of it. For the rest of the year, that little hunk of metal and fiberglass is my best friend and will be well taken care of.

15 SEPT 66

...My platoon went on an ambush patrol last night. We set up along the railroad tracks south of the village we searched last week, hoping the VC would come our way. We sat in the rice paddies from 8:00 yesterday evening until 4:30 this morning and did not accomplish a thing except get cold, wet, and miserable. I sure wish we could find some bad guys. It gets frustrating going out day after day and not finding anything...

19 SEPT 66

...The 101st Airborne lost a bunch of people last night, including the company commander, executive officer, and first sergeant. They are the ones that looked out for us when we first came to Tuy Hoa. Their perimeter was overrun and everyone in the command post was killed. From what we hear, it was something that could have been avoided - they let their security down and the VC got them. It just proves once again you can never be too careful over here.

We have a new pastime. The Vietnamese kids sneak through the perimeter during the day and rummage through the trash dump. Our job is to keep them out, which is an impossible task. We cannot shoot them unless they have a weapon.

We have tried shooting in front of them and over their heads but that does not scare them. So on Saturday, First Sergeant MacDonald and I decided the best way to get them out of here is to catch them and spank them. We went out in a jeep and chased them down, got out of the jeep, chased and caught them on foot, and then spanked them with our belts.

It is impossible to catch them all but if you get two or three boys about ten or twelve years old, the rest of the kids get the idea and "dee-dee" (Vietnamese word for "go"). They will usually stay away for at least half a day before they try to come back. About once or twice a day since then, someone from the company goes out and runs them off. It is like herding cattle. Get them started out of the area, cut a nice big yearling out of the herd, catch him, and brand him.

I have been spanked harder than we hit them so do not think we are beating these kids to death. It is for the good of all concerned, the kids and our troops. There are all sorts of grenades and ammo laying around the area that the South Vietnamese left. One of the kids could get hurt or killed if he started messing with something he did not know anything about.

Another, and more important reason as far as we are concerned, is they could take this outside the perimeter and get it into the hands of the VC. I will spank a million kids before I will let them take ammo out for the VC to use against us. Besides, it's good exercise chasing the kids down. They are real sprinters running across the sand.

21 SEPT 66

I have been places since my last letter. (See story on "A Night in a Whorehouse")...

Another patrol – and poor discipline on keeping spread out.
Fortunately, we didn't get hurt from this mistake

A Night in a Whorehouse

On my first mission after our move to Tuy Hoa, I lost my military ID card. As the month of September progressed, several other men also lost theirs. The closest place to get one made was in Nha Trang, a half hour flight south.

One day, when we were providing perimeter security for the 101st Airborne's base camp, we decided things were slow enough that we could spare a day to get new ID cards made. About noon, I boarded a plane with six of our troops for the short trip down the coast to Nha Trang.

After the flight, we started the simple process of filling out the paper work, getting our pictures made, and waiting for the ID cards to be laminated. By mid afternoon we were finished.

Since we were hitchhiking and did not have any priority to get onto an aircraft, I decided to spend the night in Nha Trang and start early the next morning trying to find a flight with seven empty seats. The men were still my responsibility so I took them to a replacement company, got them checked in for the night and then went downtown to MACV headquarters to find a place for myself.

After eating supper in the officer's mess, which was very elaborate compared to anything else I had seen in Vietnam, I went to the housing desk to sign up for sleeping quarters. "Sorry, Lieutenant, everything here is full.

I suggest you go down the street to a hotel. A lot of the permanent party people live there, they should have a vacancy."

For 700 piasters (about $5.50), I checked into a room with a double bed, electric lights, a fan, and little else. It did not have a bathroom, that was down the hall. It was not plush but it was the first chance I had had to sleep on a bed since I got off the ship almost two months earlier.

The Vietnamese hotel clerk suggested I check my rifle and field gear in with him. He assured me the area was secure and I would not need it. "Thanks, but no thanks," was my reply. "Wherever I go, my rifle goes with me."

Lying across the bed, I surveyed the room. Despite its relative comfort, I got the feeling it was closing in on me. Even though I had been assured Nha Trang was a secure city, I was not comfortable being by myself outside a perimeter secured by American troops.

The longer I lay there, the more uncomfortable I became. Finally, I got up and went downstairs to the bar where a number of Americans and Vietnamese girls were drinking. I had decided to be real brave and leave my rifle in my locked room. As I walked into the bar, I was joined by a Vietnamese girl who asked if I would buy her a drink. I declined the offer and found a seat at the bar next to an Army First Sergeant who was drinking alone.

As we talked, I asked him if there were always this many Vietnamese girls in the bar. He looked at me like I had just asked the most stupid question he had ever heard. "Lieutenant, where else do you think the girls would be? Don't you know this is a government inspected whorehouse?"

Again, my straight laced, small town morality (coupled with a large dose of naivety) was shocked. I knew there were a lot of whorehouses, but I did not know American GI's lived permanently in some of them. The uncomfortable feeling I had just being in that place, coupled with my totally naive view of the world, made up my mind for me. I finished my drink, went straight back to my room, picked up my rifle, field gear, and shaving kit and left the hotel. It was just getting dark as I walked out into the streets of Nha Trang. I had no idea where I was going to spend the night but I knew it was not going to be in that hotel.

Nha Trang was different from any place I had seen in Vietnam. There were several large four and five story modern buildings, very much unlike the tin shacks that made up Pleiku and Tuy Hoa. It was a modern city with electric lights in all the buildings, even street lights.

After the Americans got off duty, they put on civilian clothes and were allowed in town until midnight. They could stay in town after midnight but had to be off the streets. You can guess where they went.

I was the only person with a rifle and steel helmet standing on the street and looked pretty conspicuous to the GIs starting their night of partying. Rather than stand on the street corner, I boarded an Army bus taking troops to town for their evening of fun.

Riding the bus through the streets of Nha Trang gave me a different view of the war. There were bars and girls and cheap souvenir stands on every street corner. The American GIs, in civilian clothes, were having a great time as they moved in and out of the bars and hooked up with the Vietnamese prostitutes.

The marked contrast of the life those GIs were living to the conditions we infantrymen knew was appalling to me. I am sure some of those GIs were living a lot better life than they had known in the States. And, they sure did not seem to worry about the VC. (But, that was not unique to Vietnam. Some soldiers have lived and acted that way in every war since the Stone Ages.)

After three hours aimlessly riding the bus as it made its circuit around Nha Trang, I got off at the replacement company where I had left my men. I found a tent with rows of cots, honest to goodness real mattresses, and pillows. I stripped off my field gear and boots, propped my rifle by the side of the cot, lay down and slept like a baby, alone. The next day we caught helicopters back to Tuy Hoa. We were on perimeter security living the life of an infantryman by nightfall.

I never did tell anyone about the 700 piasters I paid for a room in a whorehouse and left empty all night.

25 SEPT 66

We went on a patrol all day yesterday. General Collins was supposed to be around the area so all three platoons went out to make sure no VC took a pot shot at him. It rained most of the day and the General did not show. We all got soaked again. Such is the life of the Infantry...

26 SEPT 66

Last night we had a good bull session sitting around our hootch. Walt, some of the NCOs from our platoons, and I sat around and talked about life in the States until about 10:00. It sure did make us all homesick. You really do not appreciate all the advantages and luxuries of living in the United States until you have been away from them for awhile.

To top off my feeling of homesickness, I crawled into my bunk with my new poncho liner for the first time. A poncho liner is a light-weight, quilted blanket that feels about like our blue bedspread. That was the first time since I left the States that I had slept under something that reminded me of anything besides canvas...

Walt got three letters yesterday from some sixth graders in Georgia. It might be an interesting project for your homeroom to try writing letters to some of my guys. If you like the idea, I can give you some names to write to. It would be a good morale factor for my men and an interesting project for your students...

27 SEPT 66

I spent the day doing nothing and listening on the radio to a firefight Charlie Company was having north of here. They had a fight yesterday afternoon and had to break contact when it got dark. This morning, they went back to the same place and made contact with an undetermined number of VC. Pinned down most of the day, they had three men killed and eleven wounded and never did get close enough to the VC to see if they had killed any of them. They called in air strikes and armed choppers so maybe they killed some of the little slant-eyed bastards.

We continue to be extremely cautious. Sandy Fiacco has deeply ingrained in all four platoon leaders and all our troops the value of caution and fire power. We have never moved into a possible enemy area without first blowing it apart with artillery fire. Because of this, we have not gotten into trouble...

29 SEPT 66

I'm tired. We went on a patrol today and spent the day climbing up and down mountains. We did not find a blasted thing but we sure did go over some tough terrain. We were out from early morning until late afternoon.

(From Letter to my Folks) - ... Today I wasted several thousand dollars worth of artillery and mortar shells blowing rocks around on the mountains. I do not know if I killed any VC but at least I brought back all the people I took out with me. As long as I can do that, I will feel like I am doing a good job...

30 SEPT 66

We went patrolling again today. We were climbing mountains all day again and all I have to show for it is a torn pair of pants and a tired, aching body. I usually fall at least two or three times a day...

(See story "Another Leadership Challenge").

ANOTHER LEADERSHIP CHALLENGE

We had started patrolling through the marshes and rocky foothills of Mosquito Valley early, before the sun became so hot. Now the mid morning sun was beating down on us unmercifully. The boredom that comes from a hot day of slogging through marshes and across huge boulders and not finding anything was beginning to set in.

As we approached a fairly large stream, the point squad stopped and motioned for me to come forward. I could see excitement on the face of Mark Petrino, the point man, as I approached where he and Sergeant Benge, his squad leader, were crouched talking. "What's up?" I asked. "There's a great big assed snake out there in the water and I'm not going in with it!" was the immediate response from Mark.

As if to punctuate his remark, the six foot long snake surfaced for just a few seconds before it went back under. Near the opposite bank of the stream, about twenty five yards away, it was directly in our path. Shooting it would have been the obvious thing but that would have given our position away to the VC. And, it was under water and you can not shoot what you can not see.

Once again the classic Army question, "What you gonna do now, Lieutenant," came to my mind as my men looked at me to see how I would handle this challenge.

My options were limited. There was no way to go around the stream so we had to cross it. This looked like a spot that was shallow enough for our non swimmers to get across without too much problem. No one had volunteered to go in after the snake. (There was no question in my mind Sergeant Benge or Petrino would have gone if I had said to.)

The answer was obvious to me as I started stripping off my web gear and equipment. I had to be the one to set the example and go into the water first. "Sergeant Benge, have your people ready to move when I get rid of that damned snake." With that, I picked up my M16 rifle, put an extra magazine of ammunition in my helmet camouflage band, grabbed a machete, and started into the water. "Keep a close eye on me and let me know if you see anything," I shouted over my shoulder as I eased into the waist deep water.

My eyes kept searching the water in front of me as I eased deeper and deeper into it. At any moment, I expected to get bitten by the unseen snake that was lurking in wait. My machete wielding right arm stayed tense as I prepared to slash at anything that moved. My jungle boots delicately felt their way along the bottom of the stream.

I soon realized our problem was more than just a snake. I was shoulder deep in the water, it was still getting deeper, and it was another ten yards to the other bank. This was not going to be a suitable crossing site for several of my men. Most were shorter than my 6'2", would have on all their equipment, and some could not swim.

I worked my way downstream trying to find a shallow spot to cross, still anticipating a visit from the snake. "Look here, sir!" Sergeant Benge yelled. I quickly whirled around, ready to cut the snake in half, only to see Sergeant Benge had taken my camera out of the ammo pouch where I always carried it, and was taking my picture.

After gingerly working fifty yards downstream and never getting out of shoulder deep water, I decided to head back upstream and see if there was a shallow spot above where I had entered. All of my senses and reflexes were at full alert as I approached and then passed the spot where we had last seen the snake.

As I moved upstream, the water became shallow and I soon found a suitable crossing site for the patrol - fifty yards upstream from the snake. After retrieving my web gear and equipment, I led the way across the stream. This time, I was the one on the bank taking a picture as Sergeant Benge and his squad waded quickly through the waist deep water.

We never did see the snake again but each man in the platoon was fully alert and wasted no time as he crossed to the relative safety of the opposite bank. Now all we had to worry about were the VC as we continued the patrol. I moved a little prouder knowing I had successfully passed another test of leadership in the eyes of my men (and in my own eyes as well.)

Bob looking for the snake in the river.

1 Oct 66

Greetings from a First Lieutenant! As of today, I am no longer a "shave tail."

Have you sent my new Playboy yet? A bunch of us are anxiously awaiting its arrival...

2 Oct 66

This afternoon I gave my best friend a thorough cleaning for the first time in over a week. After I finished that I wrote letters. Speaking of my best friend (my rifle), I have named it after you. I scratched your name into the stock so every time I pick it up I can see your name...

Ron Marksity moved out of the company today. He earned a great deal, he's going to be aide to General Byers, assistant Division Commander.

3 Oct 66

I took a patrol out again today. We did not go very far and were back by mid afternoon. "Rawhide" wanted us to check out a mountain ridge which overlooks Highway #1. Our First Brigade lands tomorrow and it would be rather embarrassing if someone shot at them. It poured down rain all day long, we got soaked, but we are used to that.

I'm having a hard time concentrating tonight because there is so much traffic on the radio. Second platoon has two ambush patrols out. They think they have spotted something. They keep calling in on the radio every few minutes and I have to serve as a relay station to Lieutenant - now Captain - Fiacco. He is over in the artillery area getting a fire mission plotted and ready to fire if needed...

4 Oct 66

My platoon spent the day out on small three and four man outposts along Highway #1 securing it for the First Brigade. After we spent most of the day there, you guessed it, battalion finally remembered to tell us the First Brigade was not landing here today. They decided to have them dock at Nha Trang and then fly them to Tuy Hoa.

Consequently, my people spent the day sitting out in the rain for no reason. But, such is life. If they were not doing that they would be doing something else just as military so it is six of one and half a dozen of the other, just another day in Vietnam.

Sandy, First Sergeant MacDonald, and I were returning from Tuy Hoa after dark and had a pretty big scare. (See story on "A Murdered Woman?")...

The Second platoon thinks they killed four VC by artillery fire last night. This is the right way to fight a war, sit in hiding and let the artillery do the killing for you. (See story on "The Buffalo Hunters")...

A MURDERED WOMAN?

A cold chill coursed down my spine as I heard the terror filled shriek of a woman coming from the mountainside. It brought everyone on the outpost out of his sleep and grabbing for his rifle. The noise seemed to have come from an outcropping of boulders about one hundred yards away that rose from the side of Highway #1.

As I tried to decide for myself what the noise could be, I remembered back to a Sunday night in high school. Phyllis and I had been driving out in the country (or maybe we were parked) after church when we had heard the same type of scream. We had driven home as fast as we could to report a potential murder to my parents. After describing the sound, my Dad assured us it was the shriek of a mountain lion, not a woman. He had frequently heard them while running a freight train through the mountains south of home.

I had a hard time convincing the men and myself we had heard a mountain lion, not a woman being murdered. Whatever it was, we were all convinced something was up on the mountain we did not want to tangle with.

Everyone stayed on full alert for the next hour, listening intently and scanning the darkness to try to determine the source of the scream. Only darkness and quiet engulfed us so we finally went back to our normal security and tried to get some sleep. None of us slept very well the rest of the night. Soon after daylight, I took a patrol up on the mountain to see what we could find. After an hour of searching for a body, cat tracks, drag marks, or anything to give us a clue as to the source of the scream, we gave up and returned to our outpost.

No screams were heard the next night as we listened intently to all noises. Two nights later, we heard it again. It came from the same place and sounded just as much like a woman screaming in terror. Again, we spent a restless night listening and wondering what caused the scream. Sergeant Roath led a patrol up into the mountains the next morning and looked more intently for animal tracks, blood trails, a body, or drag marks. Sure enough, they found some large pug marks made by what we assumed to be a mountain lion.

It relieved us to know a murder ritual was not being performed outside our outpost. It did not make us feel any better, however, to know we now had to worry about a mountain lion sneaking up on us. We were probably less concerned about the VC hitting our six man outpost than we were the mountain lion.

We had heard nothing more from the mountain lion until three nights later. Captain Fiacco, his driver Harry Troutman, First Sergeant MacDonald, and I were returning after dark to Mosquito Valley from the base camp at Tuy Hoa. As our jeep rounded a curve in the road, we saw a huge mountain lion bound across the road and spring up into the large rocks leading into the mountains. Like a phantom, the cat was gone before we could get our rifles to our shoulders.

The next day, our mission changed and we moved from the outpost, never to return. The mountain lion was only seen by four of us, but for several nights it had added a new dimension of concern to many soldiers as we sat in outposts along the road.

THE BUFFALO HUNTERS

It seemed like a good idea at the time. While patrolling close to the mountains along the edge of Mosquito Valley, the second platoon had come across a water buffalo that had been killed by artillery fire. It was an ideal place to leave an ambush patrol to see if the VC would come down from the hills to cut it up and haul it off to supplement their rice rations.

Stars sparkled brightly as the ambush patrol lay patiently in waiting. Soon after midnight, a squad of VC came down and started carving up the buffalo. Sergeant Moody, the patrol leader, keyed his radio handset and, in a barely audible whisper, called for the prearranged artillery barrage, "Redleg, this is Oscar 60 Bravo, concentration 42, fire for effect. Out."

The area around the water buffalo soon exploded as Charlie Battery, 4/42 Artillery rapidly responded to the fire mission. As the dust settled, Sergeant Moody scanned the area through his starlight scope. Four VC lay, unmoving, on the ground. With their mission accomplished, the patrol quietly withdrew and stealthily made their way back to the artillery fire base.

The bodies had been dragged off before the ambush patrol returned to the area at daylight. Drag marks and blood trails indicated the artillery barrage had done significant damage. Not a single rifle shot had been fired.

The patrol was ecstatic as they relaxed inside the safety of the fire base. With that taste of success, they wanted to get some more the next night. Their logic was simple. If they could kill four VC with one dead water buffalo, they should be able to kill a lot more with several.

The next day, the second platoon herded four more water buffalo from the field where they were grazing to the edge of the mountain. An M16 round between the eyes dropped each buffalo in his tracks in a carefully selected ambush site. After dark, four ambush patrols quietly worked their way out of the fire base and took their positions to watch all the likely approaches. Claymore mines were carefully set out in front of each patrol.

The bright starlight of the previous night gave way to clouds. The rains of the approaching monsoon pelted the waiting men as they lay motionless, listening for movement. Daylight found four patrols of wet and miserable soldiers who had lain out all night in a driving rainstorm without seeing a thing. After returning to the fire base, they spent the day resting to be ready to go out and try their luck again.

The weather was more cooperative the next night but the mosquitoes and VC were not. Mosquitoes mercilessly dive bombed the men throughout the night and the VC again stayed away. It was a weary bunch of soldiers who radioed in at daybreak their mission had, again, been unsuccessful.

"It was a good idea, the VC just did not cooperate," Walt Ferguson, the platoon leader, told Captain Fiacco as he recommended calling the mission off. Captain Fiacco agreed with Walt but added, "You are going to have to destroy those buffalo, we can not leave all that meat out there. That is enough food to feed a company of VC for a month."

Walt had a challenge. How could he destroy four water buffalo that weighed close to a ton each? He sure could not pick them up and carry them away. After telling the patrols to hold their positions, Walt keyed his radio handset to call Sergeant Angulo, the mess sergeant.

"Do you have any rat poison?" Walt asked. Surprised at the request, Sergeant Angulo responded, "Sure, but what in the hell do you want rat poison for?" Not wanting to divulge his plan over the radio, Walt responded, "I will tell you when you get here. Just throw a twenty five pound bag on the mess truck when you bring the chow out this morning."

As the mess truck pulled into the fire base, Sergeant Angulo jumped down and quickly hunted down Walt to find out what he planned to do with the rat poison. When Sergeant Angulo heard the plan, he volunteered to go along on the mission to provide his expertise on how to destroy meat.

By the time Walt, Sergeant Angulo, and the rat poison patrol had arrived at the dead water buffalo, the ambush patrols had been busily at work with their machetes. They had learned how thick and tough the hide of a water buffalo is. Despite all their hacking, the four water buffalo were still pretty much intact.

After three nights of ambush and two hours of hacking on the buffalo, the men were anxious to get the mission over and get back to where they could get some rest. They quickly started spreading the white rat poison over the buffalo.

Sergeant Angulo turned to Walt and said, "It's your call, Sir, but that rat poison is not going to do a bit of good like that. You have to get it down deep into the meat, not just on the surface. The first rain will wash all of that away." Walt agreed and told his men to keep hacking so they could really spoil the meat.

Figuring there was surely a faster and easier way to accomplish the mission, one of the men suggested, "Sir, it would be a lot quicker if you let me shoot an M79 grenade round into each buffalo to split it open." That made sense, an M79 grenade packed more of a wallop than a machete. Everyone moved behind a small rise in the ground while the grenadier aimed his M79 at the gut of the first water buffalo.

His shot was right on target. The explosion burst the bloating stomach open but the cry, "Medic!" diverted everyone's attention. They turned to see the grenadier lying on the ground clutching his leg in agony. Even though he was well outside the ten yard bursting radius of the grenade round, a stray fragment had slashed through the air to where he stood some fifty yards away.

"Oscar 6, this is Oscar 60, we need a dust-off, over," was Walt's calm call to Captain Fiacco. Captain Fiacco was in his tent briefing Colonel "Rawhide" Morley when the call came in. Always quick to help his troops, Rawhide told

Sandy, "Jump in my helicopter, we can get there a lot faster than a medevac chopper from Tuy Hoa." Rawhide and Captain Fiacco were quickly on their way to the ambush site to pick up the wounded man.

"He isn't hurt too badly, he just can't walk," Walt shouted over the roar of the helicopter as Captain Fiacco and Rawhide jumped to the ground. Walt's men quickly loaded their wounded comrade on the helicopter.

"What happened, Walt?" Rawhide asked. "And what are all those dead water buffalo doing around here? And what is that white stuff all over them?" As Walt explained his platoon's operation of the past three nights, Rawhide became visibly upset. "Damn, Walt! Don't you know that using poison is against the laws of the Geneva Convention? I can just see my picture on the front page of the Hanoi newspaper under the headline 'American Colonel Uses Rat Poison Against VC'".

Turning to Captain Fiacco, he said, "Sandy, stay out here. I want these water buffalo buried. Now!" And with that, Rawhide got into his helicopter and left to take the wounded man to the aid station.

An infantry company is not equipped to bury four water buffalo in the middle of a hard, dry field. As Sandy and Walt pondered how they were going to accomplish the mission, Sandy radioed Russ Zink, the company executive officer. "Oscar 5, this is Oscar 6. Let's see what you are made of. I need two front end loaders from the engineers out to my position immediately. Out." With a perplexed look on his face, Russ left his tent, jumped into his jeep, and started looking for an engineer unit.

Soon Sandy received a call from Russ, "Mission accomplished. We're on the way, see you in thirty minutes." Fortunately, the position was not too far off Highway #1 and Russ and his convoy of front end loaders made it from the road to the field without any problems and right on schedule.

Rather than bury the buffalo where they lay, in full sight of any potential VC snipers in the hills, Sandy decided to dig a hole behind a tree line which screened the work party from any lurking danger.

Word spread quickly about the mission that was underway. I took a small patrol and walked out to watch the event. Walt still failed to see any humor in what was happening as his platoon provided security for the burial detail. It was late afternoon before the front end loaders dragged the last buffalo across the field and plopped it unceremoniously into the mass grave.

Rawhide got over his anger and agreed that even though Walt's "intentions" were good; his "judgment" was somewhat questionable. Would he have fallen into the same trap, night after night, himself? Even though the VC lived like animals, it did not mean their reasoning processes were not finely honed.

The U.S. government paid the Vietnamese villagers for the dead water buffalo. The wounded man was patched up and returned to his platoon. Walt regained his sense of humor and the second platoon became permanently known as the "Buffalo Hunters".

7 Oct 66

We've moved again but this time it was to a life of ease. We traded places with the First Platoon who has been guarding a pontoon bridge a few miles north of where we were. Our sole mission is to guard the bridge, so we do not have to send out any patrols. We have a machine gun position at each end of the bridge twenty-four hours a day and two men walking on the bridge at night.

My platoon CP is in a house along the river bank. The roof does not leak so we can stay dry when it rains, which is most of the time except for today. There is an old woman and two kids who live in one room of the house. She keeps the place pretty clean and also does our laundry for us. She charges 30 piasters (25 cents) to do a set of fatigues, socks, and underwear.

We give her and all the kids around here the food we do not eat. There are some real cute kids who come around selling Cokes, shining boots, and picking up our trash. They are cleaner and nicer than any others we have run into. I do not mind feeding them and helping them any way we can...

10 Oct 66

... I found out today I am going to a school. I have to fly back to Pleiku tomorrow afternoon. The school starts on 14 October at Cu Chi, the 25th Infantry Division headquarters. From what I understand, it is a two week school on ambush techniques...

11 OCT 66

Greetings from Pleiku. This place has really changed since we left. It has grown a lot since division headquarters is now here. The defense perimeter is complete with five rows of barbed wire fence and concertina wire all around. Quite a change from our first nights sitting in the monsoon rains on the edge of the jungle. You would never know now there ever was any jungle around the camp.

They have started making wooden frames for the tents, complete with screened in windows and wooden floors. There is a good network of roads all over the camp. It has stopped raining and the mud has dried up. The people say it gets cold at night and you have to have a sleeping bag to keep warm. It's 9:00PM now and the air already has a little chill in it, like an early fall day.

12 OCT 66

I damn near froze to death last night! It never entered my mind it would ever get cold over here. Well, it really is not cold (between 50 - 60 degrees, I guess) but it sure did seem cold after spending the previous night sweating on the beach at Tuy Hoa. It is like the fall of the year here at Pleiku. It gets hot during the day but definitely starts cooling off at night.

13 OCT 66

Here I am at ambush school or, as the 25th Infantry Division calls it, "The Lightning Ambush Academy". From the initial looks of things, it is going to be a pretty good school. It will last four and a half days...

I am going to do my best to get in to Saigon when I leave here and head back to Pleiku.

It was a good but uneventful school. I refreshed myself on ambush techniques and enjoyed the opportunity to be a student and not the guy in charge.

19 OCT 66

...We flew by helicopter from Cu Chi to Saigon, en route to Pleiku. We could not get a flight out of Saigon yesterday, so we went to the officer's club on top of the Brink's Hotel for supper. Talk about feeling out of place. We were the only ones in the place in jungle fatigues. They made us check our rifles before we went in. Everyone else was in either khakis or civilian clothes. They live a totally different life in Saigon than we infantrymen do in the field. A female Philippino band provided live entertainment - quite a change from the ambush patrol two nights ago.

It is a good thing I came to Pleiku instead of Tuy Hoa. The company came back the day after I left for Cu Chi and are already securing another position, Highway #19 this time.

It was great talking to you yesterday. I never thought I would get the chance but when I walked by the USO, I jumped at the opportunity. I waited about three hours for my turn but it was well worth the wait. It was so good to hear your voice, I only wish we could have talked longer...

21 OCT 66

As I told you, our company lucked out again and we are guarding another highway. We are under the control of the 1st Squadron, 10th Cavalry (same as a battalion). The task force is divided into three groups consisting of one infantry platoon, one tank platoon (five tanks), and one cavalry platoon in each group.

It is really nice to have all these tanks around. They sure do make you feel secure. The VC are afraid of tanks and will not mess around an area where they are located. Our mission is to secure this area along Highway #19. My platoon sends out one patrol during the day and two ambush patrols at night. There has not been any contact at all since we have been here. I am going out tomorrow on a mounted patrol with two tanks and two Armored Personnel Carriers (APC's).

The enclosed card is the new calling card of my platoon. (See story on "Babcock's Bastard's")...

"BABCOCK'S BASTARDS"
MY PLATOON ROSTER

I was very fortunate to have a platoon of men who became a close knit unit and took intense pride in themselves. An indication of this is the name they gave themselves, "Babcock's Bastards".

The Second platoon had become known as the "Buffalo Hunters" after their episode with the water buffaloes (see chapter by that name). To the best of my knowledge, the First and Weapons platoons never did give themselves a name.

There was a healthy competition between my Third platoon and Walt's Second platoon. We both seemed to get more than our fair share of challenging missions from the company and the battalion.

PFC Wilbur Miller, in my second squad, is the man who gets the credit for naming my platoon. Wilbur had worked for a print shop before being drafted. Unknown to me, he had designed and ordered a platoon calling card from his old boss. One day, a package came in the mail and "Babcock's Bastards" was born and had officially become our name.

The card was the size and format of a playing card. It was a red ace of hearts with the words "Babcock's" printed across the top and "Bastards" printed across the bottom of the card in black. The idea had come from a much publicized news story that came from the 25th Infantry Division, written by war correspondent and author Tom Tiede.

In part, the article said, "Some time ago they had determined the ace of spades, long an ominous symbol in the poker-playing nations of the world, is even more so among some of the enemy. The Viet Cong, they conceived, have a thing about the card and avoid it like a mortar shell."

Rather than do like many units had done and copy the ace of spades idea intact, Wilbur decided the ace of hearts would prove to be just as ominous. To make sure the VC knew who to be afraid of, he added our personalization to it.

From then on, our calling cards were left everywhere we went. The cards were left on dead VC and NVA soldiers, around burned out huts, in bars and brothels, sent home to friends and family, and in various other places around Vietnam.

Later in the year, I had my Dad make engraved, personalized key chains with the logo on the back to give to each of my men. I still have mine and bet the other guys have stuck theirs somewhere in their stockpile of memorabilia.

The original "Babcock's Bastards" with their ranks as of October 1, 1966:

PLATOON HEADQUARTERS -
    First Lieutenant Robert O. Babcock, Platoon Leader
    Staff Sergeant Frank E. Roath, Platoon Sergeant
    Private First Class (PFC) Stanley Cameron, Radio Operator
    PFC Moses Jackson, Medic
    PFC Kennie Nelson, Mortar Forward Observer
    PFC Roy Martinez, Radio Operator for Mortar FO
FIRST SQUAD -
    Staff Sergeant Raul Baez, Squad Leader
    PFC Pete Militano
    PFC Ernest Redin
    PFC Ronald Norton
    PFC Ronald Dixon

Second Squad -
   Spec Fourth Class (SP4) Edward D. Muller, Squad Leader
   PFC Wilbur Miller
   PFC David Padilla
   PFC Jorge Frases
   SP4 Aubrey Thomas
   PFC Ervin McGee
   PFC David Shell
   SP4 Clifford Pfeffer
Third Squad -
   Staff Sergeant James Benge, Squad Leader
   PFC Mark Petrino
   PFC Ralph Duncan
   PFC Charles Marrano
   SP4 Charles Heath
   SP4 Willie Cheatham
   SP4 Danny Hughes
   SP4 William Bukovec
Weapons Squad -
   Sergeant Albert Burruel, Squad Leader
   SP4 Calixtro Espinoza
   PFC Roberto Garza
   PFC Peter Nikulin
   PFC David Harris
   PFC George Benjamin
   PFC Johnny Ross
   PFC Donald Gilbert
   PFC Charles Boswell
   SP4 Paul Metoyer
   PFC Earlie Moore

*Babcock's Bastards luggage tag made by Bob's dad
and sent to all members of Bob's platoon.*

21 OCT 66 (CONT'D)

... I distributed the letters from your class among my men. They all really enjoyed the letters and are writing back. It will probably be a couple of days before they get them all finished but I will mail them ASAP. I will send them to you so you can read them before giving them to the class. I do not think there will be any problem of them writing bad letters. Everyone seems to be really enthusiastic about writing. Please send me a roster of all the members of your class so I can be sure we write letters to all of them. (See story on "Pen Pals")...

... Have you sent Playboy to me yet? I never have gotten the October issue. Please send it and the November issue as soon as you can. Everyone in the platoon looks forward to seeing it...

25 Oct 66

... I have been on a couple of patrols. It is still raining off and on all the time. This is the wettest dry season I have ever seen (of course it is the only dry season I have ever seen). It seems the rain is just following us around the country.

Let me tell you about a little almost morbid entertainment we have been having. The stretch of Highway #19 we are securing is at the bottom of a small hill. The road comes around a curve just as it starts down the hill. Our tanks and APC's have been crossing the highway and leaving a lot of slick, red mud on the highway.

The Vietnamese come rounding the curve and start down the hill in their little three wheeled Lambretta's or overloaded trucks, hit the wet mud, and start sliding all over the place. We sit at the bottom of the hill and watch it like you would a demolition derby. So far no one has been hurt. I am sure we are not doing anything to improve the relationship between our two countries but it does make a great spectator sport.

Rest assured, we did not put the mud on the road on purpose, it can not be avoided, and we do not have any way to clean it up.

My candle has burned out and my flashlight batteries are about gone so I had better draw this to a close...

28 Oct 66

I am tired! My platoon went on a patrol today and we climbed one of the steepest mountains I have ever seen. It seems like we were climbing uphill all day long. I wonder why it seems as if it is uphill both ways...

PEN PALS

An Army reporter interviewed me and wrote the following story which appeared in several Stateside newspapers:

GIs AND KIDS BOTH ENJOY LETTER IDEA

Plei Djereng, Vietnam – "I don't know how to write to a brave man, but I'll try," was the beginning of a letter to 1st Lieutenant Robert O. Babcock of Company B, 1st Battalion, 22nd Infantry.

It is typical of many letters Lieutenant Babcock and the men of the 4th Infantry Division receive regularly from junior high school students in Topeka, Kansas. Lieutenant Babcock's wife, Phyllis, thought the letter writing would be an interesting current events project for the seventh grade class she teaches.

After a few blind letters, written by the students to "anyone" in the company, many warm friendships were formed.

Now on a first name basis with the kids they write, many of the men send examples of Chieu Hoi leaflets, post cards, and local money. In addition, Lieutenant Babcock sends color slides of the men who write. Other items such as Montagnard crossbows have also been mailed to the students.

"These kids are really curious," he says, "and are always asking questions."

"How does it feel to be at war?" and "Sleep on the ground?" or, as one puts it, "What do C rashons taste like?" are typical questions.

Although the reality of Vietnam has taken much of the glamour out of war, Lieutenant Babcock remembers when he was a kid. "I used to think 'boy an Army man's really something, fighting in a war' so I appreciate the feeling behind the letters."

The students, in turn, have expressed their own enthusiasm by starting a bulletin board full of memorabilia from Vietnam.

According to Lieutenant Babcock, "It's a good morale builder for us and a good current events project for them. Another boy wrote and asked if he could start a similar program in his Scout troop."

While reading one of the letters, Lieutenant Babcock summed up his feelings about the project and the kids, "I think it makes them glad they're Americans," he said.

29 Oct 66

I would give anything in the world if we were together tonight. I need to have you to talk to. We had our first accident today. Specialist 4 Thomas, my man from the West Indies, caught a piece of shrapnel from an M-79 grenade in his left eye. They were out on patrol and were firing into a VC bunker when the fragment hit him. They brought him back to our position and we called in medevac to take him to the hospital. We are afraid he might lose his eye. It really made me sick. It was just a freak accident that could not be helped but it is terrible. He is without a doubt one of the best men in the battalion. I am certain he will not be back so we will just have to do without him.

Tomorrow we are moving again. We are going back under the control of our own battalion. I do not know what they are doing now. I think they are working as the reserve battalion for the brigade west of Pleiku. I do not know whether we will go directly from here to them or if we will stop by base camp. I might not get to write for awhile until we get reorganized but I will write again as soon as I can...

1 Nov 66

While I am waiting to make my next move, I will try to scratch out another letter to let you know what is happening. We are operating west of Pleiku toward the Cambodian border. We went from our mission of securing Highway #19 back to base camp about noon on Sunday. We were scheduled to come out here early yesterday morning.

At 8:30 Sunday night, just as I was starting to write you, we got word to move out immediately. We were to move 30 miles southwest of our base camp to reinforce the Special Forces camp at Plei Me. (See story on "Relief of Plei Me").

RELIEF OF PLEI ME

October 31, 1966 was not only the day before pay day, it was one of the few days the troops had had off since we arrived in Vietnam on August 6. I am not sure anyone even remembered it was also Halloween. Most of the troops and NCOs had spent the afternoon at "Dodge City", the US government inspected bar and brothel district that had sprung up outside the Fourth Infantry Division's base camp at Dragon Mountain.

By suppertime, a large number of the troops and NCOs were "feeling no pain" as they prepared to spend one of the few nights of their tour in a tent, sleeping on a cot. Tales of their exploits in "Dodge City" were exaggerated by the drunken state many found themselves in.

My platoon was loud and boisterous as they proclaimed their presence had been made known in every bar and whorehouse in "Dodge City". Their "Babcock's Bastards" calling cards had been tacked up in a prominent place in every establishment they visited.

No one was prepared for the mission we were about to get when Captain Fiacco was urgently called to battalion headquarters. "Get the troops saddled up and ready to move out in an hour. Have the platoon leaders in my tent for a briefing in ten minutes," was the message he called back to the company.

You can imagine the disbelief and disgruntled comments coming from the entire company when First Sergeant MacDonald sent runners to all the platoon areas to alert them to the upcoming mission. However, as good infantrymen, they started checking their weapons and ammunition to be sure they were ready for whatever faced them.

"What's up, Sir?" was our first question when Captain Fiacco walked into his tent where the four platoon leaders were assembled. "We are going to Plei Me," was his reply. "The Special Forces camp has strong intelligence reports they are going to be attacked by an NVA regiment tonight. We're going down to help them out."

"When do we fly out?" was our next question. "We are not flying," was the unexpected response. "We are going to ride down there on 'deuce and a halfs' (two and a half ton trucks). We will be accompanied by B Troop of the Tenth Cavalry plus a battery of 155 millimeter self propelled howitzers..." Then he explained the rest of the mission.

Plei Me. We had all heard of it. What we knew did not give us a good feeling. Plei Me was one of the Special Forces camps that had made national news in the days before America had committed large troop forces in Vietnam.

Only a year earlier, in October 1965, it had survived a several week siege with a handful of Special Forces troops and a unit of Montagnard irregulars who had been mortared and attacked incessantly by a large NVA force.

(General Norman Schwartzkopf, of Desert Storm fame, had been an advisor to the South Vietnamese Ranger battalion who had come to the aid of the beleaguered outpost. Peter Arnett, then an AP reporter who later reported on Desert Storm from Baghdad, was also in the relief unit.)

It was also close to the area in the Ia Drang valley where the First Cavalry Division (Airmobile) had suffered heavy casualties in the first large scale battle of the war in November of 1965. The relaxation we had enjoyed all that day quickly gave way to deep feelings of concern.

I tried not to show my concern as I assembled my squad leaders to brief them on what lay ahead. It had long been my belief to tell my squad leaders everything I knew - a belief not universally accepted by other platoon leaders. (Many people thought soldiers only needed to be told what to do and did not need to be filled in on the background or why of the orders. In the event of capture, troops can not divulge what they do not know. My belief was (and still is) people work better when they know why they are doing it. The risk of divulging information to the enemy was less a concern to me than keeping my troops informed.)

"Plei Me is about thirty miles southwest of here off Highway 14. B Troop of the Tenth Cavalry will lead the way with their tanks. We will follow in trucks. B Troop's armored personnel carriers will be mixed in with our column to give us some additional armored protection in the event of an ambush. We will travel under blackout conditions. As things develop, we will be given further orders..."

I answered as best I could the questions the squad leaders and Sergeant Roath asked. "Travel light but be sure everyone has plenty of ammo. The trucks should be here shortly so go get your people ready."

It was pitch dark as the troops loaded into the trucks. I climbed into the cab of our platoon's lead truck to ride "shotgun". It eased my mind a little as I noted the floorboard had been covered with sandbags. That would, hopefully, absorb much of the blast if we hit a mine on the road. All of the canvas had been taken off the trucks so nothing would impede our visibility or get in our way if we had to make a rapid exit. The troops, as they had been trained, sat facing outward, ready to react to anything that happened.

The tanks, armored personnel carriers, and self propelled howitzers joined our column as we exited the main gate and safety of our base camp. Damn, I did not want to do this. Riding the roads in Vietnam was undesirable in daylight, doing it at night under these circumstances seemed like a sure way to get into trouble.

Stars sparkled brightly in the clear sky but there was no moon to brighten the night. The silhouette of the armored personnel carrier in front of us was barely visible except for the dim red blackout lights that showed like cat's eyes to mark its position. Nothing was on the road except for us as the relief column moved slowly toward Plei Me.

My mind was alert and my body tense as we moved through the darkness. The driver's eyes strained forward as he followed the pinpoints of light in front of us, making sure we did not get too close or lag too far behind. It was really a helpless feeling sitting in the truck not knowing what was in store. I did not know whether to worry more about a possible ambush along the road or to worry about the "large NVA force" that supposedly waited for us around Plei Me.

The column stopped frequently as it snaked through the night. Each time we stopped, several of the troops jumped off to relieve themselves of the beer they had consumed all afternoon. We were under radio silence orders so we had no idea why we were stopping. The absence of gunfire let us know no one had been ambushed yet. That did not relieve my tension as I peered out into the darkness along the side of the road. After several hours of stop and go movement, we began to see the flash and hear the rumble of artillery fire in the distance.

Occasionally we heard the drone of jet fighters overhead. The brighter, longer lasting flashes as they dropped napalm and the louder rumble as they dropped their thousand pound bombs gave us a strong indication something big was going on ahead of us. Radio silence was still in effect so we could only guess what was happening.

It was almost BMNT (Beginning of Morning Nautical Twilight or, as civilians call it, the first light of dawn) as my radio crackled to life with the first message of the night. We were pulling off the road and were to create a defensive perimeter around our attached artillery unit. The artillery fire we had been hearing throughout the night had eased up except for an occasional explosion that now had a more distinct roar. We were obviously getting very close to our objective.

As the early morning light eased away the darkness, we could see the Plei Me Special Forces camp across the mist covered valley. It sat on a small hill about one thousand yards away and was surrounded by rows of barbed wire. There was no sign of activity, either inside the camp or in the countryside around it.

As the light burned away the mist, the terrain came more into focus. The entire area around the camp was pock marked from the untold number of artillery shells and bombs that had exploded during the night and in the months and years before. The yellow and red South Vietnamese flag was clearly visible flying from the flagpole in the center of the camp.

Captain Fiacco assembled the platoon leaders around his jeep that served as his mobile command post and told us what was going on. An all night artillery barrage had been fired around the camp by both American and South Vietnamese artillery units. Bombing attacks had added to the wall of steel and fire created by the artillery.

No NVA troops had dared brave the constant bombardment. Montagnard patrols had uncovered no signs of enemy activity. Before calling off the alert, additional patrols were being sent out from the Special Forces camp. We were to stand by with the artillery, ready to go help them if we were needed.

As we stood around contemplating the situation, we noticed a number of Montagnard children moving toward us. Unlike the Vietnamese children we had run into at Tuy Hoa and Pleiku, we felt comfortable with the presence of the Montagnard kids. They ranged in age from toddlers up to kids who were probably ten or twelve. Knowing they had lived through a lot more war than we had, we all felt a strong compassion for them.

As they came into our perimeter, we kept our eyes on them but quickly did what all GI's in all wars have done - we responded to their warm smiles and started giving them food and other things we dug out of our rucksacks.

Sergeant Reynolds, the acting weapons platoon leader, started using American ingenuity to bring even brighter smiles to the kids' faces. With his pocket knife, he cut neck and arm holes in empty sand bags and put them on the kids. Before long, he had a line of kids waiting to be outfitted in one of the fashionable GI sandbag dresses.

As several of the troops started helping him bring smiles to the kids' faces, I thought of the irony of the whole situation. We had driven all night long expecting to get into a major battle at any minute and instead, here we stood making sand bag dresses for a bunch of kids who were having the time of their lives.

The sun was beating down fiercely when we got word from the Special Forces camp their patrols had still not found anything. Our mission was cancelled and we loaded back into the trucks for the ride back to base camp. The trip back was uneventful and non stop. But, our night of sleeping on cots in the relative safety of base camp was not to be. Later that day, we loaded into trucks again and headed west to the Special Forces camp at Plei Djereng to start our participation in Operation Paul Revere IV.

(Twenty years later, when I met two of my men in Connecticut, this experience came up in our conversation. I remembered how scared I was all that night. It really surprised me to hear both of them say they were not scared at all. They did not know where we were going, why we were doing it, and had not really cared. They just did what they were told, and tried to get as much sleep as they could during the all night truck ride. They left the rest of it to their leaders. The first they knew of the purpose of our mission was when I told them that night twenty years later).

SFC Reynolds making sandbag dresses for Montagnard kids

1 NOV 66 (CONT'D)

... When we got back to base camp, we got paid, loaded back in trucks, and headed west to the brigade forward base camp. It is about thirty miles northwest of Pleiku and five miles south of the Special Forces camp at Plei Djereng.

We got in there late this afternoon and then moved about five miles farther west to an artillery position that Alpha Company was securing. Luckily, they realized we had not slept the night before so we got to sleep all night while they guarded the perimeter.

Later... We have moved again, this time about a mile and a half farther west, securing the same artillery battery. Tomorrow we are going to move out about five miles from the Cambodian border and start on Operation Paul Revere IV.

This will be a real large operation. All three battalions in our brigade and two from the 25th Infantry Division will be sweeping north. Letter writing time will be limited so please bear with me if I do not get to write as often as I have been doing.

2 Nov 66

... On this operation there will be about 5,000 American troops in the area with another 10,000 on call from the First Cavalry Division (Airmobile). There is no way in hell the North Vietnamese Army (NVA) can have enough power to give us much trouble.

You would not believe how much artillery and air power we have supporting us. We will probably get shot at but we are smart enough and good enough to handle whatever they throw our way without getting hurt. Captain Fiacco is the best company commander in the business, I am pretty damn good at what I do, and my platoon is great. When you hear about contact with the enemy, do not think it is always me involved...

I will close for now. Keep writing me and I will do the same whenever possible. I do not have any idea how long this operation will last. We are starting now to do what we were sent over here to do. Remember I am always thinking of you.

The next day we flew to the Cambodian border and started the next phase of my year in Vietnam - Operation Paul Revere IV, a two month long search and destroy mission through dense jungle forests.

Just before we boarded helicopters to start our combat assault to begin
Operation Paul Revere IV – 3 November 1966

SECTION FOUR

Operation Paul Revere IV - In The Jungle

November 3, 1966 - December 31, 1966

OPERATION PAUL REVERE IV
11/3/66 TO 12/31/66

Like the section on "Tuy Hoa & Highway Security", this section is a collection of the letters I wrote to Phyllis and my parents while I was living through the time period described. Also included is a collection of short stories describing key events of that period.

Operation Paul Revere IV, a division sized operation, was designed to search for and destroy the North Vietnamese Army regulars who had infiltrated down the Ho Chi Minh trail through Laos and Cambodia.

This two month period probably has created as many strong memories and done more to shape my ability to lead men (and subsequently women) than any other time in my life.

Time constraints did not allow me to write as often as I had written during the earlier part of my tour, but I still tried to level with Phyllis as much as possible on my feelings and what I was experiencing during what, until this stage, had been the most dangerous part of my tour.

All of the letters are to Phyllis unless otherwise noted.

4 Nov 66

I'll bet you didn't expect to hear from me again this soon. We have moved to a fire base and are waiting to move out on foot tomorrow morning on Operation Paul Revere IV. The area we will be moving through was saturated with artillery barrages and B52 bomb strikes just before we came out here. As it looks now, we will be moving north about ten miles during the operation trying to find anything in the area. It should take two weeks, more or less.

7 Nov 66

Alpha Company got hit the other day and Lieutenant Dick Collins was killed. I really hated to hear about it. (See story on "Trust the Dog")...

We are going great out here in the jungle. We had some excitement our first night out and have found some abandoned base camp positions. (See story on "They Said What?")...

Today is the first day we have had a chopper landing zone. They have been dropping our C-rations to us. We had to chop down trees for two hours to get an LZ but it was worth it to get hot chow for a change.

10 Nov 66

We are still plugging along here in the wilderness. We travel about 1500 yards a day as an average. We found an old Montagnard man, woman, and boy out here one day and some more abandoned NVA base camps. (See story on the "The Old Man and Old Woman")...

TRUST THE DOG

Our first experience working with Army scout dogs had been while securing Highway 19 east of Pleiku. After working with them and their handlers, we became strong believers in their ability to sniff out the enemy. With this background, I was delighted to have a scout dog working with us as we started into the jungle on the first day of Operation Paul Revere IV. I felt certain we would be running into seasoned NVA troops and any edge we could get was fine with me.

We were all more than a little apprehensive as we left the assumed safety of the battalion fire base and started on our search and destroy mission through the dense, twisted jungle. My platoon had been given the dubious "honor" of being the point platoon. We saddled up and started moving into the jungle, the dog and his handler leading the way, followed closely by our point squad.

I wondered what made a man volunteer to be a dog handler. I knew our platoon would be rotating between point and further to the rear of the column each day. He and his dog would be in the lead day after day after day.

We had moved without incident through the morning and into the early afternoon. The rough terrain and heavy load we carried had us sweating profusely, forcing frequent rest stops. As the month progressed, we would be in better shape for the rugged terrain and load. But, on this day, we were just plain tired as we moved cautiously through the virgin jungle.

About mid afternoon, the dog stopped and perked up its ears. His handler immediately dropped to the ground and pulled the dog down with him. He motioned for the point squad to come forward to see what the dog had sensed.

The adrenalin pumping through my body made my ears feel as though two bass drums were dueling. I moved up close to the dog and waited for Sergeant Benge's point squad to check out the area. Were we going to fight our first NVA today?

"Oscar 61, this is Oscar 6. What's the delay? Over." came crackling over the radio.

"This is 61, the dog has spotted something, we're checking it out, I'll keep you informed. Out." was my reply. As the point squad returned, they each reported nothing out of the ordinary had been seen. We started to move forward again, this time with even more caution.

Fifteen minutes later, the dog alerted again. The handler dropped immediately with the dog and once again motioned the point squad forward. As the squad moved out, I again got a call from Oscar 6.

"Oscar 61, this is Oscar 6. Have you found anything? Over."

"This is 61, negative. I will keep you informed. Out." The point squad returned and again reported finding no trace of enemy activity. Cautiously, we continued our advance. We had not been moving five minutes when the dog alerted again. The same procedure was repeated as my point man led the point squad past the dog to find out what was causing his alert.

Again, the radio crackled. This time I could sense a tone of impatience as Captain Fiacco spoke. "Oscar 61, this is 6. We have got to get moving. We need to make another 400 yards so we can have a good spot to stop for the night. Let me know what's wrong. Over."

"6, this is 61. I am checking things out as quickly as I can. I will keep you informed. Out." Once again, the point squad found nothing. We had barely started to move when the dog handler went down again as his dog alerted. After the last alert, I had changed point squads. A fresh squad moved forward to check the area to our front.

"61, this is 6. Cut out the delay, we have got to move so we can set up for the night! Over." I was starting to feel the pressure as I debated with myself whether to listen to the dog or ignore him and go on without checking out his alert.

"This is 61, we are checking it out as fast as we can. We will be moving shortly. Out." For the fourth time in less than an hour, the point squad came back without having found a trace of anything. Again the column moved forward. After moving another fifty yards, the dog alerted once more. I had moved up closer to the front of the column to watch the dog. I could see the visible alerting of his ears and head as his senses picked up something.

For the fifth time, we dropped to the ground and the point squad advanced to check it out. Sergeant Roath, my platoon sergeant, accompanied them to insure they were not missing anything. The voice on the radio came immediately. "61, move out! Quit stopping! That's an order! Out!"

The first thing that came to my mind was we were in a combat zone. The penalty was severe for disregarding a direct order under combat conditions. "What you gonna do now, Lieutenant?" flashed through my mind.

It was a terse voice that crackled over the radio waves as my reply went back. "6, this is 61. If you want to run this unit, come on up and run it. If not, I will continue to make the decisions. When we move! When we stop! I am checking the dog's alert! Out." The point squad and Sergeant Roath again found nothing.

I was very concerned as we started to move forward. I had gotten no reply from my response to Captain Fiacco. I knew the other platoons had heard it on their radios. I was sweating, not entirely from the heat or the NVA that seemed to be staying just out of our reach, but what awaited me when we finally stopped for the night.

We moved up a hill and I radioed back to Captain Fiacco, "Oscar 6, this is Oscar 61. I am on a good place to set up for the night. Do you want to stop? Over." His reply was curt, "Affirmative, secure the area and I will move the rest of the people up to your position. Out."

As we set about digging foxholes and cutting trees to build bunkers and clear fields of fire, I was still very worried about the consequences I expected from Captain Fiacco. Disregarding a direct order was bad, saying what I had said over the radio was much worse. But I was convinced I had done the right thing.

As Captain Fiacco came around to check the progress of the work on the defensive perimeter, he motioned for me to come away from the men I was with and talk to him. "Here it comes," I thought.

"Bob, I got a little tough on you this afternoon. I was in a hurry. You did the right thing. Thanks for standing up to me." Man, was I relieved to hear those words! Sandy had shown one of the character traits that made him such a great leader. If I had had any questions before, I knew then I was working with a man who had the welfare of his troops always in the front of his mind.

Two days later, the dog and handler were working with Alpha Company. Lieutenant Dick Collins, the West Point officer who had beaten my platoon in the platoon tests at Fort Lewis, was dealing with a similar situation where the dog kept alerting frequently.

As he, his point squad leader, and the dog handler were talking about what to do, they were all three killed by an NVA ambush. The dog was not hurt. I still shudder as I wonder what would have happened to us if I had not trusted the dog.

Richard Collins' name is engraved on panel 12E, line 27 on the Vietnam Memorial Wall in Washington, D. C.

One of the dogs we worked with, not the one involved in this story

"THEY SAID WHAT?"

It was our first night in the jungles along the Cambodian border. Even though we had been in country for three months, we still felt green and scared in this new environment. Our previous work had been against the Viet Cong, now we would be facing the North Vietnamese Army (NVA) regular troops who had traveled down the Ho Chi Minh trail. We knew they were better trained, better disciplined, and better equipped than the VC.

To heighten our concern on that first night of Operation Paul Revere IV, we had been working with the dog that had kept alerting all afternoon. There had to be something out there the dog was sensing. Our movement had been slowed as we checked out the terrain each time the dog alerted. By the time we finally stopped for the night, evening was approaching and we had not had as much time to build good, strong bunkers and clear fields of fire as was to become the norm for us.

We kept working to improve our positions as the day's light began to disappear. As dusk was about to turn into darkness, Captain Fiacco called us on the radio. "Oscar, this is Oscar 6. Make sure everyone is in his bunker. I'm about to adjust in the def-cons."

We all knew that "def-cons" was short for "defensive concentrations" of artillery. By pre- registering the def-cons, the artillery knew where to fire if we were attacked. Def-cons filled all the likely avenues of attack and also covered the low spots in the terrain where the enemy could hide and not be hit by direct rifle or machinegun fire.

Methodically, he and his artillery and mortar forward observers adjusted the 105mm artillery fire and 4.2 inch and 81mm mortar fire until it fell in a nice iron curtain around our perimeter. This became an every night ritual throughout the remainder of Paul Revere IV.

"Oscar, this is Oscar 6. All's clear. Make sure everyone eats and then let me know when your listening posts are going out."

Most of the men had already eaten their C-rations while on break from their bunker digging chores. Hacking through the jungle, carrying all our worldly possessions on our backs was back breaking work. Add digging foxholes and chopping down trees to make strong bunkers and you have a recipe for ravenous troops. Even C-rations had the flair of a seven course dinner.

Several of the men moved forward of the bunker line to set out claymore mines. Like the def-cons, this became a nightly ritual. We always set up claymores in depth.

There were three claymores in front of each bunker, staggered at distances from approximately five yards on out to twenty-five yards in front of our positions. Trip flares were rigged on some to alert us if the NVA tried to crawl up and turn the claymores around to fire at us rather than toward the enemy approaches.

The men took great care in making sure that everything was set just right before they returned to the bunkers. We were not in VC territory any longer, we were in NVA territory and nothing was left to chance.

As full darkness settled in, we sent our listening posts out. Listening posts (LP) consisted of three or four men with a radio and several claymores.

They went out in front of our perimeter along the most likely avenues of approach to listen for the enemy and give us early warning if anyone tried to sneak up on us during the night. Each platoon typically sent out one LP in front of its defensive sector. It was not good duty but everyone had to do it when his turn came. It gave a great sense of security to know someone was out front to give advance warning of an NVA attack.

When a listening post confirmed they heard NVA, they could blow their claymore mines and high tail it back to the perimeter, or lay low and hope they were not seen or heard. The decision was up to the LP leader.

All was quiet for about an hour when the jungle night was shattered with a loud, "F**K YOU". Everyone immediately tensed up and scrambled for their bunkers, not believing what we had just heard.

My listening post was the first one to break radio silence, "Oscar 61, this is Oscar 61 Bravo, did you hear what we just heard? Over." "I sure did. Stay quiet and be alert. Let us know if you hear any movement. Out." I had already heard the other platoons call Captain Fiacco on the company radio net to report what they had heard.

"F**K YOU," came the sound again. My adrenalin was pumping full speed. I knew the NVA were better than the VC but I did not think they were so good they would stand out in the jungle and taunt us in English.

"Oscar 61 Bravo, this is Oscar 61. Do you hear any movement? Over." "Negative. Where are they yelling from? Can we come in? Over." "Stay where you are. I will advise. Out."

Rather than add to the already high level of radio traffic, I crawled out of my bunker and half ran, half crawled to Captain Fiacco's command bunker 25 yards away.

"What in the world do you think they are doing?" I asked Sandy, hoping he could shed some light on what was scaring my men and me to death. He was as bewildered and concerned as we were as we heard another, "F**K YOU," come out of the jungle.

"Babcock, bring your listening post in. Harry, call the other platoons and tell them to bring in their LP's. Let me know when everyone is in. We're going to put some firepower out there. And do not let anyone fire his weapon or give away his position. Keep everyone alert and in his bunker."

I scrambled back to my bunker and called my listening post in. It took no time for them to come thrashing up through the jungle thickets.

As they neared the perimeter, you could hear a loud whisper with the challenge, "Green!" "Bean," came the whispered password as the men crashed through the perimeter and flung themselves into the bunkers along the platoon front. I reported to Captain Fiacco that they were safely in and soon heard reports the other LP's were also in.

I could hear Captain Fiacco calling the battalion fire base. "This is Oscar 6. We have bad guys around us. Request a fire mission, over."

"How many and where are they?" came the reply. "I don't know how many or where they are, they're hollering at us. I need a fire mission, over."

"What are they saying? Over." came the reply. "They said 'F**k You.' Now quit asking questions and get me some fire out here, over." "Say again. They said what?" was the astonished reply.

"F**k you!. Damn it, get some artillery fire going out here! NOW! Fire the def-cons! Out."

Soon the welcome sound of artillery shells whistling through the air and exploding around us filled the jungle. We all stayed hunkered down in our bunkers and peered out into the darkness waiting for the inevitable attack.

The safeties were taken off the claymore charger handles. Rifles and machine guns were checked to make sure rounds were in the chambers and ready to fire. A curtain of steel was exploding around our perimeter as we continued to wait in anxious anticipation.

Finally, the artillery fire stopped and silence engulfed the jungle night once more. The NVA still had not attacked. Maybe the artillery fire had worked. It should have. It was hard to see how anyone or anything could have lived through that bombardment.

After what seemed like an eternity peering out into the darkness, listening for any sound of movement, I once again crawled up to the command post bunker to talk to Captain Fiacco.

"Keep your troops on 50% alert. Send your listening posts back out. Let me know if you hear anything," were Sandy's instructions to the platoon leaders.

Keeping our troops on 50% alert was not a problem. Getting the listening posts to go back out could have been. But, the troops responded like the true professionals they were and moved back out into the darkness.

If any one of the more than 120 men we had with us that night got more than fifteen minutes sleep, it was highly unusual. We lay awake all night long, looking, listening, and wondering what kind of monsters the NVA were that would scream at us saying, "F**K YOU." They had to be some kind of tough fighting men!

Only men who have lived through combat can understand how happy we were to see daylight. The listening posts came in at first light. Each platoon sent a squad sized patrol out to check the area in front of its position. None of the patrols found anything except a lot of leaves and branches that had been blown down by the intense artillery firepower.

We kept outposts outside the perimeter as we broke camp and prepared to move out on our next day's trek through the jungle. Caution was our byword as we cleared out of our night position and started plowing through virgin jungle forests again.

After moving all morning, we were more than happy to stop for a lunch and rest break. After security was posted, the rest of the troops leaned up against trees or plopped down on the ground to catch a few winks of sleep to make up for the sleepless night. As we rested there in the jungle, we heard it again. "F**K YOU."

This time we found the culprit immediately. Perched on the side of a tree next to one of our men was a little green lizard. From then on we ignored the sound of the Vietnamese F**k You lizard. We heard its cry many times in the weeks and months ahead. Never again did it bring fear into the hearts of so many men as it did that first night in the jungle.

The Old Man and
Old Woman

For the second week, our search and destroy mission moved through the dense, triple canopied Vietnamese jungle. The area had been declared a "free fire zone" by the South Vietnamese government. Several months earlier, they had warned all their citizens to get out of this area. Anyone left was to be considered enemy.

Cautiously, we moved down a slope, toward one of the many small streams we crossed each day. The small trail we were following made us stay more alert than if we had been moving through untracked jungle. My platoon was the point platoon and, as always, I was positioned behind my lead squad.

Three rapid rifle shots from Ernie Redin, my point man, ruptured the jungle calm. Without thinking, our instincts drove us to the ground as we quickly scanned the jungle around us. Was this going to be our first fight with the NVA? Half crawling, half crouching, I moved to the front of the column to see what was happening. Quiet again engulfed the jungle.

Ernie was pointing his rifle at an old Montagnard man and woman standing by the stream with their hands in the air. Sergeant Benge had moved the rest of his squad up to form a hasty skirmish line on either side of Ernie. "What's up?" I asked Ernie. "A Montagnard boy ran up that hill when he saw me. I fired at him but don't think I hit him", was his reply. "How big was he? Did you see anyone else?" I asked. "I would guess he was about twelve and I didn't see anyone else."

As I radioed the information back to Captain Fiacco, I sent the point squad across the stream and up the hill to see what they could find. They cautiously worked their way up the hill, alert to any sign of an enemy ambush. I led the old man and old woman back to where the rest of my platoon had formed a defensive perimeter. We waited to see if our squad found the boy, or anything else.

The squad soon returned, having found nothing. In the meantime, our Vietnamese interpreter, Sergeant Quann, was trying to question the captives. As Montagnards, they had their own language and did not speak Vietnamese. (The nomadic Montagnard tribes roamed the highlands of Vietnam, living a very primitive, almost prehistoric existence. They were frequently discriminated against by the Vietnamese).

None of us, including Sergeant Quann, understood their jabbering, punctuated with a lot of pointing in the way the boy had run. Looks of anguish clouded their faces.

The old woman's teeth were stained from the beetle nuts that were chewed by so many of the Montagnards. (It had a numbing effect on the gums and helped ease the pain from bad teeth that had never seen a toothbrush or dentist).

They were a pathetic site, old and weak, scared to death, and obviously not a threat to anyone. We were not so sure about the boy who had run away, however.

They caused us a real dilemma. It was mid-afternoon and we needed to get moving to find a defensive position for the night. The man and woman were too old and slow to be able to move with us and keep up. The thick, triple canopied jungle precluded us getting a helicopter in to take them out. And, they had been with a fighting aged boy who ran away when he saw us coming. What were our options?

Though Captain Fiacco had the ultimate decision, I talked our options over with him. The obvious thing was to shoot them and move on. The

Vietnamese government had said that anything in this area could be considered to be enemy. They had been with a healthy boy, old enough to lead enemy troops to us, who had run away. That option was immediately dismissed. They were, at worst case, now our prisoners of war and protected by the Geneva Convention.

We also could have moved them with us, knowing that it would slow us down. If they were innocent civilians, we would have left the young boy out in the jungle to fend for himself and that option did not appeal to us. Since the jungle was so thick, cutting a helicopter landing zone would have been impossible. Our only other choice was to let them go.

Sandy and I concluded they were innocent civilians and, hopefully, were not going to hurt anyone. And, we really did not like the idea of leaving that boy out there in the jungle by himself. So, we decided to let them go.

As I gave the command to saddle up and move out, they looked very confused when we started to move out and left them standing there. We veered off from the trail and took a different route towards what looked like a good hill to set up on for the night. All our senses were alert as we resumed our movement through the jungle.

A squad from the second platoon stayed a little further behind than rear security would normally stay, just to make sure nothing moved in behind us. They radioed, "The old man and old woman are following us." Sandy radioed back, "Fire a few warning shots into the air and try to scare them off." The warning shots worked and we moved on out of their sight.

As we moved up the hill to prepare our nightly defensive position, we posted security outposts on all sides. Our nightly artillery and mortar defensive concentrations were registered especially close to our perimeter. It was a restless night; none of us were comfortable we were not still being followed. Staying awake was easy when it was your turn to be on guard duty.

As the last shadows of night disappeared, and the first waves of daylight started to creep into our perimeter, we breathed a collective sigh of relief. Before we started breaking down our defensive positions, patrols swept the surrounding area in search of ambushes that might have been set up around us during the night. Nothing was found. Fully aware that a unit is most vulnerable when it first starts moving, we moved out with extra caution. (The troops tend to be clustered together and confusion seems to be the norm.)

We continued with our habit of filling in the bunkers so they could not be used by the enemy at a later time. That was good for the future, but it did not give us any retreat options if we were hit as we moved out.

By noon, we were convinced nothing was going to come from our encounter with the old man and old woman. We had put quite a distance between us and the spot where we had left them. We started to breathe easier.

I have often thought about that incident. It never crossed my mind to shoot them. I'm sure Captain Fiacco felt the same way. When someone was armed and capable of hurting us, it was a different story. But, when we had taken away the means to fight and had them as a captive, my heart always went out to them with compassion as a human being. I could only guess how frightened they must have been.

And, I also wonder how I would have handled it later in life if either Sandy or I had decided to shoot them. I am sure there are veterans of all wars, not just Vietnam, who have had to live with decisions made under adverse circumstances.

Much has been written about the atrocities, real or alleged, that were committed by our servicemen during the Vietnam war. Fortunately, I was never a party to, nor a witness of, any of the things that the press seemed to think made good news stories.

I firmly believe there are more stories similar to the one I have written than there are of the headline grabbing spectacles that the press corps so frequently pounced on. The way we conducted ourselves on this occasion makes me very proud of Sandy Fiacco and of myself. I am sure most of our comrades would have made the same decision. It would have been difficult to live with any decision other than the one we made that day.

The beginning of Operation Paul Revere IV – fortunately it was a cold LZ

10 NOV 66 (CONT'D)

We should finish our mission in four or five days unless they extend our area of operation. Time goes pretty fast out here so I guess I'd just as soon be here as any place else in Vietnam.

The unit that was hit with the human wave attacks a couple of weeks ago was C Company, 2nd Battalion of the 8th Infantry Regiment. They killed 54 NVA by body count and probably killed twice that many. They lost seven of their own men killed and many wounded. I do not think this could happen to us the way we set up every night.

We always stop before 3:00 in the afternoon to dig foxholes and build good, strong, heavy bunkers. This is what our defensive perimeter looks like:

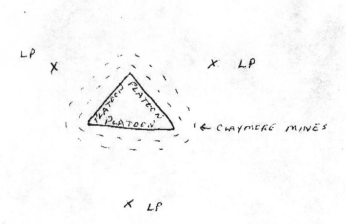

By setting up in a triangular defensive position, we have maximum firepower aimed at the most likely avenues of approach. We always put out at least three listening posts to cover the best routes of approach for an NVA attack.

I got my November Playboy yesterday. I never did get the October issue but I read someone else's.

We are cutting an LZ this morning so we can get a helicopter in to take out a couple of guys who are sick.

11 Nov 66

Surprise again! We are holding in position at the LZ we prepared yesterday and are sending out small squad sized patrols today and tomorrow. It is a welcome relief to get to stay in one place and rest up a little.

Alpha Company got hit again last night. They were hit by mortars about 7:00 and then were hit by a ground attack, which they repelled. The report we heard today is they lost two men killed and fourteen wounded. They killed quite a few NVA and captured two. It seems they are not stopping early enough to get into good, dug-in positions before dark. They are also moving real slow and on low ground where it is easy to be trailed.

P.S. I guess the NVA have not gone back to Cambodia like I thought a few days ago.

12 Nov 66 - (Letter written to my folks)

Happy Birthday, Jim! I am thinking about you on your birthday even though I am not in a place to celebrate with you.

We have been held up a couple of days in our movement northward. Our company is getting out of range of our supporting artillery, and too far ahead of the rest of the battalion. It would be foolhardy to outreach the range of our support. We are waiting for the other companies to catch up and for the artillery to move up closer to our rear. We will then move out again.

It has been a welcome relief to get some rest instead of moving all the time. We all went down to a water filled bomb crater, took a bath, and washed our clothes. We were all ready for it. It had been nine days since our last bath and we all smelled pretty ripe.

We are still maintaining our standards of early stops, deep holes, solid bunkers, and "with a little bit of luck", have had no action. I think the NVA recon patrols have passed the word along, "Don't screw around with Bravo Company". I think the def-cons we fire each evening have a psychological effect on the NVA. Who would want to try to penetrate a wall of flying pieces of steel? There is action on both sides of us but nothing in our area. (One of my men did shoot a wild turkey a few days ago but I don't think it will last until Thanksgiving.)

Night before last, Alpha Company of our battalion was attacked by an NVA force about a mile southeast of us. We could hear the shooting but nothing came near. They caught a prisoner who reported they had chopped up an NVA battalion. He said they were the only NVA force around.

There has been a lot of fighting three or four miles to our left for the last couple of days. We can hear artillery and air strikes hitting constantly. I think it is a South Vietnamese force doing the fighting with a unit from our 25th Infantry Division moving in to help them out.

Seldom do we hear what is going on in the outside world. We sleep on the ground, drink creek water, get chewed on by ants, mosquitoes, and leeches, and dig foxholes every night. In spite of all this, our spirits are real high and we are as happy as if we had good sense. Since we are over here, this is as good a way to live as any...

14 Nov 66

We are still at it. We keep hunting the little slant-eyed bastards but just can not seem to find them. Everyone around us has made contact but we just keep looking and they seem to elude or avoid us.

For the last three days and nights we have been listening to artillery fire, air strikes, and B-52 bombing raids between us and the Cambodian border. The 1st of the 12th Infantry is over there and are really tearing up the NVA. I heard today they estimate they have killed or wounded at least 1,500. They are just about two or three miles from the Cambodian border.

We moved yesterday from our old position and set up in another place closer to the river. Today I took my platoon on a patrol along the riverbank and found some NVA river crossing sites. We destroyed three rafts and found two graves. (See story "Get the Body Count")...

I am doing just fine. The chopper is coming in so I have to draw this to a close. (See story on "Michelle Ray's Visit")...

"Get the Body Count"

Some lessons you learn the hard way. Vietnam was a war with no front lines. Success was measured, not in real estate occupied, but by the body count of enemy you could report. Every day the newspapers carried accounts of how many NVA and VC had been killed while losing a much smaller number of our own soldiers. Even though the body count reports often got embellished before they were reported to the newspapers, they all started with the people out in the field reporting the results of what they had done.

We learned our body count lesson one day on a patrol along the Nam Sathay river. We had discovered a major NVA crossing site and had destroyed three bamboo rafts. The location of an underwater bridge was marked on my map. Later in the day, I would call an air strike to destroy it.

B-52 bombers out of Guam had been saturating the area with one thousand and two thousand pounders. After leaving the river, we patrolled up a path of tangled bamboo and trees torn in the jungle by the bombs. Huge craters pock marked the jungle floor. The splintered trees and bamboo tore at our clothes and bodies as we picked our way through the razor sharp hazards. It was in this path of destruction we discovered what appeared to be freshly dug graves.

As we had been taught, I called in the find to Captain Fiacco who relayed it to battalion headquarters. We were not ready for the response. "Oscar 61, this is Oscar 6. You have been requested to dig up the graves and see how many NVA are in them. Let me know the results when you are through. Out."

"Nuts! Why had we reported this find," I thought. From the appearance of the dead bamboo and trees, we guessed the strike had hit this area a week earlier. We did not relish the idea of digging up graves, especially with people who had been in them a week or more. But, the government wanted a report on how many NVA they killed with their bombing strikes and it was our job to tell them. As the old saying goes, "It's not for me to reason why, it's but for me to do or die." We started to dig.

After sweating over the graves for an hour, we had unearthed four bodies. With that, I told my men to cover them back up and we would call it in. We reported four dead NVA soldiers from the scene of the action. I have always wondered how big the number had grown to by the time it reached Saigon and was reported to the press.

In the future, when we found a grave, we waited until we were well past its location before we reported its existence. After that experience, we let the people who wanted to report body counts guess how many NVA had been in the graves we found. One job of digging up graves was all "Babcock's Bastards" was going to do.

MICHELLE RAY'S VISIT

Imagine, if you will, the plight of a company of GI's who had been moving through dense jungles on a constant search and destroy mission for almost two weeks. Life had become a ritual of meeting the basic needs and not much else.

Little things that were almost meaningless previously had now taken on great importance. Things like mail from home, how long the moon was up each night before the jungle reverted to total darkness, and the daily C-rations that had begun to taste better all the time. Baths, shaving, and other common daily rituals like brushing your teeth became things to look forward to when there was time, usually every three or four days. To stop for those things were luxuries not afforded a combat infantryman.

The men focused on the really important things - making sure they and their buddies stayed alert, digging deep foxholes and building strong bunkers when they stopped for the night. They focused on memorizing the terrain features in front of them so that when the inevitable darkness fell, they could replay in their mind what was out there.

Some days we were fortunate and could prepare a helicopter landing zone. Other days, we had to rely on aerial drops to resupply our needs. Aerial drops meant staying alert to avoid the cases of C-rations that came falling through the trees as they were kicked from the slow flying helicopters. On occasion, it even meant having to scout several hundred yards outside the perimeter to find the yellow mail sack that fell off target because a chopper pilot would not slow his craft down enough to insure all the supplies fell inside the perimeter.

When there was a helicopter landing zone, it meant hot chow, and visits from people who lived and worked in the rear area. A sick man who had had to walk with the company for several days despite his fever could be evacuated to a hospital. And, on this one occasion, it provided a strong shot in the arm for the entire company.

It was a routine day, late in the afternoon. Most of the bunkers had been dug, fields of fire had been cleared, and men were busy cleaning their weapons or writing letters to be sent out on the last chopper of the day.

I was sitting at the company command bunker talking to Captain Fiacco when we got word that "Rawhide", Colonel Morley, was coming in for a visit. As the down thrust of the landing helicopter blew dirt into our faces, we walked out to greet him. As he got off the chopper, he turned to help another person down. I could not believe my eyes! Instead of a man, it was a woman getting off the chopper.

Rather than a steel helmet, she wore a floppy jungle hat with pigtails draping over her shoulders. Instead of a fatigue shirt, a well fitting army green tee shirt showed curves we had not seen in what seemed like months. Her fatigue pants could not hide the curve of her hips. In normal times, she would have been considered a good looking woman (she had been a model for Coco Chanel in France for two and a half years.) To us, she looked like Miss America! (Or, in more modern day terms, she was a true Bo Derek "10".)

"Sandy, Bob, I would like you to meet Michelle Ray, a French correspondent who is here to take a look at what you are doing."

The word spread like wildfire as the men saw Michelle get off the helicopter. As she walked up to the command bunker with Sandy, I reluctantly headed back to my platoon area to get back to work. When I got there, everyone wanted to know, "Who is the girl and why is she here?"

The next question was, "Can we go up and see her?" Sergeant Roath knew how to get volunteers, "We need men to go up and unload C-rations from the chopper, who wants to go?" We had more volunteers than ever before.

All of us were junior high kids again, wanting to get close to the cheerleader tryouts. Everyone, including myself, looked for excuses to go by the company command post to get another look at this honest to goodness, real life, round eyed, beautiful woman. When we were not roaming up toward the command post, all our eyes turned that way, trying to get another glimpse of this beauty. It would have been a great time for the NVA to hit us, we were not paying attention to them.

In less than an hour, she got back on the helicopter with "Rawhide" and headed back to the rear. I am sure she did not realize what a shot in the arm she had given to so many of us by her mere presence. As the song says, "Little things mean a lot".

Two months later, Michele was captured by the Viet Cong and spent several weeks as their captive. She wrote a book, "The Two Shores of Hell, A French journalist's life among the Vietcong and the G.I.'s in Vietnam".

In the book, she mentioned Colonel Morley but not her visit to our company. I am sure she made a bigger impression on us than we did on her. I can still picture her getting off that chopper and remember the spark it gave me.

Popping smoke to call in a helicopter with resupply

15 Nov 66

We still do not have any idea how long this operation will last and I still do not know anything about R&R. Maybe I will find out when this operation is finished. It may be over in a few days and it might last another month or more. We just do what we are told and never hear anything about what is going on now or what is being planned for the future. I feel like we will be back to the base camp for Christmas.

P.S. Have you heard anything about how the war is going? We never hear any news.

17 Nov 66

Just a short note to tell you about your hero, the "Snake Killer". (See story on "The Boa Constrictor").

...We are still moving north and have no idea when the operation will be over. We had some contact yesterday. (See story on "Hoboes").

THE BOA CONSTRICTOR

Another day of moving through the jungle. Soon after we had broken camp that morning, Ernie Redin, on point again, found a fairly well used trail. Cautiously, we followed it to see what could be found. We normally stayed off trails but were getting highly frustrated by not finding any NVA. After moving uneventfully for a couple of hours, Stanley Cameron, my radio operator, walking close behind me as he always did shouted, "Look out, Sir!"

I wheeled around and saw him pointing at the ground I had just walked over. Crawling across the trail was the biggest snake I had ever seen - a twelve foot boa constrictor! My heart was pounding as I backed away. I am sure it was crossing the trail when I stepped over it. (Stanley was always more observant than I and never missed the slightest little detail.)

Since the whole company had to pass that point, I decided to save them the scare it had given me and kill it. I keyed the radio handset and called the CO, Sandy Fiacco. "Oscar 6, this is Oscar 61. Don't be alarmed by the gunfire you are going to hear. We just found a great big snake up here and I'm going to kill it. Out."

My intention was to put a single bullet into its head and be done with it. I fired right on target but the snake did not even slow down. Two more times I fired into its head and it still kept moving, but slower now. Our artillery forward observer decided to help me, so he, too, started shooting. Between the two of us, we put twenty rounds into the snake. It finally lay still except for the occasional twitching of a muscle.

About that time, the radio crackled, "Oscar 61, this is Oscar 6. That better be a damn big snake! You are wasting a lot of our time! Get moving!" I replied, "It is - when you get up here, let me know what you think." With that, we continued our cautious movement down the trail.

About fifteen minutes later, when the rear of the company got to the dead snake, I got another radio call, "Oscar 61, this is 6. Hold up and break for lunch. I want to get the skin off this snake you killed, it is the biggest one I have ever seen."

It was hardly 10:30 in the morning, but, what the heck, no one ever said we had to wait until noon to eat, especially if the CO said to do it.

His next radio call was to the first platoon, bringing up the rear. He told Lieutenant Dinetz, "Oscar 59, this is Oscar 6, send 'Snake Man' up here to my position. I've got a job for him.'

Two months earlier, Sergeant Watson, one of the first platoon squad leaders, had picked up a live cobra and brought it to First Sergeant MacDonald, knowing full well that Mac had a deadly fear of snakes. After making him kill the snake and threatening him with his life if he ever did something like that again, Mac issued an order to the NCOs that no one was to mess with snakes. But, Sandy wanted a snake skin and Sergeant Watson got the job of skinning it.

Before long, we got the call to, "Saddle up and move out."

The rest of the day passed without incident. We made sure we picked a defensive position for the night where we could get a resupply helicopter to land. When it brought in our supplies, Captain Fiacco put the snake skin, which he had been carrying all day in a sand bag, into the helicopter. He told the pilot, "Be sure to give it to Sergeant Angulo, our mess sergeant, and have him salt it down to preserve it." The chopper lifted off with the snake skin and headed back to the rear.

A couple of weeks later, Sergeant Angulo flew out to bring us hot chow. He told the story of an ungodly smell that had started coming from the supply tent. The snake skin had made it back to the company area, but the instructions about who was supposed to get it and what they were supposed to do with it, never made it.

When the guys in the rear took the sandbag off the chopper, they assumed it was some excess equipment and threw it in the pile of other stuff that was kept for us in the supply tent. It was beyond hope when they found out what it was.

Captain Fiacco did not get his snake skin souvenir. Fortunately, we never saw another one like it to take its place.

"HOBOES"

Our trained reaction to the first crack of a rifle shot brought us all to the ground. The sound was followed by intense gunfire as we immediately responded to the enemy fire with our own. My heart was pounding. Adrenalin pumped through my body at an ear throbbing rate. I had tried to overcome the initial mass confusion, assess the situation, and determine what to do next. ("What you gonna do now, Lieutenant?")

We had found a number of abandoned enemy bunkers earlier in the afternoon. As I observed where the gunfire had started, it appeared there was another line of bunkers on the small rise in front of us. From where we were, it was impossible to tell how many there were and how many people were occupying them. The sound of the radio interrupted my thoughts.

"Oscar 61, this is Oscar 6. What is the situation? Over." "We have a bunker line in front of us and have received fire. We need a fire mission, over." It took no time to get our supporting 105mm howitzers called into action. The jungle soon shook from the exploding artillery blasts fired by our faithful artillerymen of C/4-42 Field Artillery.

As we lay watching the area, and continued to direct our rifle and machine gun fire at the bunker line, we got a radio call. "Oscar 6, this is Birddog 19. I have a flight of Hoboes on station. Do you need them? Over."

"Hobo" was the radio call sign for the 1950's vintage, propeller driven, Douglas A1E Skyraiders stationed at Pleiku Air Force Base. "Birddog 19" was the Air Force Forward Air Controller (FAC) whose job it was to direct the fire of all the airplanes in the area.

"Roger," was my reply. "We will shift the artillery and you can come in on target." As soon as I called to adjust the artillery fire to the rear of the target area, we could hear the first Hobo screaming toward us from right to left.

The FAC had marked the target with a white phosphorus marking rocket and the A1E released his bomb load right on target. His bombs were Cluster Bomb Units (CBUs) that exploded before they hit the ground, throwing thousands of tiny BB size projectiles across the target area.

Our position was scarcely 75 yards from where the CBUs were hitting. The shrapnel was ricocheting through the trees above us as well as on the target area. The sound of the metal ripping through the trees gave the saying, "Make myself one with Mother Earth" new meaning. The first Hobo was followed closely by a second and then a third as they saturated the bunker line with their CBUs. I had never heard anything like the clatter made as the projectiles ricocheted through the trees.

As quickly as they came, they were gone. As we were getting up to move across the bunker line, we got another call from Birddog 19. "The Hoboes have some 20mm cannons they can help you with. Do you want them to strafe the area before you go in? Over." Again, "Roger," was my reply. (No one ever accused me of not using all the firepower I had at my disposal).

This time the Hoboes came from our rear and flew directly overhead as they peppered the area to our front with their 20mm cannons. Another reality of war hit me as a hail of spent 20mm cartridge hulls came raining down on our heads. Training had never included getting pelted with the four inch long brass cartridge hulls which fell through the trees as the Hoboes flew over.

I pulled my steel helmet down tightly. Those things would have hurt if they had hit you directly on the head. Not only that, they were still hot as hell.

As the third Hobo completed his strafing run, we got up and quickly swept across the bunker line, firing into each bunker as we advanced. We moved through without stopping and took up defensive positions fifty yards past the bunkers, waiting for the rest of the company to join us.

As was so frequently the case, all we found were blood trails leading away from the bunker complex. We never knew whether or not we had killed any of the NVA. Fortunately, none of us were hurt.

We gained a better appreciation for the Hoboes. We knew they were usually on station to come to our aid when we needed them. They were slow and ugly in comparison to the sleek jets, but they had more staying power and could fly in much nastier weather.

When I went on R&R, I met one of the Hobo pilots from Pleiku. While sitting at the Cam Ranh Bay officer's club waiting for our R&R flight, I bought all his drinks. It was a small way to thank him for the close support which gave us infantrymen so much peace of mind as we walked through the jungle.

17 Nov 66 (CONT'D) (Letter to my folks)

All is still quiet on the Western front. We have been out here for two weeks and are continuing to sweep north. We have moved a little to the west and are traveling generally along the east side of the Nam Sathay River.

All of our days are about the same. We get up at 6:00, roll up our bedrolls, eat our C-ration breakfast, tear down our bunkers, and get ready to move out. We usually start moving about 7:30 and move until around noon when we stop for another C-ration meal. About 2:00 in the afternoon, we start looking for a place to spend the night. We try to find a hill that is easy to defend, has water close to it, and has a place where we can cut a suitable LZ.

When we stop, everyone starts digging foxholes, cutting down trees to build bunkers, and putting up poncho hootches to sleep under. If we have an LZ, a chopper brings in hot chow for supper. If not, one flies over and drops C-rations. Mail is brought in at supper time or is dropped to us. All packages are saved until we have an LZ.

It gets dark around 6:30 so everyone starts preparing for it. One man stays awake in each position and everyone else sleeps until it is his turn for guard. Occasionally, we spend two or three days in one place and get a rest from the routine. This routine gets old after a while but that is what we are getting paid to do. As long as we stay alert and do not make mistakes, we are fairly safe. We do save money out here. The month is over half gone and I have not spent a cent...

19 Nov 66

We are still running around out here in the jungle with no relief in sight. Yesterday was a little more interesting than some of our other days have been. We found a major NVA river crossing site and destroyed 15 rafts, a canoe, a foot bridge, and other miscellaneous stuff. We also found an NVA rifle that someone had left. He ran away just as we were approaching. We shot at him but missed.

Last night a three man listening post from my platoon ran into an NVA soldier on a trail outside our defensive perimeter. (See story on "Survival of the Fittest").

SURVIVAL OF THE FITTEST

The concerns common to fighting men since the beginning of time started to come to light on the troop ship en route to Vietnam. We were on our way to do a job that our government was asking us to do. That job involved killing other human beings. The very thought of killing someone went against the grain of what we had been taught all our lives.

I was visiting with several of my troops on the ship when John Jones (not his real name) brought up the idea that was in all of our minds. "Sir, I don't think I can kill anyone. It just isn't right."

That was a tough one. My answer to him went something like this, "I understand your concerns and you are not alone in feeling that way. I have had the same thought. But keep one thing in mind, we are not going over there to indiscriminately kill helpless people. We will be asked to kill people who will do everything in their power to kill us. Keep in mind that we will be operating at the most basic of levels - survival of the fittest."

Our first three months in country consisted of long range shots at people who were shooting at us from caves up in the hills. We never did know whether or not we had hit any of them, and if we did, we did not know whose shot had done the damage.

Things changed one night in the jungle. We had followed a good sized trail all day and had set up our defensive perimeter across it. As darkness engulfed us, I sent my three man listening post out to their position in front of our defensive bunkers.

They had not been outside the perimeter more than a minute when the loud cracks of rifle fire shattered the quiet. After five rapid shots, we heard loud rustling in the underbrush as people ran toward our perimeter. "It's us! Don't shoot! We're coming in!" was the unmistakable sound of John's voice.

He and the other two members of the listening post burst into the perimeter. I scrambled over to where they were to see what was going on. Captain Fiacco had already called me on the radio to get a situation report. "I killed the son of a bitch! I know I did! I got the son of a bitch!" Excitement and adrenalin were running wild through Jone's body.

I tried to calm him down, "How many were there? Did any of them get away? How far outside the perimeter were you?" Still shaking with excitement, Jones replied, "I know there was one and I got that son of a bitch. He wasn't three feet away from me and I blew him to hell. I don't think there were any more but I know I got one."

Sergeant Benge, my third squad leader, was squatted down beside me listening to the report. "I'll take some men and go check it out. Be right back." "Okay, be careful, we'll cover you." In less than ten minutes, Sergeant Benge was back inside the perimeter. He brought back the rucksack and rifle from the dead NVA soldier that lay not twenty yards outside our bunker line. "I didn't see any sign of anyone else but I didn't stop very long to listen for noises. That one is dead."

As I reported our results to Captain Fiacco, he decided to take the cautious approach and call in artillery fire to plaster the area. If there were any more NVA out there, they would have been either killed or scared away by the barrage of artillery and mortar fire that soon peppered down from the sky.

As quiet again returned to the jungle, I decided to send out another listening post. Jones and the other two men were still too excited to go back out. Three other men got the dubious honor and cautiously worked their way past the relative safety of the perimeter into the dark jungle. Nerves were frazzled as we stayed on 50% alert throughout the rest of the night.

As dawn was breaking, Sergeant Benge was again ready with his squad to go do a more thorough search of the area. Jones had calmed down and was ready to join the patrol. The dead man lay where he had been shot. No further sign of enemy activity was found. As full light returned to the jungle, most of the men in the company paraded by the dead NVA to see what had caused the commotion.

I later thought it ironic that I had stood by the body and nonchalantly talked to people while eating my breakfast C-rations, giving little thought that we had just killed a man. Jones described to anyone who would listen how he had, "blown that son of a bitch to kingdom come."

John Jones, like most American soldiers since the days of George Washington, had done what his government sent him to do. As was normally the case, training and the survival instinct had taken the place of making moral judgments, good allies to have when competing at the most basic level of "survival of the fittest".

I have changed the name of this soldier involved since I did not receive his permission to use it. I do not know whether this is something he has told his family or others about so I am not going to disclose a name without his permission.

Typical backpack load carried through the jungle –
this was CPT Buck Ator, the company commander
during the last half of our tour.

19 NOV 66 (CONT'D)

That little action last night was what we needed to emphasize there are enemy in the area. We should not have any trouble keeping the troops alert for the next week or so. (See story on "Cavalry Charge!")...

We really got into a hornet's nest today, literally. Sergeant Savard, squad leader in the first platoon, stumbled into the biggest hornet's nest I have ever seen. While he was trying to get away from them, he broke his glasses and got stings all over his face and arms. I know he was hurting but it was really comical to watch him flailing around trying to get away. We had to evacuate him, he is almost blind without his glasses and his face was swollen pretty badly...

"Cavalry, Charge!"

We had moved for several days through the jungle and were getting closer to the Cambodian border. Second Platoon was in the lead, the Command Group was following them, First Platoon was next and we had the luxury of almost a day off by bringing up the rear. The toughest and most dangerous job was to be the lead platoon as we moved in column, or usually in file, through the jungle. I had more than my fair share of being lead platoon so I was enjoying the day's leisurely stroll through the jungle.

We were moving up a ridge line with a parallel ridge running to our left. The two ridges joined and continued on up the slope of the hill. As the Second Platoon came to the junction of the two ridges, the point man almost collided with three NVA soldiers moving toward them.

He raised his rifle and fired from the hip, but missed. The NVA soldiers ran down the ridge to our left as the remainder of the second platoon raked the ridgeline with fire. Our leisurely walk in the sun was abruptly interrupted when we heard the firing. We hit the ground and established a hasty perimeter, making sure nothing moved in around us. The radio crackled, "Oscar 61, this is Oscar 6, over." I responded and he said, "Take your unit across the valley and cut them off before they get away!"

Damn! We knew the easy part of our day was over. I gave the command and we got up and started to move rapidly down the hill and through the dense vegetation filling the valley separating the two ridges. We had just started moving when the sound of a loud bugle burst through the jungle canopy. The classic "Cavalry, Charge" we had heard in western movies when we were kids could be heard over and over as we moved down the valley and up the ridge to cut off the NVA.

We looked up and saw the bugle call was coming from a "psyops" plane circling overhead. The pilot had been listening on our radio frequency and decided to add a little class to our charge across the valley. We got a renewed bounce in our step as we thrashed through the underbrush and up the hill. We felt like the cavalry coming over the hill to rescue the wagon train.

As we came over the crest of the ridge and hit the trail the NVA had run down, we spread out and set up a hasty ambush. Still fired up from the bugle music, we waited to wipe out the little slant eyed devils. After waiting a few minutes without results, we decided to head up the trail after them.

Despite the rush of excitement, we moved with extreme caution. I wanted to get them but I was not going to take a chance of walking into an ambush. Maybe the cavalry could ride to the rescue with reckless abandon but I was not going to take unnecessary risks as we tried to flush them out.

The afternoon shadows were starting to lengthen and I realized we had to accomplish this mission quickly. We were rapidly closing in on the time when we needed to be finding a position to set up our nightly perimeter.

Higher and higher we moved up the ridge until we heard voices. As we set up another hasty ambush, we realized the voices we were hearing were American, not Vietnamese. Our Second Platoon had set up an ambush across the trail. Somehow, the NVA soldiers had escaped the cavalry charge and our drive back up the ridge.

As we resumed our company movement up the ridge line, we could not hide an occasional smile or chuckle as we remembered the bugle charge that inspired us on our dash through the valley and up the ridge to get the bad guys.

19 NOV 66 (CONT'D)

...A few of our people are starting to get sick. We have sent in eight or ten men within the last week with fever. LT Lou Dinetz went in yesterday morning with 103 temp. I am still feeling just fine...

(Letter to my folks) - No, Mother, that is not me in the picture you cut out of the newspaper. As Dale said, the face is too full. I have no idea where the picture was taken or who it is. I told you I am okay, why don't you believe me? Also, just because his pants leg is torn, that is no sign he is injured. There are a million thorn bushes over here that just love to tear GI's pants. They have already torn one pair off me during this operation and I am starting to get rips in the new ones I got just a week ago.

His facial expression is not of pain, either. It gets tiresome running around these hills. He is probably just plain bone tired and has sore feet or something. Besides, that guy is too sloppy for me. He has his helmet chin strap hanging loose and I never do that, I keep it tied up on my helmet...

... Think positive and don't worry about me. Quit letting your imagination run away with you, Mother. I am safe, just tired and dirty.

21 Nov 66

Your past 24 hours has to have been more pleasant than mine. We had a tragic thing happen yesterday afternoon. (See story on "November 20, 1966").

NOVEMBER 20, 1966

The jungle air was thick with tension as we trudged along under its thick, triple canopy. All morning we had been monitoring radio reports of first one and then another of our sister units as they made contact with the NVA. Muffled explosions could be heard as artillery and air strikes pounded the jungle.

For seventeen days, our luck had held. We had moved along unscathed as units to our right and left took casualties regularly. Since we did not have to stop, regroup, and lick our wounds like Alpha and Charlie Companies, we were far in front of them in our movement northward through the Nam Sathay river valley. Two days earlier, we had run out of our supporting artillery battery's range.

Rather than halt our progress, we had been attached temporarily to a battalion of the Third Brigade of the 25th Infantry Division. They were to provide artillery support for us while we were under their operational control.

Just as we stopped for noon chow, Sandy Fiacco received a radio call from the battalion commander. "Oscar 6, this is Cactus 6. We have a unit in heavy contact with a large NVA unit to your right flank. I want you to move over and provide a blocking position to cut the bad guys off if they try to withdraw toward Cambodia. Over."

Sandy and I studied his map as he replied, "This is Oscar 6. Roger. We will be moving in five minutes. Out." We continued studying the map coordinates to determine the best blocking position for straddling their most likely avenue of retreat.

The troops grumbled as they gulped down the C-rations they had hoped to enjoy while relaxing. The tension continued to mount as we made a right turn and headed toward the ridge line where we would set up our position. It was mid afternoon when we reached our objective. Security outposts moved forward as we started to build our normal triangular defensive position. The muffled sounds of artillery and air strikes continued to vibrate through the thick jungle. The radio traffic indicated the unit was still slugging it out with the NVA as we started to dig in.

None of us needed encouragement to dig deep and cut down large trees for overhead protection on our bunkers. We knew that something bad was happening to the unit we were setting up to help. Now we were between the NVA and their sanctuary in Cambodia.

Suddenly, the artillery and mortar rounds started hitting closer to us. Our artillery forward observer grabbed his radio, called the fire base, and told them to, "Cease fire! You are getting dangerously close to our position."

The response from the fire base was quick, "Get off this frequency! We are on a fire mission!" Before a warning could be shouted to our troops, the next round landed with a deafening roar in the trees directly above where the second platoon was digging in.

Shrapnel clattered through the trees as we all dived for cover and tried to get as much protection as possible in the holes we were digging, behind big trees, or just flat on the ground. As the ricocheting shrapnel fell to the ground, we heard the cry, "Medic, medic!" I had dived into a hole beside our platoon medic. I told him, "Get up and go help out." He lay there with two big wide eyes looking up at me. He was not about to get out of that hole.

As I started crawling out, I grabbed him and his aid bag. "Come on, let's go see who is hurt." As I pulled on him, he took his aid bag and followed me to the second platoon. As we ran the interminably long forty yards from my position to where the round had hit, Sergeant Roath started checking our platoon position for dead or wounded and to make sure they were maintaining tight security.

We did not know whether we would get hit with another round or not. We could hear our artillery forward observer screaming into his radio, "Cease fire! Cease fire! Cease fire! You are dropping rounds right on top of us! Cease fire, Dammit!"

As I ran into the second platoon area, many of the troops were still in their holes feeling the shock of what had happened. The smell of explosives hung heavy in the air. Green leaves littered the ground. Walking with a severe limp, Walt Ferguson, the platoon leader, was up checking his people. Blood from a piece of shrapnel oozed from his knee. Walt and I got to David Mendez, his radio operator, at about the same time.

Walt said, "Get up, Mendez, and tell Fiacco to call in a Dust-off." There was no response from Mendez. I reached down and turned him over. Blood oozed from a small hole where shrapnel had gone into his heart. He never knew what hit him.

We kept looking around to find out who else had been wounded. Stanley Cameron ran over to report, "None of our men were hit." "Good, tell Sergeant Roath to keep them alert and I will stay here and help Walt's platoon."

We heard a call for, "Medic!" come from the headquarters area. Sergeant Reynolds, our communications sergeant, had been hit in the chest by a large piece of shrapnel. Air whooshed from the sucking chest wound.

The medics responded rapidly. They covered the hole with a piece of foil and wrapped it tightly with combat dressings. That stopped the bleeding and cut out the air escaping through his chest.

As we took inventory of the injured, we found that ten men had been wounded and Mendez had been killed. We directed the troops to keep digging and to maintain security. While monitoring the radio, we heard the NVA had broken contact with the unit to our east. We expected them to be withdrawing through our area at any time.

Sandy Fiacco called for a Dust-off. We had one major problem. We were still in triple canopy jungle and there was no place for a helicopter to land. We knew we had to get Sergeant Reynolds evacuated immediately. Three or four others needed to get out as quickly as possible.

Finally, a Chinook helicopter hovered above the jungle canopy and lowered a line with a stretcher down through the trees. In no time, we had Sergeant Reynolds sandwiched between the two pieces of the stretcher and strapped in securely. He was pale from fright and loss of blood as the chopper crew started winching him up through the trees.

It was getting dark and the chopper pilot, understandably, did not like hovering up there like a sitting duck with all the NVA around. We still had not seen any of them but we knew they were close at hand.

"Do you have any more that are critical? If not, I am going to take this guy and get the hell out of here." The rest could wait a little longer so we released him. Quiet returned as the Chinook headed for the 18th Surgical Hospital. Within minutes, Sergeant Reynolds would be on the operating table.

We knew we had to have an LZ. Sandy had been on the radio trying to get help in creating one. A helicopter flew over, hovered momentarily, and dropped two chain saws, some C4 plastic explosive, and rope charges. The fall through the trees broke the chain saws. Despite our efforts, we never could get them to work.

The C4 and rope charges were quickly put to use knocking down big trees. It was totally dark and took several hours, but we blew down trees until it looked like we could get a helicopter in. We called again for a Dust-off.

Within twenty minutes, we heard a chopper approaching. Harry Troutman fired a flare through the hole in the jungle canopy to mark our position. "Oscar 6, this is Mercy 2. I see your flare. Is your LZ hot or is it secure? Over."

So far we had not seen or heard from any of the NVA but we knew they could not be too far away. "This is Oscar 6, at this time it is secure. We can not promise you how long it will stay that way. Over."

The pilot responded, "I'm coming in with my lights on," as he circled trying to find the widest part of the LZ. The bright lights formed strange shadows which danced across the LZ as he started his descent.

The main rotor blades chopped leaves and branches off the trees that seemed to try to reach out and snatch him from the air. He continued his descent, "How tall are those stumps sticking up down there?"

"They are four or five feet tall, watch me and I will let you know when you are down as far as you can go," responded Captain Fiacco. He had personally taken responsibility for guiding the chopper down. He stood in the LZ, bathed in the light from the chopper, a perfect target for a NVA sniper.

As Sandy guided the chopper down, several of us moved under it with the most seriously wounded man. The down-thrust from the chopper rotors at full power blew dirt, leaves, and twigs into our faces as we waited for it to ease down. I was one of the tallest men and had to extend my arms as high as I could to reach the floor of the chopper.

With the help of the crew inside, we got the stretcher and the wounded man loaded. The pilot circled up out of the hole and radioed, "I will take him to the 18th Surg and then be right back to get another one."

In less than an hour, he was back and repeated his feat. His rotor blades again clipped branches and leaves as he brought his bird down into the clearing with his lights on. The enemy still had not shown his face. We knew we were pushing our luck. They would hit us when he came in again for sure.

He made a total of three trips to take out the most seriously wounded and offered to come back for more! We told him, "The others are not as serious. They can wait until daylight. Thanks for the help, we owe you a drink."

Words can not describe the admiration we had for that courageous pilot.

After midnight, we finally settled down. All afternoon and evening we had not even stopped long enough to eat. It was a tired, sad, and tense bunch of GI's that settled in for the night, waiting for an attack, or waiting to see daylight.

David Mendez, our KIA, had been wrapped in a poncho and placed across the top of my bunker. It was a strange feeling to be lying in a bunker with a dead man laying across the sandbags that made up our roof. What we had learned in training was now crystal clear - the order of evacuation is most wounded to least wounded. When all of those are out, you worry about evacuating the dead.

Daylight had barely broken when we heard a chopper approaching. "Oscar 6, this is Mercy 2. Do you have any more folks that need a ride out of there?" The same pilot was coming back in to get the rest of our wounded.

In daylight and with walking wounded, he could take two men out at a time. In three trips, the wounded were all out. The sun was starting to bathe the LZ as he picked up LT Walt Ferguson and David Mendez' body on his final trip.

Later that morning, a small observation helicopter circled over our position. "Oscar 6, this is Rawhide. I want to come down and see you but my pilot says your LZ is too small. Knock down some more trees so I can come in."

You can imagine our disgust. This pilot had a bird about half the size of the Dust-off chopper, it was broad daylight, and we had to enlarge the LZ for him. We finally got the LZ enlarged and Rawhide landed.

His first words as he got out of his chopper, wearing his freshly starched fatigues, were, "Damn, you guys sure do stink." It had been a week or more since we had stopped for a bath. He did not win any friends with us that day.

After he had talked to Sandy for a while, he took me aside and said, "Bob, you have got to get Sandy to calm down, he gets too excited."

Rawhide did not realize how personally Sandy cared for each of his men and how upset he was to lose Mendez and the wounded. Sandy had done a fantastic job in insuring we got help when we needed it. My hat was off to him for the leadership he had shown throughout the ordeal.

Disgusted with the way he had handled that very traumatic event, we were all glad to see Rawhide finally get back in his chopper and leave.

In retrospect, Rawhide was probably correct in his actions. As a professional soldier, he knew in order to get our company back on track, there had to be a diversion. His order to enlarge the LZ and his taunts did that. Now, we had someone to be angry at, instead of dwelling in our own misery and sorrow. Rawhide was an outstanding Battalion Commander - by far the best of the three we had that year.

David Mendez' name is engraved on panel 12E, line 96 on the Vietnam Memorial Wall in Washington, D. C.

21 Nov 66 (CONT'D)

... The only officers left now are Captain Fiacco and I. Lou is still sick with fever and is in the hospital, I think. Do not write Sandra about Walt getting hit. I do not know whether he will tell her about it or not.

Today we are staying in position and not moving. We really need it, too. We have been constantly on the go since the end of October and everyone is getting physically pooped. That accident yesterday took a lot out of the men emotionally. It is bad to be here four months without serious injury and then lose eleven men because a friendly unit made a stupid mistake. It makes you wonder if it is all worth it. Fortunately, none of the men in my platoon were hurt.

It is difficult not to feel a sense of depression after our "friendly fire" incident. Tomorrow will be much better. I will sure be glad when they get us out of this damn jungle for a few days. If they would just give us two days off so we could relax, we would be ready to go another twenty days. Well, maybe they will before too much longer.

... Your letters mean an awful lot to me. The letter I got from you today helped perk up my spirits.

I'll close and fix a C-ration meal. Don't worry. I'm just trying to talk to you in this letter since we can not talk in person...

24 Nov 66 (THANKSGIVING DAY)

Happy Thanksgiving! We are not moving today and I am thankful. I have an awful lot to be thankful for, even though I am out here in the middle of nowhere. Most of all, I am thankful I am alive, in good health, and have you.

My spirits are much better than they were my last letter. We have moved for two days and things are going pretty good. Day before yesterday, my platoon was on a patrol and saw four NVA soldiers on a trail. They saw us about the same time we saw them and ran before we could get a shot at them. We then set an ambush on the trail and about an hour later two of them came back. We really shot up some trees, too bad we missed the NVA.

Rumor has it that we will be lifted out of here within the next few days to go back to guard the battalion artillery fire base. We sure hope so. It will be a relief to get away from walking for a change...

(Letter to my folks) - Today is cooler and cloudy, just like Thanksgiving at home, but the conditions are a little different... They have promised us a Thanksgiving dinner with all the trimmings if we can get an LZ. The men are working hard because we have not had hot chow since the 15th of November.

We get mad at these chopper pilots. We cut an LZ big enough for Jim to land a DC-8 and the pilots say it is not big enough. They hover and throw C-rations to us. C-ration cans get pretty bent up when they're thrown from 150 feet in the air.

Well, we are going to get turkey dinner in here today if we have to cut down every tree from the Mekong Delta to the DMZ, and then shoot the chopper down ourselves. We feel like we deserve hot chow... (See story on "Thanksgiving, 1966").

THANKSGIVING, 1966

"Every American fighting man serving in Vietnam will have a turkey dinner with all the trimmings on this Thanksgiving day," was what President Lyndon Johnson had committed in a press conference to the American people.

Thanksgiving. The uniquely American holiday where we take time to reflect on what we are thankful for. A time to spend with family, watch football games, and eat a turkey dinner.

On Thanksgiving day of 1966, there was nothing that could be done about getting us with our families or watching a football game but it was well within the capabilities of the American government to provide us with a traditional Thanksgiving dinner. It was a great idea for those in the rear areas and also for those in the forward combat zones who had ready access to helicopter landing zones. For those of us in the dense, triple canopied jungles of the central highlands, it meant a lot of work.

It had been only three days since we had spent most of the night blowing down trees to evacuate our men wounded in the mortar accident on November 20. Thanksgiving dinner sounded good but we would just as soon have waited until we were in a place where it would have been easier to prepare a landing zone. That was not to be.

"Oscar 6, this is Rawhide. We have a complete turkey dinner for you today. When do you want it sent in? Over." "This is Oscar 6. We do not have an LZ. Let's hold it and try it another day. Over." "This is Rawhide. Negative. When the President says we are going to have a Thanksgiving dinner, we are going to have a Thanksgiving dinner. Start preparing an LZ. Keep me informed. Out."

After scouting around, we found the side of a hill where we could clear an LZ without having to knock down too many big trees. But, it was not going to be an easy task.

I dreaded the thought of having to clear an LZ but welcomed the chance not to have to walk all day. For the past two days, I had progressively been getting sicker. That morning I had a 103.4 fever when the medic checked me. My job would be to supervise, and I could do that sitting down without having to exert myself very much.

After security was set up, the men started to work on the LZ. Our engineers wrapped rope explosives and C4 around the largest trees and dropped them with loud explosions. As they did every night, the men went to work on the smaller trees with their machetes. By early afternoon, we had prepared a decent LZ. "Rawhide, this is Oscar 6. LZ is prepared, send the turkey. Over." "Turkey is on the way. Out," was the reply.

Soon, two helicopters, loaded with mermite cans full of hot food, approached our position. Harry Troutman threw a smoke grenade into the LZ and the lead pilot identified the red smoke. Rather than swoop in for a landing, he slowly circled the area.

"Oscar 6, your LZ is unsafe, we can not land there. Over." "What do you mean it's unsafe? We have had choppers come into smaller places than this. Bring one bird in at a time and we will guide you in. Over." "Negative. You are on the side of a hill and we can not set down on a place that unlevel. You are going to have to clear some more trees off the top of the hill. We are going back. Out."

Sandy was furious as the last sound of the helicopters disappeared into the distance. I was not much help in the situation. I was feeling worse as the day progressed. My fever continued to hover between 103-104. Sandy's next radio call was to Rawhide. "Rawhide, we have an LZ. Those pilots are chicken! Request your help in talking to them. We are not going to knock down any more trees! Over." "Oscar 6, this is Rawhide. Stand by, I will see what I can do. Out."

In about an hour, a single helicopter could be heard approaching our position. Once again Harry threw smoke into the LZ and the pilot, a different voice from the one we had talked to earlier, identified our purple smoke.

Without hesitation, the pilot circled down into the small clearing and hovered his chopper with one skid on the side of the hill and the other still in the air. Our troops hurried to offload the cans of hot food, being careful not to walk into the whirling rotor blade as it barely missed the side of the hill.

"I will be back with another load in a few minutes. Stand by," were his parting words as he went back to get the second load of Thanksgiving dinner. As we waited for the second load, First Sergeant MacDonald started assembling a chow line. The troops were eager to help. Not only had they really worked up an appetite clearing the LZ, we hadn't had hot food in ten days.

Soon, the pilot repeated his hovering landing and the rest of the food was added to the chow line. "Let me know when you are through and I will be back to pick up the empty containers. Out."

What a treat! We had the works. The menu consisted of shrimp cocktail with cocktail sauce and crackers, roast tom turkey, giblet gravy, poultry dressing, snow flaked potatoes, glazed sweet potatoes, cranberry sauce, buttered peas and corn, crisp relish tray, Parker house rolls, butter, pumpkin pie with whipped cream, mincemeat pie, old fashion fruit cake, fresh chilled fruit, mixed nuts, assorted candy, tea, coffee, and ICE CREAM.

Real paper napkins added a further touch of civilization to the feast. We did not have to use our pants leg as a napkin as we had done for many weeks. I was too sick to enjoy it but forced myself to eat everything on my plate. We had worked too hard for this meal to pass it up.

We had not expected anything near this magnitude as we had been preparing the LZ. I had always heard there were those people who flew flying machines and those who were "pilots". This unknown "pilot" had selflessly gone that 'extra mile' to create an unforgettable Thanksgiving for a bunch of tired, hungry, homesick GI's so far away from home. And Sergeant Angulo and his team of cooks had outdone themselves in preparing a feast fit for a king.

Another touch of class that capped off the meal was a printed menu with a prayer on the back page and a message from our commander on the inside front page. The message read as follows:

"This Thanksgiving Day we find ourselves in a foreign land assisting in the defense of the rights of free men. On this day we should offer our grateful thanks for the abundant life which we and our loved ones have been provided."

"May we each pray for continued blessings and guidance upon our endeavors to assist the Vietnamese people in their struggle to attain an everlasting peace within a free society." Signed, William C. Westmoreland, General, United States Army, Commanding.

If I am ever asked for my most memorable Thanksgiving, that Thanksgiving dinner in the middle of the jungle is the one that will always stand out in my mind.

24 NOV 66 (CONT'D)

... From the sound of things, we seem to be cleaning up on the NVA. The unit operating about 800 yards to our east has killed forty in the last two days and captured a bunch of weapons, including some machine guns.

When they start leaving machine guns behind, you know they are really getting hurt and are running. I just heard on the radio that an NVA surrendered by waving his shirt to a helicopter flying over. They dropped a rope, pulled him out, and are taking him back to the rear area. He will probably give them some valuable information...

I have gotten used to all the shooting around me, or as used to it as I can. When the artillery rounds and air strikes whistle over us and land close, I just hug the ground a little closer and try to find a bigger tree to get behind. I sure am glad we have the artillery and air power on our side and they do not. That stuff keeps the NVA on the run. When we run into him, we have all the support we can use on call at a moment's notice.

26 Nov 66

We captured a prisoner yesterday. The second platoon was on point and ran into some NVA... (See story on "First Sergeant MacDonald's Bronze Star").

First Sergeant MacDonald's Bronze Star

The sound of automatic rifle fire shattered the jungle air. The rapid staccato sound of the American M16 rifle was answered by the slower, more deliberate fire of the Russian made AK-47. At the first sound, our instincts and training forced us to drop to the ground, crawl behind cover of the nearest tree or rise in the ground, and start scanning the jungle to our flanks for any sign of NVA. Every muscle in our bodies tensed as we pulled our rifles to our shoulders, ready to repel anything that came our way.

"Oscar 6, this is Oscar 60. We have contact, over," came from the second platoon. "This is 6, how many are out there, over." "I don't know, looks like five or six at least, over." "Keep me informed, out." The radio traffic gave us an idea of what was in front of us.

After the initial burst of fire, things were quiet except for an occasional burst of automatic rifle fire from an M16 or an AK-47. Everyone stayed close to the ground waiting for the new platoon leader, Steve Cush, to maneuver his second platoon into a position where they could eliminate the NVA ambush. Mortar rounds began to fall to our front as Steve's forward observer called in fire on the NVA position.

Laying on the jungle floor, tense, ready for anything to happen for what seemed like an eternity, but probably only a few minutes, I heard a noise coming through the jungle from behind us. As I looked over my shoulder toward the source of the noise, First Sergeant MacDonald came walking through the column of troops lying on the ground. He showed no caution but just kept walking forward toward the front of the column to where the action was.

When he got to where I lay, he asked, "What's the holdup, why aren't we moving?" "We're waiting for second platoon to clear out the NVA," was my reply. "Bull sh*t, we can't wait all day, let's go see what the problem is," he growled as he continued to walk forward, his 12 gauge shotgun crooked over his arm.

Getting up to follow him, I stayed down in a low crouch, taking every opportunity to get behind trees as I followed him forward. My heart was pounding as I rapidly scanned the jungle, looking for any telltale sign of movement or danger. Mac still walked like he was on a Sunday stroll.

As Mac walked up on the rear of the second platoon's position, one of the men looked up at him with wide eyed surprise and motioned at a tree twenty yards to his flank. "There's one over there, First Sergeant," he whispered.

Without hesitating, First Sergeant MacDonald turned to his left and started walking, still upright, toward the tree. His eyes were riveted to the top of the trees in front of him. It was a common NVA tactic to fire from the ground, retreat, and let a sniper in the tree shoot unwary troops who moved into the area. His shotgun moved to the ready position as he closed the distance between himself and the unseen enemy. Kneeling beside a tree, I snapped my rifle to my shoulder, ready to fire at the first thing that moved.

As First Sergeant MacDonald rounded a large tree, an NVA soldier lay on the ground with his AK-47 rifle pointed menacingly at the First Sergeant's stomach! During the brief instant of truth as the soldier looked at him, AK-47 at the ready, First Sergeant MacDonald responded with his shotgun. "WHAM! WHAM! WHAM!" Mac emptied his shotgun into the NVA as rapidly as he could pump another round into the chamber and pull the trigger.

"Now let's move!" the First Sergeant shouted to the awe struck second platoon members. Without hesitation, each man got up and moved rapidly into the jungle, firing from the hip, to clear out any remaining NVA.

As I walked to where First Sergeant MacDonald stood over the lifeless, bloody pulp that had been a live human being only seconds before, I noticed an empty AK-47 magazine lying beside the body. The NVA soldier had emptied his magazine in the first burst of activity and had loaded a fresh magazine into his weapon. Why he froze when First Sergeant MacDonald walked up on him will never be known.

In addition to Mac's kill, one NVA was captured and several blood trails were seen leading into the jungle but the NVA had withdrawn and contact had been broken. We soon continued our movement on our search and destroy mission through the jungle. Mac picked up the AK-47 and slung it over his shoulder as he rejoined Captain Fiacco and the company command group.

When we stopped for the night, Mac meticulously cleaned the enemy weapon. After he had it spotless (he is one of the cleanest, neatest men I ever met), he called the platoon leaders together for a close examination of the assault rifle. After we had each handled and fired it, we each took it to our platoon area to give an up close firing demonstration to our platoon. Mac never passed up the opportunity to train his men, knowing that one day we might be forced to pick up an AK-47 and fight with it.

First Sergeant MacDonald appeared un-phased by his day's experience. All of us had known he was good. As a Korean War veteran, one of eighteen survivors when his battalion of the First Cavalry Division had been overrun, a prisoner of war for eight days before he escaped his captors, he possessed all the instincts of a combat infantryman.

We now held him in even higher esteem as the story of his heroics quickly spread through the company. His leadership by example had put a spark into our company which few of us would ever forget. Later in the year, General Ray Peers awarded Mac the Bronze Star for Valor during a battalion awards ceremony.

After twenty-four years without knowing where he was, I renewed my friendship with retired First Sergeant Bob MacDonald in May, 1991 and we relived this experience. To this day, he still does not know why he was not cut in two by the NVA with the AK-47. His only conclusion is that it was not his time to go. The AK-47 was donated to a military museum in Hawaii.

26 Nov 66 (CONT'D)

After Mac got us going again, we called in artillery fire and an air strike. One guy came out of the woods and surrendered. I felt sorry for him, he was scared to death. We questioned him through our interpreter and then sent him on a chopper back to battalion. This morning they brought him back and he led the first platoon to a possible rice cache. They just came back and did not find anything. He seemed to be starved so I fed him my C rations.

See, I am not such a hard hearted guy after all. I even have compassion for the people who are responsible for me being in this God forsaken place. This poor guy is just like us, he doesn't want to be here. All he wants to do is go home, grow rice, and make babies, not necessarily in that order. (See story on "A Night in a Typhoon").

27 Nov 66

It got dark on me yesterday so I will try to finish this letter today. We have been set up here in one position for two days and are sending out patrols. Tomorrow or the next day we will probably start moving again. (See story on "B-52 Bomber Attack")...

A Night in the Typhoon

For two days we had been hearing reports on the battalion radio net of a typhoon approaching the coast of Vietnam. Since we were inland, working on the Cambodian border, we were not worried about the wind effects of the typhoon. Our worry was from the thick clouds and heavy rain we would experience. Getting wet did not bother us, we were used to that. What we did not like was the impact the weather would have on helicopter and fighter plane support. We had learned to rely on the ready availability of air support.

Since the jungle trees were so tall, we seldom got a glimpse of the sky. Except for a little gnawing concern on the part of the officers, we ignored the typhoon warnings. When we stopped for the night, the evening weather report told us to expect heavy rains. We passed the warning on to the troops so they could be a little more cautious about where and how they built their hootches.

On a dry night, it was common to build a hootch wherever a relatively flat piece of ground could be found close to your bunker. When we expected rain, we tried to find little rises so the water would run away. We also took the time to dig a small drainage trench around the hootch, a practice that was ignored most nights.

Harry Troutman, Captain Fiacco's radio operator, always built the hootch where he and Captain Fiacco slept. Sandy and I were watching Harry build the hootch as we talked.

"Harry, you better make sure that thing is water tight. I don't want to get wet tonight." "Sir, you're insulting me. You know I build the best damned hootch in the Army. Don't worry. We'll stay dry."

As we continued to talk, it got dark. We were both feeling melancholy and a little nostalgic. We were the only two experienced officers left in the company after Walt had gotten wounded and Lou had gone in with a high fever. As we talked, Harry interrupted.

"When are you two going to stop jabbering? I need to get some sleep. I've got radio watch at midnight." "Harry, you go on down and sleep in Babcock's hootch. He can stay up here with me tonight and we won't bother you." Harry grabbed his equipment, walked the fifteen yards to my hootch, and went to sleep.

We finally stopped talking just as the first drops of rain started to fall. We settled down under the hootch and quickly went to sleep, ignoring the patter of rain. We had grown accustomed to sleeping when we could, knowing we would be awakened later for our turns at radio watch.

The rain continued to fall harder as we slept, when suddenly, we were awakened by an instant drenching. Harry, the great hootch builder, had not put the proper slope on the poncho roof. Instead of repelling water, it had collected it until its weight broke the poncho and doused us with what felt like a bathtub full of cold water!

As we sat up with a start, Sandy ignored all the rules of sound discipline and yelled, "Harry, get your ass up here! Damn it, I thought you knew how to build a hootch." His voice was heard all over the perimeter. Even the listening posts could hear the commotion from their positions out in the jungle.

Harry stirred and poked his head out from where he was sleeping, "What's the problem, Sir?" "You damn near drowned us! Now get your butt up here and fix this thing." Knowing he had screwed up, Harry quickly put on his boots and crawled out into the torrential rain to fix the hootch he had guaranteed to be water tight. Stanley Cameron, my radio operator, took pity on Harry's plight and crawled out into the rain to help him.

Once you have been drenched, it is impossible to get comfortable again. Sandy, Harry, Stanley, and I spent the rest of the night huddled up trying to stay warm and cursing the typhoon. The problem with air support did not cross our minds as we worried more about how to get dry.

The next day, the rest of the company did not pass up the opportunity to needle Harry as many of them volunteered to build a "real hootch" for the company commander the next night.

B-52 Bomber Attack

"Oscar 6, this is Rawhide. Coded message follows." The coded message was deciphered to read, "Set up your night position at least 2000 yards from Hill 645 tonight. A B-52 bomber strike is scheduled to hit there at 10:00 PM. Be prepared to move into the strike area at first light to assess the damage."

Our sense of adventure and anticipation increased. We were going to experience up close what a B52 strike was like. We had been hearing them at a distance for several weeks. The rumble of the bombs exploding was awesome. At that stage of the war, 2000 yards was the minimum distance troops could be to a planned B-52 strike. (Later in the war, at places like Khe Sanh, B-52 strikes went in as close as 500 yards or closer to American positions.)

A typical B-52 strike consisted of up to eighteen of the large, eight engines, long range bombers flying in formation from their base in Guam. They dropped their payload of 1000 and 2000 pound bombs from high altitude on a predetermined target, causing incredible damage. Huge craters were created in the ground. Giant trees, 100 feet tall and taller, were crumbled and splintered like toothpicks. The bamboo and other jungle underbrush was twisted and gnarled from the force of the explosions.

Any enemy in the area was decimated unless they happened to be in well built underground bunkers. Even those troops were badly shaken, most with shattered eardrums.

It was with great anticipation that we dug in for the night. There was a little concern that the bombs might be off target so we made sure our holes were a little deeper and our bunkers built a little stronger than on most nights.

As the hour for the attack approached, every man was awake. We had tuned all our radios onto the battalion frequency and listened intently as they relayed what they heard from the forward air controllers about the progress of the B-52s. They were right on time and at 9:55, Rawhide called us. "Oscar 6, this is Rawhide. The big boys are on their final approach. Get your people down and stand by for impact. Over." "This is Oscar 6. Wilco. Out."

We all scrambled into our bunkers to await the impact. Captain Fiacco crawled over to my position to get a better view of the fireworks. We listened for the drone of planes as the hands on our watches swept up to 10:00.

Suddenly, flashes brightened the jungle like daylight. Seconds later, the ground trembled and the night was shattered by the deafening sounds of exploding bombs. The power of the devastation we were hearing, seeing, and feeling was incredible. From their bunkers around the perimeter, we could hear the awe filled comments from our troops as they encouraged the bombs to, "blow those little slant eyed bastards to hell".

As quickly as the strike had started, it was over. Quiet engulfed the jungle once more. The moon and stars provided the only light. The B-52s had come and gone and we had never heard them, just their destructive power.

At daylight, we were saddled up ready to move into the strike area to assess the damage. Since the target had been on a hill assumed to be an NVA headquarters, all our senses were alert as we made our way up the hill. Entering the path of the strike, we found total devastation.

Twisted trees and underbrush made it almost impassable. Frequently, we had to change direction to get through areas that were too clogged to cut through with a machete. We spent the entire morning fighting the tangled mess but found no sign of the NVA, either dead or alive. As we worked our way back down the hill, thinking the strike had been wasted, we found an NVA soldier lying in a hammock suspended between two trees. He was too weak from malaria to even reach for the SKS rifle that lay beside him.

Our interpreter, Sergeant Quann, questioned him as we carried him back to our defensive position. He had been on the hill during the attack and had heard people screaming. They had left him as they evacuated during the night. Fortunately for him, he had been just outside the area where the bombs landed.

The next day, we stayed in the same defensive position. Ambush patrols lay in wait to catch anyone coming down the hill. After an uneventful morning, the afternoon quiet was shattered by the staccato burst of M-16 fire from the position where one of my squads lay waiting in ambush. I scrambled to my radio to find out what was going on.

"Oscar 61, this is 61 Bravo. We have captured one bad guy with an AK-47 rifle. Request a fire mission to see if we can get any more where he came from. Over." I replied, "Call your fire mission. Keep me informed. Out."

Quickly our always reliable Charlie Battery of 4-42 Field Artillery responded by pounding the hillside in front of the ambush site with high explosive rounds. After patrolling through the area to see what was hit, the squad leader, Sergeant Doug Muller, called and said they were returning to our position.

It was a comical looking procession that came back into our defensive position. SP4 Kenny Nelson led the prisoner like he would a pet dog, with a small piece of twine tied loosely around his neck. The prisoner was young, we guessed him to be no more than eighteen years old, and he appeared very happy. Sergeant Muller was carrying his AK-47 rifle. "Tell me what happened," I asked. "How did you capture him with that weapon?" The story of his capture was a classic.

As they lay in ambush alongside the trail, they saw the NVA approaching, his AK-47 rifle slung across his shoulder. They all knew from their training to wait until he reached the center of the killing zone and then all were to open fire at once. In theory, the plan was good, but in reality, the human factor came into play.

Kenny Nelson lay concealed in bushes at the front end of the ambush. As soon as the soldier came even with his position, Kenny raised his M-16 to his shoulder to shoot him. As he pulled the trigger, he heard nothing but a click. He had forgotten to put a round in the chamber.

Kenny was as startled as the NVA. Rather than jack a round into the chamber and try to fire again, he lunged forward the three yards and tackled him!

The NVA offered no resistance as he was wrestled to the ground. As Kenny pulled him off the trail, the rest of the squad opened fire up the trail to get anyone else who might have been with him. As they checked out the area, it appeared the man had been alone.

When they searched him, among other things, they found American C-rations. It really angered them that some stupid Americans had left food out there for the NVA to eat. (It was our practice to puncture any C-ration cans we did not want to eat or carry and then bury everything we discarded. Obviously, other companies working in the area did not have that same level of discipline.) The find reiterated in our minds that little things like burying garbage were important to keep from aiding the enemy.

We got an interesting account as Sergeant Quann questioned the prisoner. He had been on the hill when the B-52 attack had hit but had been out of the path of the bombs. He had walked down the Ho Chi Minh trail from North Vietnam and was tired of the war. Many of his comrades were sick from malaria and wanted to go home.

He had picked up a "chieu hoi" leaflet in the jungle and had decided to turn himself in to the Americans. "Chieu hoi" was an "open arms" offer to the NVA and VC that was advertised through leaflets dropped across the countryside. It offered safe passage and a monetary reward for turning in a weapon. Little did the man know we had no idea he wanted to turn himself in. Except for the empty chamber in Nelson's M-16, he would have been a dead man.

Evacuating a soldier who had cut his leg with a machete –
we didn't have an LZ so had to wench him out

28 Nov 66

Tomorrow I get a break and get to go back to base camp. Since Russ Zink has been promoted to HQ Company CO, I'm the unofficial XO, which also makes me pay officer. It is my job to get the money for the troops. Even though there is no place to spend it, they still want to be paid...

(Letter to my folks) - ... Our luck is still holding out. Day before yesterday the second platoon captured an NVA, and today a squad from my platoon caught another one, complete with AK-47 rifle. We have been out here a month. People on our right and left have been getting hit and we just move through the middle and come out smelling like a rose. We have been working hard and doing the right things. Because of this, we are not getting hurt.

29 Nov 66

I am out of the field! Yesterday I went from the company to the brigade forward base camp on the chow chopper and then this morning came into base camp...

When I flew over the area we have been operating in, I was awestruck! We have been in some of the most rugged terrain I have ever seen. Looking at it from the air, you would swear that no human could travel through it, let alone for thirty days, and go as far as we have.

As far as you could see, there was trackless jungle. Mountain peaks jutted up through low hanging clouds laying in some of the valleys. I am glad I did not see what it looked like before we started or it probably would have scared me to death. It made me feel proud to look down and know I had traveled through it. We went through a hell of a lot walking through that crap.

... Tonight I am getting on a cot so maybe I can catch up on some of the sleep I have been missing the last month...

2 Dec 66

I hope you do not mind the typewriter but I thought it would be easier and faster to type than write in the poor light we have in the tent tonight. I just came back to base camp this evening after getting all the troops in the field paid.

I went out yesterday morning to the battalion fire base where the company is. When I got there I found out they had had a little more action the day after I came in. They killed one NVA and captured one. They also captured a rifle, a light machine-gun, a field telephone, some commo wire, and a bunch of anti-aircraft ammo.

Yesterday afternoon when I was getting ready to leave the fire base and go back to the forward base camp at Plei Djereng, they had another freak accident. (See story on "The Dangers of Retreat Ceremonies")...

THE DANGERS OF RETREAT CEREMONIES

Tradition has long been an important part of the Army. In the jungles of Vietnam, it was hard to maintain anything traditional but when an opportunity presented itself, it was jumped at. The practice in Vietnam was to never fly the American flag unless the South Vietnamese flag was flying with it. This showed we were over there, not alone, but standing as allies with the government of South Vietnam.

As we finished the first month of Operation Paul Revere IV, there was not a sign of a South Vietnamese soldier or civilian anywhere near us. While they were back in the relative safety of the rear area, we were out in the jungle doing their dirty work. Colonel Morley probably had that in mind when he decided to proudly fly the American flag, alone, over his artillery fire base. The South Vietnamese flag, like the South Vietnamese army, was no where in sight.

With all the ceremony and tradition that it received at a Stateside Army post, the American flag was proudly raised each morning and lowered each evening. The flag lowering ceremony was held at 6:00 each afternoon. A skeleton force of troops manned the defensive perimeter, while the rest of the people participated in the ceremony. Each soldier stood at attention, wherever they were, and saluted as the flag was lowered from its pole next to the command bunker. The ceremony had a special meaning to each participant under these combat conditions.

To complete the ceremony, two 81mm mortar rounds were fired in salute. As the rounds landed with a loud explosion outside the fire base perimeter, the ceremony came to an end and everyone returned to their normal duties.

On December 1, Bravo Company had finally been brought in out of the jungle and was securing the fire base. It was payday; I had paid all the troops, and was ready to return to base camp on the evening chow chopper to turn in the payroll. As 6:00 PM approached, the command was given to prepare for retiring the colors. Since we had constantly been out in the jungle, this was our first chance to participate in this special ceremony. The thrill that coursed down my spine each time I stood at attention and saluted the American flag was only intensified under these conditions in the middle of the jungle, defending the flag that fluttered so proudly in the breeze.

Right on schedule, the ceremony began. One man provided security at each bunker, the rest of us stood proudly at rigid attention as the retreat ceremony began. The flag was lowered and the two round mortar salute was fired as the color guard began folding the flag.

I watched the rounds rise rapidly into the sky, stop, turn over and begin their fall back to earth. One was quickly followed by the other as they landed outside the perimeter with an ear shattering explosion. As the second round exploded, we heard a scream, "Medic! Medic!" As the dismissal command was given, several of us sprinted over to see what the problem was.

Lieutenant Lou Dinetz, our first platoon leader, fresh back from his bout with fever and the hospital, was lying on the ground with a medic working over him. As the mortar rounds had exploded, an errant piece of shrapnel had hurtled across the fire base and slashed into his head, hitting him above the right eye. As he had reached up instinctively to touch the pain, the searing hot mortar fragment had blistered the palm of his hand.

Lou had been extremely lucky. If the fragment had hit him an inch lower, it would have put out his eye. If it had been an inch to the right, it would have hit him in the temple and probably killed him. As it was, he had a thumbnail sized piece of shrapnel to cut out of his head, a black eye from the impact, and a blister in the palm of his right hand.

He was almost embarrassed as he rode the chow chopper with me into base camp to get the fragment taken out and the cut stitched up. Later in the month, he was awarded the Purple Heart in a battalion awards ceremony.

That little accident did not put a damper on retreat ceremonies in Rawhide's fire base. The only change was the mandatory wearing of steel helmets during the ceremony. Lou, of course, got his share of good natured kidding when he returned to duty a few days later.

*The area where Operation Paul Revere IV was conducted –
awesome jungle and mountains*

2 DEC 66 (CONT'D)

...That was among the funniest accidents in Army history, I think... It will be a story well worth telling our grandkids.

We received a letter from Walt a couple of days ago. He is in the 36th Evac Hospital at Vung Tau, close to Saigon. He thinks he will be back to the company in ten to fifteen days but will not be able to hump the hills for quite a while yet...

3 DEC 66

... I spent an hour this evening talking to eight replacements. I tried to answer their questions and dispel some of the rumors they have heard. They are about as shaken up as we were when we first got here. After they have been out in the field with us for a couple of weeks, they will get over it and replace their fear with caution.

8 DEC 66

I am back at the fire base. I came out on the 5th of December and have been on several patrols. This morning we are moving out on a five to ten day operation, a sweep to the south and then working back into the fire base. Alpha Company will be going with us.

As usual, we got screwed. Charlie Company was supposed to be going but they are keeping them in the fire base and sending us. We always have to hump the hills and never stay back to secure the artillery.

12 DEC 66

I am sitting on top of a mountain in the middle of a jungle listening to jets blow the hell out of the next mountain to the north. It sure is music to my ears to hear those planes screaming overhead and then feel the ground shake as the bombs hit the ground on a suspected NVA battalion base camp.

We are still on an operation and do not know when we will head back toward the fire base. Alpha Company is still working with us. It is nice to have two companies together instead of working by ourselves. We have had pretty good success so far. Our company has killed two NVA and captured one. Alpha Company has matched our results.

I now know what it means when someone gets his brains blown out. One of the NVA we killed caught an M16 round in the head and his brain was laying on the ground beside him. It was an interesting, although somewhat gory sight. These people we are picking up seem to be stragglers. They are all pretty sickly. (See story on "Chapel Services on the Cambodian Border")...

CHAPEL SERVICE ON THE
CAMBODIAN BORDER

It was mid December, 1966. We had been on a constant search and destroy mission since November 3. On this day, we were as close to Cambodia as anyone was supposed to be. II Corps headquarters had established the rule that no American unit could set up an overnight defensive position any closer than three kilometers from the border.

The day before, as we cautiously followed a well traveled, high speed trail through the jungle, we had found a large enemy base camp. Moving into it, we had killed one NVA soldier and were sure many more had heard us and fled. Small fires were burning, pots of water still boiled. The latrines stunk from fresh human waste.

With relish, we started the "destroy" part of our mission. The well constructed bamboo huts were torched and a large rice cache burned. A classroom with wooden models of our helicopters, strung on string between two trees, was destroyed. This was, obviously, a class for anti-aircraft gunner training.

After leaving the base camp in ruins, we moved west trying to find the NVA force that had fled. Before long, as I read the terrain features on my map, I knew we had crossed over the border and were in Cambodia. There were no signs that said, "Welcome to Cambodia," or, "You are now leaving Vietnam." It all looked the same - dense jungle.

We patrolled another hour deeper into Cambodia. Our senses stayed razor sharp as we probed further and further into this known NVA sanctuary. Trails were numerous but we found no sign of the NVA. When we called our position back to battalion headquarters, they became irate when they heard where we were. Our orders were to turn around and get out of there, "Right Now!"

We retraced our steps and found a small hill about three kilometers inside Vietnam. The terrain suited Captain Fiacco so he ordered us to stop and build our nightly, triangular defensive position. Security was just a little tighter and bunkers just a little stronger than normal. It raised your "pucker factor" considerably to be that close to Cambodia and to have found a major base camp. There was no question in our minds the NVA were close at hand and could come swarming up on us at any minute.

After a tense night, the first light of the new day brought a sigh of relief. Rather than move out again, we decided to stick around, send out some small patrols, and see what we stumbled on to. By cutting down only a few trees, we cleared a spot that allowed a helicopter to come in to resupply us.

When the helicopter arrived, Captain Sauer, our battalion chaplain, jumped off. The helicopter crew quickly threw off C-rations, ammunition, radio batteries, mail, and other supplies we needed to keep going.

We were as happy to see Chaplain Sauer as we were to get the yellow mail sacks. Chapel was held whenever and wherever we could do it. I do not remember what day it was, but I know it was not a Sunday. It really did not matter. Chaplain Sauer showed up every chance he got and we always welcomed his presence.

Chapel services in the jungle were always well attended. That day, with Cambodia and who knows how many NVA not too far away (probably listening), the service was a little better attended than normal. (I can not think of too many chapel services I missed while in Vietnam. My faith in God was, and is still today, a big help to me.)

Captain Sauer carried his portable chapel set everywhere he went. It consisted of a briefcase size fold up alter - complete with cross and alter cloth. A battery powered tape recorder provided the church music. Song books were carried in an empty ammo can. It was a well thought out portable unit that made any place take on the feeling of a church.

That particular day, as usual, we maintained listening posts and security around the perimeter. If more people wanted to go to church than could be accommodated without taking too many off security, the chaplain always had two services.

We were sitting on the side of the hill about ten minutes into the service, singing with the accompaniment of the organ on the tape recorder, when the sound of a single rifle shot rang through the jungle. As we all hit the ground, the chaplain calmly said, as if he had rehearsed it many times before, "Men, go to your posts!"

You never saw so many men scatter to the safety of their bunkers so fast. I do not know what the chaplain did, none of us looked back to see.

As we sprinted the short distance to our bunkers, we heard one of the men on the line shout out, "As you were! False alarm! Take it easy!" As we investigated the source of the shot, a man in the second platoon admitted sheepishly what he had done. While cleaning his rifle, he had forgotten to take the round out of the chamber, and it went off. Fortunately, neither he nor anyone else was hurt.

Chapel service resumed but the attendance fell off. Some of the men decided it made more sense to stay close to their bunkers and listen from a safer location.

When the helicopter came back early that afternoon to pick up the Chaplain, I think he was more relieved than normal to be getting out of there and heading back to the relative safety of the brigade forward base camp.

12 DEC 66 (CONT'D)

We got another new second lieutenant in yesterday, Roy Dean. He is an OCS graduate, has nine years previous Army service, is married, and has one boy. He is 29 years old and seems like he is really going to be a good officer.

He is running the 1st platoon now. As soon as Lou gets back to the field, which should be within the next few days, he is taking over my platoon and I officially take over as XO. Isn't that great!?

Sergeant Hankins brought all the officers and NCOs some "medicinal cough syrup" when he came back from the rear area yesterday. The bottles were regulation cough syrup bottles but the contents tasted suspiciously like bourbon. I have not coughed all day so it must have worked ...

It is going to be dark before long so I had better stop and get my equipment organized. More later. (See story on "My Greatest Compliment")...

P.S. I got a letter from Thomas. He did lose his left eye and is back in the States now. If you want to send him a Christmas card, his address is...

My Greatest Compliment

All my life, I have been fortunate to have had more than my fair share of good fortune and compliments. One compliment I received deep in the jungles of Vietnam still stands out.

We had located and destroyed a large NVA base camp that afternoon. After destroying the camp and the rice cache, we had pursued the NVA into Cambodia before our battalion found out where we were and ordered us to return to the Vietnamese side of the border. It had been a hard and tense day.

We were returning from our unauthorized foray into Cambodia. As we stopped to rest, I sat down and leaned up against a tree beside Ernie Redin, my point man. Ernie had been on point nearly all day long. He was so good and dependable I put him there much more than anyone else, especially when we were in tough situations. I had often wondered how he could continue to do the point man job as often as he did, without a hint of a complaint about how frequently he was called on.

The point man was the man who led our movement through the jungle. He was the most vulnerable, first to make enemy contact, first to get shot because of that "first contact," first to catch a trip wire, and first to step into a pit of punji stakes. It required skill, courage, and stamina as he led us through the untracked jungle.

I asked him as we were sitting there, "Redin, how can you take point day after day? I have a map, a compass, and a radio so I can hear everything that is going on. All you have is your rifle. I would feel naked if I did not have everything I have, and had to lead the way like you do."

Without hesitation, he looked me in the eye and said, "Sir, I trust you. I know you won't let me down."

Never before or since have I gotten such a compliment. It made me renew my dedication to do everything within my power to bring all the men in my platoon home alive.

14 DEC 66

... We came back into the fire base yesterday. We walked about five or six miles through the jungle so we were definitely tired when we arrived. Luckily, Charlie Company was manning the perimeter so we got to sleep all night (except for an incident I didn't tell Phyllis about - see story on "Puff Hoses Us Down"). This morning Alpha and Charlie Companies moved out on another four or five day operation and we are getting to stay and guard the fire base. Maybe we can catch up on our letter writing.

I had quite a scare yesterday afternoon. We were walking through a bunch of NVA bunkers with everyone on full alert, ready to shoot at anything that moved. The machine gunner I keep with me at all times tripped and fired a burst of machine gun rounds into the ground not six inches from my heel. It did get my attention.

Our company's luck is still holding out. On this operation we killed five NVA, captured five, four AK-47 automatic rifles, three SKS bolt action rifles, one light machine-gun, one rocket launcher, one field telephone, commo wire, a lot of ammo, and about six tons of rice.

We still have not been hurt by the NVA. It is amazing, isn't it? I personally have killed one twelve foot boa constrictor. Our only bad luck has been when that mortar round fell short on us on 20 November...

16 DEC 66

Thank you for the Christmas stocking. It is hanging at the entrance to my tent and my Christmas tree is sitting inside the tent. The cookies were delicious and were devoured in nothing flat. As soon as the battalion pulls back to base camp, I will utilize the rest of the decorations.

Captain Fiacco went into base camp yesterday to have an infected leg treated. I am now the acting company commander. I do not have much to do except being responsible for securing the artillery and sending out patrols. It is nice to be able to send them out instead of being sent myself. As soon as Sandy gets back, I am starting work as XO, so my days as a platoon leader are gone.

I guess you are about ready for Christmas and know you are thinking about me. I hope you do not get depressed during this season of the year. I would give anything in the world if I could spend it with you. Do not worry, it does not seem like Christmas over here where it is so hot and we are so busy.

In fact, I did not realize until tonight there are only nine days left 'til Christmas. All of us feel the same. We share our goodies from home and in general keep each other's spirits up. My Christmas season will wait until we get together in Hawaii. I hope you understand why I have not sent you anything for Christmas. They have not started building shopping malls in the jungle yet...

(Letter to my folks) - My job as executive officer (XO) will be concerned mainly with supply, chow, and administration for the company. It will be my job to see the company gets all the equipment, clothes, ammo, etc. it needs when it is in the field. Any administrative or personnel problems will be mine to handle.

I will do all this from the rear area and will also be in command of the people who are not in the field. I will become, as we "combat" soldiers call them, a "rear echelon S.O.B." All of us front line troops get pretty disgusted with the people in the rear because some do not always give us the support we need. Maybe I can straighten things out since I am a front line trooper and know first hand their needs and problems...

21 DEC 66

Greetings from "Oscar 5". That's my new radio call sign since I became XO. We moved back into base camp yesterday and I took over as XO today. I definitely am going to like my new job. I think I can really do a lot to help out the company when they are in the field...

As usual, B Company got screwed when we moved. (See story on "Bob Hope")...

"Puff" Hoses Us Down

For the first night since the beginning of Operation Paul Revere IV, all three rifle companies were in the artillery fire base. After 45 days of constant search and destroy operations, we were eagerly anticipating being pulled out of the jungle before long and flown back to base camp. Charlie Company had perimeter guard duty. Alpha Company and Bravo Company had the night off and were looking forward to a full night's sleep sleep without guard duty or radio watch. A million stars filled the cloudless sky.

Since no rain was forecast, most of the troops did not even bother to build a hootch; they just curled up on the most inviting piece of ground and went to sleep. The strain of the long operation started to ease as we slept in the relative safety of the fire base. Sometime after midnight, our sleep was sharply interrupted by a loud burping noise in the sky, followed immediately by a sound like hail splattering the trees outside our perimeter.

With the reflexes we had learned in the many nights in the jungle, we all abruptly became wide awake. We also quickly identified the burping sound in the sky; it was "Puff, the Magic Dragon," one of our AC-47 attack planes.

The burping sound came from his 6,000 rounds per minute Gatlin guns. The sound of hail came from the bullets pounding the jungle outside our perimeter.

We grabbed our rifles and steel helmets and scrambled quickly to cram ourselves into the bunkers Charlie Company was occupying on the perimeter. We still did not know what was going on but that fire was too close for comfort!

"Take cover! He's coming around again! Take cover!" was the shout from the battalion command post in the middle of the fire base. I could hear the forward air controller in the command bunker feverishly trying to reach the plane on his radio and tell him to, "Cease fire!"

We found how sardines must feel as we continued to cram three companies of men into bunkers built to hold one. We started to piece together what was going on as we waited for another pass of the AC-47.

The AC-47 was a converted C-47 (or DC-3), the workhorse cargo plane of World War II and early civilian air transportation. Four Gatlin guns capable of firing 6,000 machine gun rounds per minute were mounted in the left side door with two additional guns in the left over wing windows. When the rifling was worn from the barrels, they were seldom changed. Who really cared how straight they shot as long as they left a good footprint of lead on the ground.

They were made by General Electric, fired electrically, simultaneously from the cockpit. The only reason for the guys in the rear end was to insure "an adequate and smooth flow of bullets from floor mounted containers, to the breech of each and every gun". It was said they could put a bullet into every square foot of a football field with one pull of the trigger.

The sound we heard on the ground was like a long burp. A solid stream of tracers traced the path to the ground as the bullets raced from the plane to their target. This was even more awesome when you realized only one out of every five bullets was a tracer round, the other four couldn't be seen. "Puff" was quite an impressive weapon.

We also came to the conclusion he was on an H&I mission. H&I stood for "Harassing and Interdicting". It was a nightly practice for artillery, mortars, and airplanes to drop rounds on suspected enemy targets to harass them, keep them worried, and hopefully hit something and interrupt their supply lines. All of the H&I missions were coordinated to go where American troops were not located so as not to hurt any of our people.

In theory, the practice worked. We had found a dead NVA a few days earlier at a trail intersection. We assumed he had been hit by H&I fire. On the other hand, early in this operation, our company defensive perimeter had barely been missed by a 500 pound bomb dropped by one of our airplanes. Fortunately, we were all lying down, asleep or on guard. No one had been hurt by the shrapnel that flew through our perimeter. One man had been saved by his steel helmet when a piece of shrapnel lodged into it as it lay on the ground in front of his head.

As we sat crammed into the bunkers, we heard the plane approach again and then heard the loud burp as he opened fire. This time, he did not miss us. His fire raked across the east end of our perimeter, right on top of the firing pits of our supporting artillery. The sound of his bullets pounding the ground was sobering. Abruptly the fire stopped as the forward air controller finally got through to him on the radio.

Loud cries for, "Medic!" told us Puff had done some damage. Soon a shout from the command bunker told us, "All clear, you can come out of the bunkers". For three of the artillery men, it was too late. One was killed and two others were wounded by this all too common accident of war.

The rest of us settled back down to a fitful sleep. We jumped at every little sound as our artillery continued to fire intermittent H&I fires into the night. Our sleep was not as restful as we had hoped for.

As Paul Harvey would say, here is "the rest of the story" – from an email from Dan Allred, Tucson, AZ, cousin of the man killed in this incident... Dec. 2002. I was at my desk at home looking at the pencil etching I took of my cousin's name (Kim S. Bird) from the Vietnam Memorial Wall in Washington D.C. back in 1991. All we knew is that he was killed on December 14, 1966 by friendly fire. His parents were told he was killed by a ricochet from a helicopter gun ship that was laying down machine gun fire in the surrounding jungle to keep the enemy away from his artillery fire base.

I looked his name up on the Vietnam wall web site and found he was with the 4th Infantry Division. I found their web site and left a message on the guest book asking if anyone remembered the incident. The next day I had an e-mail from a vet that gave me your name, Bob. Within three days I had the story you wrote and was talking on the phone with his former sergeant, SGT Robert Gobble. Somehow I missed the name Tom Basarab in one of the e-mails you sent me (I've saved them all) back then. Now a year later, December 2003, I sent him a letter. He called me a week later. Come to find out, he was the first one to Kim after he was hit. Kim lived only a short time after that, just minutes it sounds like. Interesting how the Internet can be such an evil thing and such a wonderful tool for good.

Kim Bird's name is listed on the Vietnam Memorial Wall, Panel 13E, Line 42.

BOB HOPE

Almost since the beginning of time, or so it seems, Bob Hope has entertained the American troops at Christmas time when they go to war. He has been as much an American institution as baseball, Mom's apple pie, and the American flag. Probably no other person has done so much for America's fighting men. My feelings have always been - if you are going to war, you have earned the right to see Bob Hope.

The governments of North Vietnam and the United States had agreed to a 24 hour cease fire on Christmas and New Year's days. Since we had done a good job of cleaning the NVA out of our area of operation, Operation Paul Revere IV was brought to a close. The entire brigade was to be flown back to our Dragon Mountain base camp on December 20 - the day Bob Hope and his troupe, including Ann Margaret, were scheduled to perform there.

Everyone was excited at the prospect of getting out of the jungle after 47 days of constant search and destroy missions. We were doubly excited when we found out about the performance that awaited us in base camp.

As acting company commander, I was summoned, along with the other company commanders, to the battalion command post the night before we were to be airlifted out of the fire base. We received our operation orders for the movement back to base camp - order of movement, security responsibilities, what to do when we got back to camp, etc. I could barely disguise my anger when I was told Bravo Company had security responsibility for the movement out.

"Damn!" I thought. "We are the company that has been out in the jungle more than anyone else and we get screwed again. Why do we have to be the last one to go in?"

I knew the odds were slim to none of getting three infantry companies, battalion headquarters, and an artillery battery with all their equipment airlifted out in time for us to make the mid afternoon Bob Hope show. Nothing could make me rationalize we were being treated fairly. But, it was not for me to reason why, it was for me to do or die.

I was livid when I called the platoon leaders and platoon sergeants together for a briefing. "We got screwed again," was my opening remark as I outlined the plan for the following day. Not only were we to be the last ones out, we also had to send out three squad sized patrols. We sure did not want to take a chance on the NVA sneaking up on us while we were breaking down the fire base.

After exercising every soldier's right to complain and commiserate on how badly we were being treated, we broke up the meeting. The leaders went back to break the news to the troops and to prepare to implement the plan like the true professionals that we were.

The morning dawned bright and clear. The choppers started moving in right on schedule. Alpha Company and Charlie Company were the first units flown out, just as we were sending out our three patrols. No one in our company, including me, was happy and our attitude showed.

A call from the Headquarters command post on my field telephone added to my bad mood. "Lieutenant Babcock, we are flying in a combo from the Fourth Division band to entertain your troops before you move back to base camp. Keep whatever security you think is needed for the perimeter and send the rest of your people up to the CP bunker in half an hour."

I was furious, "Negative! There is no way I am going to send any troops up there! Don't try to pacify us with a token! Leave the combo at base camp. At least they should get to see Bob Hope, even if we can't!"

A few minutes later, Sergeant Major Arruda came walking toward my command post and motioned for First Sergeant MacDonald. They moved away from the command post and started talking. After a few minutes of stern looks, raised voices, and arm waving, the two top sergeants turned and went back to their positions. From the look on First Sergeant MacDonald's face, I could tell he was disagreeing strongly with the Sergeant Major.

"What's up, First Sergeant?" I asked. "You don't want to know. Don't worry about it, I will take care of it," he replied as he sent a runner out to bring the platoon sergeants up to meet with him. It is a well known fact the sergeants run the day to day operations of the Army. That day was no exception. After a short meeting between First Sergeant MacDonald and the platoon sergeants, they broke up. Soon men from each platoon started walking up to the headquarters CP bunker to wait for the combo.

First Sergeant MacDonald explained it to me. "The Sergeant Major has us over a barrel. Colonel Morley is bringing Colonel Miller (the brigade commander) out to mingle with the troops while they are being entertained. If we cooperate, he will take care of us when it comes time to assign work details and guard duty in base camp. If we embarrass Colonel Morley (and the Sergeant Major) by not being good soldiers, he will screw us again when we get to base camp." The NCO network had prevailed again.

The combo played for over an hour. The troops tried to act like they enjoyed it, and maybe they did. I acted like a good officer and went up to exchange idle chatter with Colonel Morley and Colonel Miller. I had a hard time hiding my smile when an American propaganda plane kept flying over the fire base playing Christmas music over their loudspeakers. For the past several days, they had replaced the Vietnamese language propaganda they normally played with Christmas music.

As the music from the plane drowned out the combo, I chuckled to myself how the right hand never seemed to know what the left hand was doing. It brightened my day when the combo caught a ride back to base camp with Colonel Morley and Colonel Miller. I assumed they got to see Bob Hope.

As the day progressed, it got hotter and hotter. The hot air, coupled with the altitude, caused the helicopters to progressively lose some of their lifting capacity. During the morning, they had lifted out of the jungle easily with eight troops to a load. As it became harder and harder to clear the trees, they started reducing their load of troops from eight, to six, to five, then finally to three.

The reduced lift factor dashed all remaining hopes of getting back to base camp to see Bob Hope. It would take all day to lift the rest of the troops out at three to a chopper.

By mid afternoon, another concern started to weigh on my mind. As the last howitzer was lifted out of the fire base by the big Chinook helicopters, I started thinking about how vulnerable we now were to an NVA attack. Not only was our artillery battery gone, but the two batteries supporting us from the other battalions' fire bases had also been lifted out.

Our 81mm mortar platoon's three tubes were still set up but that did not give me nearly the feeling of security I had gotten knowing I had three artillery batteries ready to fire whenever I called on them. And, the NVA had to know how small a force we had left in the fire base if they had been counting the helicopter sorties that had been flying out of there all day.

It was nearly 5:00 when the choppers came in to lift out the last troops. At the last minute, I called in the last of our listening posts. We all breathed a sigh of relief as the choppers barely cleared the trees and started climbing for the ride to our forward base camp. I took one last look back at the desolate fire base and wondered how long it would be before the NVA moved in to see what we had left behind.

We were finishing Operation Paul Revere IV where we had started it 47 days earlier - at Plei Djereng. Trucks were waiting to take us back to Dragon Mountain and the security of base camp. I could feel the pressures of responsibility easing from my shoulders as I thought about returning to a semblance of normalcy in the base camp.

As we prepared to load the trucks, my radio came to life. "Oscar 5, stand by, we have a mission for you. I will be right there to tell you what it is." A jeep drove up as I wondered how else we would get screwed, and I found out.

"A helicopter hit some trees and went down lifting the last troops out of the "Red Warriors" (1st Battalion of the 12th Infantry Regiment) fire base. You are to be prepared to go in with a platoon and secure the helicopter tonight until we can get a flying crane in to lift it out tomorrow. You can send the rest of the company on back to base camp."

Damn! Just what I had always wanted to do - go out on the Cambodian border with thirty men and no telling how many NVA around and spend the night without any artillery or mortar support. This had really turned into a crappy day, and it got worse the longer it lasted. "What you gonna do now, Lieutenant?" came to mind.

It was an easy decision to pick the platoon for the mission. If I was going back into the jungle, it would be with my own third platoon. I broke the news to Sergeant Roath and the squad leaders. First Sergeant MacDonald, after arguing he wanted to go back out with me, took charge of getting the rest of the company back to base camp on the trucks.

We sat and waited for helicopters to take us back out into the jungle. The sun kept dropping lower and lower on the horizon as we waited. Not only were we going back out there, at this rate we were going to have to establish our defensive perimeter in the dark. And all we could do was sit, and wait, and worry.

"Oscar 5, this is Rawhide, over," broke the silence. "This is Oscar 5, send your message, over." "Good news. They lifted the bird out tonight and your mission has been scratched. Birds are on the way to fly you home. See you there, out." I felt like the weight of the world had been lifted off my shoulders as I told my men the good news.

It was 9:00 and pitch dark when the Chinooks settled down on the landing pad in the base camp. Captain Fiacco met us as we got off the chopper. "Sergeant Angulo has just thrown steaks on the grill for all of you. Go drop your gear in your tents and get some hot chow."

All the worries of the day quickly vanished as we savored the juicy steaks and cold beer and thought of the good night's sleep that lay ahead of us - inside a secure perimeter sleeping on cots inside a tent - a welcome change from sleeping on the ground and providing our own security.

I even got over being angry about not seeing Bob Hope.

Combo from 4ID Band playing for troops in fire base

Bob holding AK-47 that 1SG MacDonald captured

21 DEC 66 (CONT'D)

... Last night after supper we had a farewell party for Captain Fiacco. All the company officers and NCOs were there and most got drunk (not me, I only had five beers) before the night was over.

Captain Fiacco moved up to division this morning and took over as commandant of the 4th Infantry Division NCO Academy and Replacement Orientation School. He should really be a good man for the job. He will indoctrinate the replacements on what they need to know and I am sure he can teach the junior NCOs a lot in the NCO Academy.

Captain Ator took over the company today. I think he is going to be a great company commander. He knows what is happening and is not going to let battalion screw us up.

22 DEC 66

Two nights before we came in from the field, we had some action. About 6:00 that afternoon, the NVA tried to mortar the artillery fire base. They threw sixteen rounds of 82 mm mortars at us but they all landed outside the perimeter by about 100 yards.

We thought they would attack us but they never did. As you would expect, everyone was very alert on the perimeter that night. I still can not figure out why they wasted those sixteen rounds of ammo.

23 DEC 66

This afternoon, General Collins came to the battalion and conducted a critique of Operation Paul Revere IV. We got to tell him how we operated and what we learned. It was a pretty interesting session. He is a sharp man and asked some good questions. Our comments will be written into an After Action Report so others can learn from our experience and not have to learn on the job like we did...

Tomorrow is Christmas Eve. Things are "beginning to look a lot like Christmas." They decorated the mess hall yesterday and the orderly room has Christmas lights outlining its front. I used the decorations you sent me in our tent so it feels a lot more like Christmas here, too. We are listening to Christmas music on my portable radio.

CHRISTMAS EVE 66

... This Christmas Eve is different from any I have ever seen. This morning we had a battalion formation so Colonel Morley could present medals to some men. After the battalion formation, we had a company formation to present the Combat Infantryman's Badge (CIB) to all the men in the company.

We are all extremely proud to have earned the CIB. It is one award that is restricted totally to infantrymen who have served in combat. It was first awarded during World War II and has been earned by infantrymen in Korea and now, in Vietnam.

It is a distinctive medal - a long rifle on a blue background surrounded by a wreath. Sergeant Roath and First Sergeant MacDonald have a star above their rifle since they earned their first CIB in Korea. It is worn in a place of honor above all other ribbons, including the Medal of Honor. I have always been proud of my AIRBORNE wings, but I am even more proud to have earned my CIB.

We gave all our troops the afternoon off. Most of them went to a row of bars and "houses of ill repute" which have sprung up outside the base camp. They were really glad to get the opportunity to get away and throw a good drunk. I think it helped them forget how homesick they are.

This evening I've been listening to Christmas music on the radio, thinking of you, and watching the stars. Occasionally, one of the troops stops by and talks for a few minutes. All of the men who are not drunk are thinking about home. This is the first Christmas away from home for most of them.

To add the feeling of war to this Christmas Eve, we hear a few bursts of machine gun fire every once in a while from one of the guards on the perimeter who thinks he sees something.

Santa Claus just came to see me! Some of the men from my platoon (or rather my former platoon) got a Santa Claus mask from somewhere and are making the rounds of the officers' and platoon tents giving out presents. Santa gave me a rubber ball from his sandbag full of trinkets. See, the Christmas spirit is here even though we are a million miles from home...

CHRISTMAS 1966

Merry Christmas! Christmas is about over here. It is 9:00 at night and I guess now you are over at my folks on Christmas morning. (See story on "Christmas in Vietnam")...

The Combat Infantryman's Badge
The one thing I've earned in my life that I'm the most proud of.

CHRISTMAS IN VIETNAM

Maybe it is a normal human response to block out unpleasant memories, but for the life of me, I can not remember Christmas day in Vietnam like I can remember Thanksgiving, New Year's Eve, April Fool's Day, and even Buddha's Birthday.

My Christmas memories are limited to what I found in a letter I wrote to my wife:

CHRISTMAS 1966

Merry Christmas! It is 6:40 in the evening here and the day is about gone. I imagine Daddy is just now waking everyone up at home on Christmas morning. Today has been fairly enjoyable.

Captain Ator, our new company commander, and I slept until about 8:45 this morning. This was my first morning to sleep in since I have been in country. About five minutes after we got up, we got a call from battalion that General Westmoreland was coming to the battalion area at 9:15 and they wanted us up there.

You have never seen two guys shave, get dressed, and move out as fast as we did. We got up there on time and waited around until 10:30. The General never did show up so we went back to the company.

I then opened the Christmas present you had asked me to save for Christmas. As soon as I saw the piece of the puzzle with her eye on it, I knew it was my Beautiful Wife. It did not take me any time to put the puzzle together because I knew what a pretty face was contained in the pieces. Everyone who has seen it has commented on it. I sure do thank you for it...

At noon, we had Christmas dinner - turkey with all the trimmings. It was really good. After chow, we had a company formation and passed out Christmas packages from Red Cross chapters in the States to each of the men. They contained knick-knacks, books, writing paper, etc. The men really got a kick out of them.

This afternoon I loafed around and did nothing. Lieutenant Dean and I went riding around the base camp in a jeep for an hour to kill some time. Tonight I am going to try to get a start on my letter writing...

All in all, it was a very unmemorable day. I was successful in trying not to focus on that special family day of the year. I just tried to look on it as another day that counted on the 365 days I had to spend away from home.

27 Dec 66

I am freezing! It has turned cold and we are not used to it. The wind has been blowing hard for the last couple of days and is keeping the temperature down. Of course it is not nearly as cold here as it is at home. It is probably in the high 50's or low 60's but that is cold when you are not used to it.

28 Dec 66

Are you ready? Start making your plans. We are going to meet in Hawaii on our anniversary and spend the rest of the month together. The word came down this afternoon about R&R. I am scheduled to go to Hawaii from the 24th through the 31st of January. This means I will leave Nha Trang on the 24th and arrive in Hawaii sometime that day or night. We will have from then until the 30th or 31st until I have to fly back. This news makes me ecstatic...

29 DEC 66

Only 26 more days to go!... I can't think of anything to write about but R&R...

(Letter to my folks) - ... This morning I ate breakfast with General Harold K. Johnson, the Chief of Staff of the Army, who is here on an inspection tour. I sat at a table with him, Colonel Morley, and a West Point lieutenant, Jay Vaughn. I was real happy to get to eat with the highest ranking four star general in the Army.

He asked where I went to college. When I told him, he said he knew the college and how outstanding an ROTC program they have. I thought it was amazing he knew about Pittsburg or its ROTC program.

1 JAN 67

I had just started to sit down and write you a letter when all hell broke loose... (See story on "New Year's Eve, 1966").

Thus ended the first half of my tour in Vietnam. I would not take anything for the time I spent as a platoon leader but was very happy to move out of that job into my new challenge as the Company Executive Officer. Little did I realize I would have more harrowing experiences as an XO than I did as a platoon leader.

NEW YEAR'S EVE, 1966

New Year's Eve! Time to have a party! We knew the Christmas stand down would be over in a little over 24 hours and we would be going back to the field to hunt bad guys again. This was all the occasion we needed to throw a battalion officers' party in the officers' club tent.

Several things were memorable about the party. Most of us drank too much, tried to tell bigger war stories than the next guy, let our hair down, and tried to relax and have fun. Bill Saling had just returned from meeting his wife in Hong Kong on R&R and was full of stories about his trip. Many of us were eagerly anticipating the time in the not too distant future when we would be meeting our own wives on R&R.

Besides his stories, Bill brought back something else from Hong Kong. He had a copy of what he assured us was "the best 8mm porno movie we would ever see". As we continued to add to our drunken state, we all eagerly awaited the showing of the movie. But, none of us had the guts to start it while the battalion chaplain, Captain Sauer, was still at the party.

I am sure the chaplain enjoyed the party as much as we did, if not more. He stayed sober, and had to have known we could not wait for him to leave. (I feel sure he felt better in the morning than the rest of us.) I am sure he knew what was coming next when he smiled and said, "Well, I guess I will leave and turn in for the night." He was hardly out the door when a makeshift screen was put up and the movie projector turned on.

The movie did not disappoint us. Hong Kong was far advanced over the United States in porno movies in 1966. But, anticipation is half the fun, and after two or three showings, we tired of it and started drifting back to our tents. It was about 11:45 when Captain Buck Ator and I returned to our tent to write our wives before turning in.

We had hardly put pen to paper when, at the stroke of midnight, all hell broke loose! The entire perimeter started firing at once. What alarmed us even more, was the intensity of the firing coming from many places inside the perimeter, especially from the mortar positions set up to provide fire support.

We grabbed our rifles and helmets and bolted out of the tent to see what was going on. We could see tracer rounds going everywhere, mostly up in the air, but many were going just over the tops of the tents. "Babcock, you take the mortar position, I'll take the perimeter," was Buck's order as he sprinted for the perimeter.

We were fairly confident the firing was not caused by a VC or NVA attack. We strongly suspected we were dealing with a bunch of drunken American troops celebrating New Year's with loaded weapons.

As I ran the two hundred yards up the hill to the mortar position, the firing continued indiscriminately. The tracer rounds were still going mostly up in the air but some were much too close to my head. I stayed in a low crouch as I approached the mortar position. If I was going to get shot, I did not want it from a drunken GI.

"What in the hell is going on here?!" I shouted as I scrambled over the sandbag wall surrounding the mortar position. By then, the firing had stopped. "Nothing, Sir," replied the sergeant in charge of the position. Fortunately, he appeared to be sober. "Who has been firing their weapons?" I asked. "I don't know, I didn't hear anything."

As I went man to man, I grabbed their M-16 rifles. All of the barrels were too hot to touch. Still, no one admitted having done or heard anything. They had their story, and they were sticking to it. Like the sergeant, they all appeared to be sober. "Sergeant, I do not want any more firing. We will deal with you in the morning." With that, I headed for the base camp perimeter to see what Buck had found.

He had found the same thing. Every man had fired everything he could get his hands on. All the weapons were sizzling hot. Most of the bunker positions were completely out of ammunition. Buck and I methodically went from man to man and asked if he had fired his weapon. As we inspected the weapons, the men grudgingly admitted they had fired them. At the last bunker, one man, the Beetle Bailey equivalent in our company, was sound asleep on his cot.

We knew he was trying to pull a fast one on us so we unceremoniously pulled him off his cot. "Why did you fire your rifle?!" we demanded. Sleepily, he replied, "Huh, I don't know what you're talking about." As we checked his rifle, the barrel was cool and clean. In true Beetle Bailey fashion, he had slept through the entire ordeal.

After insuring the bunkers had been resupplied with ammo, we returned to our tent. It was too late to write. As we climbed onto our cots, we wondered if the rest of the New Year was going to be as exciting as the first hour had been.

My platoon, the day we were awarded the Combat Infantryman's Badge

SECTION FIVE

My Days as the Company Executive Officer

January 1, 1967 - July 5, 1967

EXECUTIVE OFFICER DAYS
1/1/67 TO 7/5/67

After spending the first half of my tour as a rifle platoon leader, I was promoted to Company Executive Officer (XO) in the same company (Bravo Company, 1st Battalion, 22nd Infantry Regiment, 4th Infantry Division). As Executive Officer, I was second in command of the company and responsible for running the daily operations in support of the troops in the field.

This is the last section I use excerpts of letters I wrote Phyllis. The subsequent chapters in this section tell some of the stories in more detail.

5 JAN 67

It sure was great talking to you yesterday! It's going to be even greater when I meet you in Hawaii in 19 days...

Rick Huizi and I got back to base camp at 6:30 this evening after our little tour around the countryside. We left here just before noon on 2 January and flew to Cam Ranh Bay to visit our troops in the 6th Convalescent Hospital. We spent the night in a BOQ at the hospital and moved out early the next morning to catch a flight to Vung Tau to visit the hospital there. Finally, at 4:00PM, we got on a flight to Saigon, never made it to Vung Tau.

It cost us 600 piasters ($5) for a room in a fairly decent hotel. We slept with loaded pistols, just to feel safe. The next morning we got up early and went to the USO to call you and Erin. I sure am glad I caught you at home.

Last night, Ron Marksity and Bob Jenkins (a friend from college) took us bar hopping. First, we ate at the "Crazy Cow", a real nice French restaurant. After supper we hit all the bars around the area where Bob hangs out. Saigon duty is quite a different lifestyle than we are used to...

Our flight left Saigon early this morning and got into Qui Nhon about 9:00. We had to circle Qui Nhon for half an hour waiting for the clouds to lift. (See "White Knuckles from Saigon to Pleiku").

The company moved back out to the field yesterday. I will probably go out to the brigade forward base camp and stay there until R&R time.

White Knuckles from Saigon to Pleiku

I learned early in my tour that flying in military aircraft under combat conditions was a lot different than stateside flying. My first hint of the different rules was when they loaded 180 men, standing, in the back of a C-130 and flew us to Pleiku from Qui Nhon on our first day in country. I never flew in a helicopter with its doors closed; few even had doors on them. But my most white knuckled flying experience happened one day flying from Saigon to Pleiku in a C-130 "Herky Bird".

As I boarded the plane at Ton Son Nhut air base in Saigon, I had a reaffirmation this was the real world. I was in a war, 8,000 miles from home - Vietnam. Several South Vietnamese soldiers and their families, complete with carry on baggage, cooking pots of assorted kinds, and a live goat, boarded with me. A body bag holding a dead soldier was loaded on the floor of the plane.

As several other GIs climbed aboard and strapped themselves into the canvas seats along the sides of the airplane, we taxied away from the ramp and began the first leg of the trip, to Qui Nhon. The Vietnamese people kept up a continual jabbering which could be heard above the noise of the four engines as we climbed to our cruising altitude.

As we started to descend through the clouds, I looked out the window to watch our landing. The plane was buffeted by strong winds and a driving rainstorm as we continued to plow down through the heavy clouds. We kept descending into the clutching murk as the rain beat a tattoo on the windows.

My concern began to rise as I started to wonder what kind of electronic gear the pilot had to assist us down through this mess. Suddenly, we broke through the clouds and I saw we were not more than twenty feet above the ocean, still going down!

Fortunately, the pilot saw where we were at the same time, slammed the thrust levers to full power, and jerked back on the control column to take us out of our descent and pull us away from the ocean that was trying to engulf us. At full power, the "Herky Bird" clawed back up through the clouds and finally came out of the soup into blue skies.

We circled for a few minutes before the pilot pointed the nose down and started down again through the murk. The loadmaster, sitting in the rear of the plane, appeared to be as concerned as I was.

The pilot made no attempt to tell us over the plane's speaker system what was going on. (All you would have heard, when he keyed the mike button, would have been the clattering of his teeth. I am sure he was as scared as we were.)

I gripped the bottom of the canvas seat tightly, made sure my seat belt was fastened snugly, and watched and worried as we were once again buffeted by the winds and heavy rains. Nothing could be seen except rain streaming across the window as I strained to get a glimpse of land. The Vietnamese people had suddenly gotten very quiet.

We were at least fifty feet above the ocean as we broke through the clouds the second time. As I braced for a crash, I caught a glimpse of land flash by just as the wheels of the plane touched down, barely on dry ground, on the end of the runway.

We pulled up to the hangar and got out in the still driving rain to stretch our legs and calm our nerves. After an hour, the rain slackened, the plane was unloaded, reloaded, and we were ready for our second leg, this time to An Khe.

By now, I was thoroughly spooked. We took off uneventfully but I was thinking forward to what lay ahead of us at An Khe. The An Khe landing strip had been built by the First Cavalry Division (Airmobile) when they first got to Vietnam in the fall of 1965. It was a short strip, built between two rather tall mountains.

When I had been there before, I had seen both mountains were littered with the wreckage of airplanes and helicopters that had been unsuccessful in taking off or landing in the tight surroundings. Based on our experience at Qui Nhon, I expected us to be the next piece of wreckage to decorate one of the mountains.

As we started to descend through the clouds, I once again gripped my seat, took another loop in my pucker string, looked out the window, prayed, and waited. This time, we broke through the clouds before we were right on the ground. I could see the wreckage on the mountain as we barely cleared it before touching down.

I relaxed for a moment as the propellers were reversed and we were thrown forward against our seat belt as we came to a hard stop. We had made it safely into An Khe but still had to clear the mountain to get out of there. My worries were not over yet.

Our stop in An Khe was short. As I waited to reboard the plane, I could not keep my eyes from the wreckage on the mountain we would be taking off over. It was white knuckle time again. The four engines went to full power as we started our takeoff roll. As soon as the wheels cleared the ground, the pilot pointed the nose up steeply, climbing rapidly. I saw the mountain, strewn with wreckage, fall away below as we went through clouds climbing to our cruising altitude.

For the first time since we had started our first descent into Qui Nhon, I breathed a sigh of relief. I knew the Pleiku airfield sat in the middle of a wide plain with no mountains or oceans to worry about. What a relief, back to the relative safety of the VC and NVA with no more plane rides for a while.

7 Jan 67

Seventeen more days until R&R. I am already getting nervous and excited with anticipation. All I can think about now is meeting you...

10 JAN 67

I was really sorry to hear about Mike Featherston getting wounded... I got a letter from him around the first of the year that said he was going out on his last mission before his transfer to the transportation corps. I guess that was when he got hit.

12 JAN 67

Twelve more days to go. Every day that passes is bringing us that much closer together...There isn't much going on around here. I am back at "3 Tango" (the code name for the brigade forward supply base near the Special Forces camp at Plei Djereng) and it is as dull as usual. I flew out to the artillery fire base this afternoon and spent about four hours. I caught the last chopper out of there and have been catching up on some reading...

14 JAN 67

Ten more days to go! Boy, I sure am getting impatient... "Rawhide" gives up command of the battalion on 23 January. Colonel Miller is giving up command of the brigade tomorrow. He is going to division chief of staff and Colonel Morley is going to division G-1 (chief of personnel).

17 JAN 67

We are down to seven more days! I hope you get this before you leave home... (See story on "R & R").

R & R

I saw my wife, Phyllis, before she saw me. As I left the rear entrance of the bus, she was standing at the front entrance, straining to find me in the mass of khaki clad GIs. We all looked alike in our uniforms but she stood out, the sight I had been waiting to see for six months. As I approached her, she finally picked me out of the crowd of GIs. We ran the few remaining steps that separated us.

For six long months we had been apart, never knowing from one day to the next whether or not we would ever see each other again. Now we were prepared to have six unforgettable days together before we had to face another six months of forced separation.

R & R - Rest and Relaxation, the one thing all GIs looked forward to from the day they set foot in Vietnam. There were a number of locations to choose from - Bangkok, Singapore, Hong Kong, Tokyo, Kuala Lumpur, the Philippines, and Hawaii. Australia was added as an option later in the war.

For me, the decision was simple. Phyllis and I had been planning to meet in Hawaii since before I left the States.

The anticipation had continued to build as I waited to get my orders giving the exact date and location. I did not want to go too early in my twelve month tour but as the six month mark approached, I was more than ready to get out of there.

The fatigue of the thirteen hour flight quickly evaporated as we both talked at once and soaked in the pleasure of being together. We sat through the indoctrination lecture that seemed to go on forever, picked up our Aloha R&R Hawaii identification card, and grabbed a cab to Honolulu.

Never had we been treated as royally as in Hawaii! The people honestly appreciated what the men in Vietnam were doing and showed their appreciation in many ways.

We stayed at the Ilikai Hotel, the one shown every week during the opening credits of the "Hawaii Five-O" television series. Even for 1967, the price we paid in that first class hotel was ridiculously low, only $15 per night, a huge discount simply because I was a Vietnam serviceman on R&R.

The six days were a blur of activity and relaxation. We toured the normal tourist places - the Polynesian Cultural Center, the USS Arizona, and the Kodak Hula Show.

We enjoyed the dining every evening, from the sunset dinner at the Fort Shafter officers club at the base of Diamond Head to the finest steak I had ever eaten, served in the charming atmosphere of the Colonel's Plantation restaurant in the International Marketplace.

Our days always included plenty of time lying on Waikiki Beach. The GIs from Vietnam were easy to spot with our GI suntans - brown faces, necks, and arms contrasting with the pale white of the rest of our bodies. It was not long before the pale skin was replaced with sunburn, but we did not mind.

We found cozy bars to sit in, danced until we got tired, and slept until we were ready to get up. I tried to catch up on all the milk I had missed for six months and seemed to always have a glass in my hand. And for six days, Phyllis and I never strayed too far away from each other.

As the time drew near for me to return to Vietnam, we tried to hide our sick feelings from each other. R&R had been something we had grasped on to and anticipated for six months. Now it was about over. The six months remaining before I returned home seemed like an eternity.

Phyllis had another emotion to deal with that I did not know about until after I got back to the States. She was a believer in omens. She felt that since we had had such a wonderful six days, something would happen to me when I got back to Vietnam. She never expected to see me again.

I did not have that concern. I was out of the field and expected the last half of my tour to be much safer than the first half had been (which did not turn out to be the case). I was not worried so much about my safety as I was about the hollow feeling inside as I faced another six months of separation.

It was a sad group of GIs and wives who finally bid each other farewell at the end of the six days. Few eyes were dry as we boarded the bus that would take us to the airplane. In thirteen flying hours, we would be back into the war in Vietnam.

It would be six long months (and the real possibility of never) before we would see our loved ones again. For some unfortunate ones, it would be the last time they ever had together.

29 JAN 67 - (FROM ILIKAI HOTEL IN HAWAII)

I am writing this while you are in the other room so you will not have to wait so long for a letter. I have had a wonderful time and hope the next five and a half months go by fast...

2 FEB 67

Back to the old grind! How was your trip home? Ours was very uneventful. It seemed to go much faster than the trip to Hawaii...

Last night I saw Captain Fiacco. We went to the division officers' club and while there met Don Meredith, Dick Bass, and Larry Wilson. These names may not mean anything to you. They are pro football players with Dallas, Los Angeles, and St. Louis, here on a good will tour. Don Meredith, especially, was a great guy. We spent the entire evening swapping lies with them...

4 FEB 67

I am about to get used to this place again. I came back out to "3 Tango" yesterday and have been pretty busy ever since. Our new battalion commander is really making a lot of changes and keeping everyone jumping. I have enough work laid out now to keep me busy for a month.

8 FEB 67

...We have been pretty busy out at "3 Tango". Last night and today I have been attending courts martial. I was assistant defense counsel on two cases last night and primary defense counsel on the case this afternoon. They were all pretty interesting. We won two and lost one...

11 FEB 67

I am in a bad mood this afternoon... We are still working back here in base camp tearing down the company area and turning equipment in to battalion. It is rather disgusting to have to tear down everything that has been built over the last six months. Nobody at battalion will make a decision on what we are supposed to turn in and when we are supposed to do it. The battalion commander has a good idea in consolidating the battalion area but the people who are supposed to be running the show are not doing their job.

But, what the heck! Another 159 days or less and I will be out of this disgusting place...

12 FEB 67

... It has turned cold here again. Tomorrow afternoon I am going to see the Nancy Sinatra show. I missed Bob Hope and there is no way in hell I am going to miss this one. I also heard Jayne Mansfield is scheduled to be out at "3 Tango" on 18 February for an appearance...

13 FEB 67

... I saw Nancy Sinatra this afternoon. She was pretty good, especially the mini-skirt...

15 FEB 67

The lull in the war seems to be over in this area. Quite a lot has happened the last 24 hours. About 10:15 last night the VC gave us a Valentine's present - they hit us with a mortar attack! I had just gone to bed when I heard a couple of rounds explode on the chopper pad about 75 yards from my tent.

Like a big, brave soldier, I tumbled out of bed and hit the floor. I crawled out of the tent and heard shrapnel flying through the air so decided I had best vacate the area and go get in our bunker. I scrambled back into the tent and picked up my pants, my steel pot, and my rifle and ran like hell - barefooted - the fifteen yards to our bunker.

Charlie walked two more volleys toward us. The last three or four rounds were too damned close - one round hit on top of Alpha Company's bunker, one hit about five yards from our bunker, and one round hit one of Charlie Company's tents. Our mortars and artillery reacted like lightning, and were throwing "outgoing" rounds back at them so we did not get any more "incoming".

We were really lucky, out of the approximately thirty rounds they hit us with, only eight men were wounded, none seriously. The only man in our company to get hit was a guy who had a piece of shrapnel graze his back. He just got a little burn. After it was all over and I finally got back to bed, I did not sleep too well. Every time one of our mortars fired, I jumped.

The battalion flew to the Cambodian border today to join Bravo Company and begin operations out there again. Just as the lead helicopters were ready to land, Bravo Company received small arms fire from around the LZ. They killed several of the NVA without suffering any casualties. They followed a blood trail for several hundred yards but found nothing to indicate a reason to continue the pursuit.

The battalion landed without opposition after that. However, the 1st Battalion, 12th Infantry has been making contact all day. The last I heard they were still at it. They have had two or three men killed and about fifteen wounded. It looks like the picnic is over.

I feel sort of helpless and useless sitting back here in the rear away from the action. In a way, I wish I was back out there with the troops but on the other hand I am glad I am not. The most important thing to me is to finish my time and come home to you...

This place is becoming more and more of a dust bowl every day. It has not rained since the last of December. The ground has turned to red, powdery dust. I am ready for the monsoon to start again. I think it would drive anyone crazy trying to decide whether the monsoon or the dust was worse.

17 FEB 67

The war is still going hot and furious. All three battalions in our brigade were in a fight yesterday and the 1st Battalion, 12th Infantry is still slugging it out today, for the third day in a row.

Alpha Company of our battalion stumbled into an ambush yesterday about 3:30 and was in contact with the NVA until 8:00 last night. There has not been any contact made today that I know of. They have been busy all morning lifting out the wounded and KIA they could not get out last night. The report we have now is Alpha Company had 17 men killed and 19 wounded...

It is a damn dirty shame these kids are getting killed over here in this worthless hell hole. I am really getting to the point where I hate this whole place. I can hardly wait until I can leave here and come home.

Charlie Company moved in to help Alpha Company just before 6:00 last night and their company commander was killed. He had just taken over the company from Captain Kerans less than a week ago. As far as I know now, he was the only casualty. I still have not heard the details. My guess is he was somewhere he should not have been or else a sniper picked him out and zapped him.

Bravo Company is still living a charmed existence. Our company is securing the artillery fire base so we did not see any action. From what I hear now, Alpha Company will pull back to the fire base and we will go out tomorrow to assume their mission. I am confident Captain Ator and the men in Bravo Company will continue their caution and professionalism and not get greased. I pray the company's luck holds out like it did the first half of our tour.

We have not been mortared any more. This morning about 2:30 someone thought they heard something so they blew the brigade alarm system and we all scrambled for the bunker. After fifteen minutes or so in the bunker, they decided they had made a mistake so sounded the all clear and we went back to a restless sleep.

Needless to say, I have not accomplished much in the past two days and my spirits are not very high. There is nothing for me to do to help so I just sit around and listen to the action on the radio. Last night's radio was like New Year's Day football on TV, every channel you switched to you could hear someone else battling it out with the NVA.

They really seem to be thick out on the border now. Even though they are hurting us, I think we are taking a heavy toll on them, too. Alpha Company has already found 43 NVA bodies and there is no telling how many more had been dragged off. I think the 1st Battalion, 12th Infantry and 2nd Battalion, 8th Infantry are also killing quite a few. Incidentally, the name of this operation is Operation Sam Houston.

Yesterday afternoon Jayne Mansfield was here in the area. She was really a disappointment. She looks like hell, her hair was like straw from all the bleach. Even all the troops said she looked like an old skag. But she does have a set of lungs...

As you can probably tell from the tone of my letter, my spirits are pretty low tonight. Do not worry about me. I will be over it in a day or two. I feel drained like when we had that mortar round fall on us in November. Well, such is life...

21 Feb 67

We are starting on our eighth month now. Seven down, less than five to go. 149 days from now and we will be back in each other's arms...

23 Feb 67

... Our battalion has not made any contact with the NVA lately. Bravo Company, 2nd Battalion, 8th Infantry was mortared yesterday and lost six killed and sixty wounded...

25 FEB 67

Walt and Sandra are proud parents now. A telegram came to the battalion today. It was a nine and a half pound boy, 22 inches long. Both are fine. I have not talked to Walt yet, but I am sure he is thrilled...

28 FEB 67

... Bad luck hit the company again yesterday. A "friendly" artillery round fell on us, killing one man and wounding two others. As was the case before, the man who was killed was a good soldier and a real fine kid. The two wounded were both medics, neither one hurt seriously, just some shrapnel in the legs and arms. It is a damn dirty shame this kind of mistake has to happen. That takes a lot out of your spirits... (See story "Friendly Fire on Hubbard: A Tough Mission").

FRIENDLY FIRE ON HUBBARD: A TOUGH MISSION

The letter was addressed to Commanding Officer, B Company, 1/22 Infantry, 4th Infantry Division, APO, San Francisco 96262. The neatly written letter, in a woman's handwriting, had been well thought out. It read:

Dear Sir,

My nephew, James R. Hubbard, a member of your unit, was recently killed in action. His family has asked that I write you to get more details concerning his death. We were not allowed to view his body prior to burial. His dog tags were not returned to us.

Recently, it was on national news that a boy in Ohio had been reported killed. As his family was preparing to bury him, it was found he was still in Vietnam, alive. There had been a terrible mix-up and the body was that of a boy from Colorado.

After hearing that news, there is now a touch of doubt in the family's mind. Was that really our boy we buried? Would you please let me know the details surrounding his death, who identified the body, and are you certain it was his body that was returned to us?

I know you are very busy but please reply to this letter. Thank you.

Signed by his Aunt

A feeling of dread swept over me as I lay down the letter and started thinking how to reply. My mind wandered back to the day Hubbard was killed...

The company had been moving through the jungle and had found several enemy bunker positions. As they approached more bunkers, Captain Ator called for artillery fire to blast the area. The first round, as usual, was fired past the target. The artillery forward observer called the correction to the fire base to walk the fire back across the bunker positions. The next round, called to land two hundred yards in front of the company, screamed in and exploded right in the middle of the company command group. The round detonated as it hit Hubbard, one of the company commander's radio operators, square in the back.

The entire force of the explosion was unleashed through Hubbard's body, blowing him into a mess that was hardly recognizable as a human. Miraculously, the other members of the command group were not hurt even though they all stood within five yards of where the round exploded.

I met the helicopter as Hubbard's body was returned to the rear. It was my responsibility to officially identify the body and turn it over to graves registration. I was not ready for the sight that greeted me as we opened the poncho containing the body. There was just enough of the head left intact for me to positively identify the body as that of Hubbard. I signed the required papers and returned to the company.

My mind continued to wrestle with my problem. How do you tell a family that their boy was blown into pieces that had to be shoveled into a poncho? I wanted to help them in their time of sorrow but I did not want to add to their grief. For several hours I sat at my desk, started a letter, and wadded it up after reading it. Finally, a thought hit me. Go see the Chaplain. He should know better than I how to write the letter.

I showed the letter to Chaplain Walt Sauer and we discussed alternative ways of responding to it. He gave me some good advice which I incorporated into the letter I mailed the next morning. It read:

Dear Mrs. Hubbard:

I hope the following information about the death of your nephew, James R. Hubbard, will help clear up your family's concerns.

James was on a company sized operation when he was hit by an artillery round. His body was badly damaged by the force of the explosion. Death was instantaneous, he did not suffer. No one else was injured by the explosion.

His body was positively identified at the site by his company commander, Captain Richard D. Ator, and by several of his friends. I provided positive identification when his body was returned to the rear.

It is a common occurrence for dog tags to be lost in the jungles. The thick undergrowth we travel through often gets tangled in the neck chain and frequently breaks it. As many as half of our men have lost their dog tags. It is not unusual that James' tags were not returned to you.

Your nephew was an outstanding soldier. His death was a great blow to all of us who knew and respected him. I hope it is some comfort to you to know he gave his life doing what his country asked him to do and doing it in an exemplary manner.

If you have any further questions, please do not hesitate to contact me.

Signed by me

Of all the things I did in Vietnam, writing that letter was undoubtedly one of the toughest. I heard nothing else from his family. I hope my letter did not add to their grief.

James Hubbard's name is engraved on panel 15E, line 105 on the Vietnam Memorial Wall in Washington, D. C.

2 MAR 67

Our perfect record has come to an end. Today we had two men in the company wounded by the NVA. I have not gotten the details yet but both men were in my old platoon. Sergeant Muller was hit twice in the back and is in fair condition. The medic, Private First Class (PFC) White, a new guy since I left the platoon, was shot in the foot while working on Muller. He is in good condition. (See story on "PFC White").

Both have been evacuated to the 18th Surgical Hospital in Pleiku. I am going back tomorrow to check on them. As is always the case, I feel drained of emotion, especially since Muller and I have become good friends. I pray he recovers okay.

Well, such is war. I am just thankful it was not any worse and pray we can start another lucky streak that will last the rest of the year... Do not let this depress you because, as always, I will bounce out of it tomorrow.

PFC WHITE

As the medevac helicopter settled onto the landing pad beside the battalion aid station, the litter bearers rushed through the swirling downdraft to lift the stretchers from its floor. I had been alerted that Bravo company had a wounded man on board and had hurried to await its arrival.

As they removed the stretchers from the helicopter, a man slid off the chopper and limped along beside one of the stretchers as it was rushed into the aid tent. When I moved alongside to see who had been wounded, I saw the pale white face of Doug Muller, a good friend and squad leader in my former platoon. Two bullets from a sniper had ripped through Doug's back.

The man limping along beside the stretcher was the platoon medic, PFC Julian White. Blood oozed from a hole in his boot where a bullet from the same sniper had hit him. Ignoring his own wound, he continued to care for Doug.

The scene continued to develop as they carried another stretcher from the chopper into the aid tent. This one carried the NVA soldier who had shot Doug and PFC White. One of our men had shot him down from his perch high up in a tree. Still alive when he fell to the ground, he became a prisoner and had to be cared for.

The doctors worked hurriedly over the two stretchers, assessing the damage, stabilizing the wounds, and preparing the men for evacuation to

18th Surgical Hospital back at Pleiku. PFC White stayed right by Sergeant Muller's side as the doctors worked to save him.

Finally, someone noticed White's limp and the blood seeping from the wound. Over his objections, he was put on a stretcher and a medic started to care for him.

While watching PFC White's obvious concern and caring for Doug Muller, I remembered an incident aboard the troop ship a few months earlier. PFC White had gone AWOL (Absent Without Leave) while we were at Fort Lewis. He had been gone for six weeks but had shown up, to everyone's surprise, the day before the ship left for Vietnam. He was placed under arrest and boarded the ship with us.

I was assigned as the prosecuting officer to bring the charges against him at his court martial. In preparing for the case, I interviewed him to find out why he had gone AWOL. He was very courteous and honest as he explained his reasons.

He had entered the Army as a conscientious objector. Since he would not carry a rifle, he had been sent to medic school. He had been wrestling with his value system throughout his time in the Army. He had no questions about his own unwillingness to kill another human being but he could not bring himself to grips with even being a part of an Army that did.

After much soul searching, he had decided he could not participate in such an organization and went AWOL. While gone, he had drifted up and down the West Coast trying to sort out his beliefs. Besides not believing in killing others, he was also a very patriotic American citizen.

His AWOL status bothered him as much as his unwillingness to participate with a killing machine. After six weeks of anguish, he had decided he could not live with himself as a deserter and had returned to Fort Lewis. He had committed himself to doing everything he could to help his fellow man without getting involved in direct conflict with the enemy.

After hearing his absolutely honest and open confession, I spent long hours trying to decide logically and objectively how I would prosecute the case. I was convinced he had already gone through enough self imposed punishment. He did not need to receive any more than the minimum allowable punishment from the Army. But, my job was to prosecute him. He had broken an Army law that had been enforced since the days of George Washington.

As I presented the facts to the court martial board, I requested they treat him with leniency. His defense council, Lieutenant Bill Saling, explained the circumstances PFC White had dealt with. Bill's eloquently presented defense argument convinced the board they were dealing with a good soldier whose value system priorities were in major conflict. After a short deliberation, the board returned a verdict of guilty.

They imposed a sentence of fourteen days confinement to quarters, a virtual non sentence under the circumstances, since we were all confined to the quarters of the ship. We knew then we had a good soldier in PFC Julian White.

He had spent the first half of his tour working in the battalion aid station and had joined my old platoon just after I had left it. All the reports I had gotten were that he was doing an outstanding job looking after the men's daily aches and pains.

When the sniper hit Doug Muller, PFC White immediately jumped up from his covered position to go to Doug's aid. Bullets pounded the area around him as he worked on Doug's wounds. When hit in the foot, he did not slow down but continued to focus all his efforts and attention on taking care of the seriously wounded man, completely ignoring his own safety.

My mind came back to the activity in the aid station. The men working on the NVA soldier stopped their activities and covered his head. He had died before they could save him. After Doug's wounds were stabilized, he was hurried out to another waiting medevac helicopter and transferred to the surgeons at 18th Surgical Hospital.

PFC White's stretcher was loaded on the same chopper. My guess was PFC White again forgot his own wound and made sure Doug was properly cared for on the short flight. I took much care and pride in writing the recommendation to award PFC Julian White a Bronze Star for Valor for his actions. He was truly a sincere human being who cared greatly for his fellow man.

General William Peers awarded PFC White his Bronze Star in a ceremony a month later.

3 MAR 67

This has been one hell of a day to say the least. It started as uneventful as usual but about mid morning things started to happen. We were monitoring the battalion radio net, as we always do, when we heard a report a helicopter was coming from "Oscar" (Bravo Company) to "3 Tango Dust-off Pad". That meant someone had been hurt so I went to the aid station.

Just as I got there, the chopper came in with Lieutenant Roy Dean, the officer who took over my old platoon. He had been hit in the side with shrapnel from a mortar round. They worked on him here then sent him on back to 18th Surgical Hospital for surgery. He is in bad shape but should pull through.

"Oscar" called in another dust-off while I was at the aid station. The chopper aborted the mission because of enemy ground fire. About an hour later, they called it out again. This time it made a pickup with no sweat.

In the meantime, Alpha Company had run into contact and had three wounded and one killed. Lieutenant Katin, who was in a helicopter serving as a radio relay station, was wounded by ground fire that came through the floor of the chopper.

So, when the next "dust-off" came in, it had Lieutenant Katin, Sergeant Cheatham from my old platoon, and Alpha Company's wounded men. Lieutenant Katin was hit in the shoulder and neck. Luckily, neither wound was serious, just flesh wounds, so he will be okay in a couple of weeks. Sergeant Cheatham took quite a bit of shrapnel in the leg and groin but he will be okay, too. The men from Alpha Company were not wounded very seriously, either.

All this activity was over by 1:00 so the rest of the afternoon was rather uneventful. I took a shower, ate supper, then it started again. A call came in from the fire base that "Regular 6" had been shot. That is the battalion commander who took over from "Rawhide".

He came in on a chopper and now has been evacuated to 18th Surg. The doctor says he is in bad shape but will survive. It seems he was in his tent and a guy in Headquarters Company was cleaning his rifle, it went off, and hit the colonel in the back.

Have you heard enough? Well, there is more. The bullet that hit the colonel went through him and hit Major Williams, the battalion executive officer, in the leg. His wound is not serious at all, in fact he did not even say he had been hit until the excitement about the colonel had died down. The bullet is still in his leg so he had to be sent back to 18th Surg to have it taken out.

So, today the battalion had four officers wounded, two seriously. Neither Alpha nor Bravo companies had any more casualties except for the ones I mentioned. I do not know how large an NVA unit they hit or how many enemy they killed.

I am beginning to get hardened to this whole war so the casualties do not bother me as much as they used to. When a wounded man comes in, I am just thankful he was not killed and pray he gets better.

It is hard to do when guys you know like Lieutenant Dean, Sergeant Muller, and Sergeant Cheatham come in hurt but I have found you just have to accept it as inevitable. I will sure be glad when this whole miserable war is over.

I guess I should not write you about all this stuff but you are the only one I can talk to. It makes me feel better to go ahead and tell you the truth...

4 Mar 67

Today was peaceful! The company came into the fire base so I went out and paid them. Their spirits are still good. They will probably be there for a week so I will get a chance to talk to them some more before they go back out.

Chaplain Sauer went to 18th Surg today and said Lieutenant Dean, Sergeant Muller, and Sergeant Cheatham are doing a little better. Tomorrow I am going to stop by to see them. Lieutenant Katin and the battalion commander are getting along okay, too.

Lieutenant Colonel Tom Roselle, the brigade executive officer, is our new battalion commander. I met him today and he seems like a much calmer, easier to get along with guy than his predecessor was. His predecessor's temper was something else. Luckily, I never did anything to bring his wrath down on my head. I hate to see anyone get hurt but I am sure glad to see that man out of the battalion...

5 MAR 67

It finally happened! It rained! This afternoon it rained for about an hour for the first time since late December. It settled the dust for tonight at least.

Today I went to 18th Surgical Hospital to see our wounded guys. They are all progressing very nicely. They will probably all be evacuated day after tomorrow. One of the nurses told me they would probably all go back to the States to recover. I sure am glad to see them making progress. Lt. Dean's wife is supposed to have a baby any day now... (See story on "Lieutenant Dexter").

LIEUTENANT DEXTER

I first saw her early in January when I went to pay our troops in the Pleiku hospital. As I entered the ward with the malaria patients, she caught my attention. Her green army fatigues could not hide her obviously well proportioned figure. Her blonde hair and pretty face added a spark to the dull hospital ward filled with American GIs. As I talked to one of my men, she approached his bed. He introduced me to her as, "My lieutenant". In our short conversation, it was apparent she was a special person who would do everything within her power to help and comfort the GIs under her care.

As I left the ward, my eyes wandered across the room for a last glimpse of Lieutenant Dexter as she made her rounds, pausing to give a smile and word of encouragement to each GI as she passed him. It seemed like forever since I had seen a beautiful American woman.

The memory of the beautiful nurse lingered with me. When I made my next trip to visit the troops in the hospital, I started looking for her as soon as I neared the hospital grounds. I saw nurses but she was not among them. After an hour of visiting with our troops, I left, disappointed that Lieutenant Dexter had not been there.

The next payday, I made my hospital visit again (we always had men in the hospital with malaria) and immediately saw her as I walked onto the ward. She was busy working with a patient across the room from where I was paying my men. It was hard to keep my mind on my pay day activities as I kept shifting my eyes to watch her work.

She had lost none of her beauty or charm since I had last seen her. I lingered for quite some time after paying the men, idly chatted with them, and finally left when she left the ward. I am sure she was totally unaware I was in the room watching her work.

In mid March, when Lieutenant Dean, Sergeant Cheatham, Sergeant Muller, and PFC White were wounded, I caught a helicopter from the fire base to the hospital to check on them. All had serious wounds and I was very worried as I walked into the ward. The first thing I saw was Lieutenant Dexter working on Sergeant Muller. He had taken two bullets through the back and was in critical condition. It immediately eased my mind when I saw who was caring for him.

I spent the morning talking to the men. Roy Dean asked me to write his wife and explain what had happened but to be certain to reassure her he was alright. She was expecting a baby at any moment and he did not want her to be unduly alarmed. An NVA mortar fragment had ripped through his side. He was in stable but still serious condition.

Sergeant Cheatham was his usual bright and chipper self despite the serious wounds to his thigh and groin area. PFC White's foot wound was not causing him too much pain. Sergeant Muller was in the worst shape. For several days prior to getting wounded, Doug had been ignoring the fever of an increasingly serious case of malaria as he continued to lead his men through the jungle. The bullet wounds, coupled with the malaria, had him in a life threatening condition.

Lieutenant Dexter continued to add a touch of warmth and professionalism to the room as she meticulously carried out her duties. She took time to stop and chat but never stopped long enough to neglect looking after anyone who needed her attention. I am sure my wounded friends appreciated her as much or more than I did. They maybe were not in shape to appreciate her beauty as much as I, but they had to enjoy the dedication of an American woman's care as they lay there, hurt and scared, so many miles away from home.

All the men were evacuated before I could get back to see them again. Except for Doug Muller, I have not seen or heard from any of them since that day. I met Doug in September 1987 at LaGuardia airport in New York City and learned about his ordeal during his long recovery period. I feel certain the rest survived their wounds, none of their names are on the Wall in Washington.

I saw Lieutenant Dexter one more time. I never did learn her first name, where she was from, or anything about her. She never even knew I existed. All I know about Lieutenant Dexter is she was a beautiful American nurse who provided a spark and a shot in the arm to me and the wounded GIs she cared for.

(On Veteran's Day, 1993 a statue honoring American women in the Vietnam War was dedicated. It stands in front of the Vietnam Memorial Wall in Washington, D.C. I attended that ceremony with Lieutenant Judi Dexter Richtsmeier, her husband, and her sister, another Vietnam nurse. More about that day in Section 7 of this book).

These women, and others like them, provided real care and comfort to many of the men who died in Vietnam and to the ones who were wounded and survived, as well as those of us who were fortunate enough to not need their care. It was a comfort to all of us to know they would have been there if we had needed them.

9 Mar 67

... Things are still pretty quiet. There has not been any contact by anyone since our company got hit on 3 March. I am keeping busy now preparing for another move. We are supposed to move back to the Oasis in about another week. I hate to think about moving but this will probably be our last one before I come home...

Premiere and Madame Ky were here today. They flew in to see MG Peers and present some awards. That has been about the extent of what is going on. We had a court martial tonight and I was on the board for a change. I have been trial or defense counsel for so long it is a welcome change to be able to sit and listen and decide whether he is innocent or guilty...

11 MAR 67

... Alpha Company found a large cache of NVA weapons and ammunition yesterday. They got eleven machine guns and beaucoup ammo of different types. Some of the stuff had Nazi markings, left over from World War II.

Yesterday I flew out to the fire base to talk to Captain Ator and get a haircut. It's something when you have to go three miles from the Cambodian border to get someone to cut your hair...

12 MAR 67

Sit down because you are not going to believe this. I can hardly believe it myself but, unfortunately, it is true. I got a letter from Ron Marksity today and Cathie wants a divorce (the couple who were our best friends at Fort Lewis). I am shocked and can not believe it...

13 MAR 67

... I got two great letters from you today. I sure was glad to get them because they have not been coming too frequently the last week or so. It makes for long days when I do not get any mail...

16 MAR 67

Sorry I have not written the last couple of days but I have been pretty busy. In fact, the past two days have been unforgettable to say the least! By now I am sure you have heard about the Second Brigade, Fourth Infantry Division forward base camp being mortared. Man, it sure was!

On the night of 13 March, a little before 11:00, I had just gone to bed when I heard something whiz over my tent and then mortar rounds started landing all over the place. (See story on "Mortar Attack on Plei Djereng")...

Mortar Attack on Plei Djereng

"Those gook mortars are lined up out there like piss tubes," joked the GIs sitting around the supply tent listening to the Chris Noel show on Armed Forces Radio. We had gotten another Army intelligence report that the NVA were going to mortar our forward base camp that night.

After Chris Noel had bid us farewell with her sultry, "Bye, love" to close out her nightly show, I headed back to my tent to write a letter before turning in. By 10:45 I had turned off the lantern, tucked the mosquito netting in around me, and was drifting off to sleep. The sound of an NVA B-40 rocket screaming over the top of my tent and exploding less than fifty yards away woke me in a flash! We had heard the intelligence reports so often we totally ignored the warning. Intelligence reports were like the little boy who cried, "wolf", we did not believe them since they had always been wrong.

My instincts were running full speed as I rolled off my cot, tearing the mosquito netting down as I fell to the floor. I instinctively grabbed for my steel helmet and rifle as I heard the explosions of mortar rounds walking across the large helicopter landing pad and toward my tent.

I huddled close to the floor, praying we did not get a direct hit. Sandbags protected the bottom two or three feet of the tent. As long as I stayed close to the ground and we did not take a direct hit, I felt as safe as you can under those circumstances.

I was pulling my pants on as we waited for a break in the explosions so we could make a run for our bunker. Sergeant George Wilhelm, my tent partner, was busy pulling his boots on, without pants. (It is funny what you consider important in a situation such as that, we really did not need either our pants or our boots.) When the rounds quit falling, we jumped up and scrambled out of the tent in a low crouch, George with no pants and me with no boots.

Several men had already made it to the bunker. As they counted noses and saw we were missing, they had assumed we had been hit. When the rounds stopped, they shined a bright flashlight from the entrance to the bunker, scanning the area trying to find us. All it did was blind me as I tried to find the door of the bunker.

"Turn out that damn light!" I shouted. "Do you want the NVA to know exactly where you are?!" With the light out, I could see the outline of the bunker entrance and dived head first into its safety as the mortar rounds started peppering the area again. George had tripped on his bootlace and twisted his knee but quickly got up and tumbled in on top of me, cursing every step he took.

The mortar fire was much more accurate this time as the rounds pounded our area. A round hit scarcely three yards from our bunker, exploding with an ear shattering blast. We were shaken by that blast but not nearly as much as by the one that hit a few seconds later, squarely on top of our bunker. The noise and concussion was deafening. Dirt and dust, along with the acrid smell of burning gunpowder, engulfed us, causing us all to start choking and coughing.

Fortunately, we always constructed good, strong bunkers and this one took the explosion without crumbling. With tears streaming down our faces from the dust and gunpowder fumes, we were all shaking as we waited to see what would happen next. Even though we wanted to hug the bottom of the bunker, we knew we had to be ready to repel any sappers who might have broken through the perimeter. The last thing we wanted was to have a satchel charge thrown in on top of us.

It was a sweet sound when we heard return fire going out from our artillery and mortar positions. Soon after our artillery started firing, the NVA mortar positions went silent. But we felt far from safe. It was pitch black, there was no moon to light up the night, and we had no idea whether any of the NVA had breached the perimeter. I posted a man on each side of the bunker to make sure no one sneaked up on us. I climbed on top so I could get a better view all around. We waited and watched but nothing happened.

Soon "Spooky" flew over dropping flares, lighting up the area like daylight. We quickly scanned the shadows and found no NVA had made it through the barbed wire perimeter, at least not in our area.

We breathed a sigh of relief and started filling sandbags to reinforce our bunker. It had taken one direct hit; we wanted it to be even stronger in case of another one. While filling sandbags, we became a cheering section as a flight of Air Force jets started working over the likely NVA mortar firing position. Each time a bomb or napalm canister exploded, a cheer went up from the GIs.

In less than half an hour, the planes had departed, the flares had burned out, and darkness crept back across the camp. It was an uneasy bunch of GIs that headed back for our tents to try to sleep through the rest of the night.

I slept with one eye open and jumped every time I heard one of our howitzers fire their random H&I fires. It was an extremely uncomfortable feeling to lay there and hope the NVA did not come back to visit.

As daylight returned, we were up surveying the damage. Amazingly, the damage had been very slight. Except for small shrapnel holes in all the tents, the heaviest damage had been to the Charlie Company supply tent. It had taken a direct hit and supplies were strewn all around but no one had been hurt. After surveying our tent area, I walked to the battalion motor pool to see if any of our vehicles had been damaged. They, too, had escaped with minor damage.

As we stood in the motor pool and marveled at the small amount of damage, we heard a sound we never expected to hear in the daylight. From just outside the perimeter, we heard the unmistakable "whump, whump, whump, whump, whump . . ." of mortar rounds being fired at us. I counted twelve "whumps" as we all screamed, "Incoming!" and dived for the nearest bunker. I scrambled into the motor pool bunker and found it already crammed with men who had reacted at the first "whump" and had not waited to count the rounds before finding shelter.

The NVA were deadly accurate. All twelve rounds landed inside the motor pool. I was barely inside the bunker and could plainly see and feel the explosions that shook the area. One round landed on top of a "deuce and a half" truck loaded with 4.2 inch mortar rounds scheduled to be carried out to the forward fire base early that morning. The truck started to burn.

I knew all hell was about to break loose. Not only was that truck loaded with mortar rounds, the one parked next to it was loaded with 81mm mortar rounds. For a brief second, I said to myself, "Babcock, if you want to earn a Silver Star for certain, go get in that truck and drive it out of the motor pool." Fortunately, my sane self took command before I made any move to do such an insane thing.

Suddenly, the mortar rounds started blowing. It sounded like high intensity popcorn as round after round exploded. Pieces of truck were hurled through the air like toys. When the truck with the 81mm mortar rounds started to explode, I decided it was time to get the hell out of that motor pool and find a bunker that was sturdier and further away from the raging inferno. Taking a deep breath, I pulled my helmet down tight on my head and ran like a sprinter to put distance between the motor pool and me. My company bunker was about fifty yards away and the distance was covered in record time.

For the second time in less than twelve hours, I dived through the entrance to the bunker as mortar explosions and pieces of truck flew through the air. Once again, several others tumbled in on top of me in a heap. They had followed my lead and had also decided to get the hell out of the motor pool area.

For the next hour, we sat in the bunker and listened to the American mortar rounds explode. As I looked out the door, I vividly remember seeing an entire truck fender hurtling through the air fifty feet above the ground. We sat in the bunker for several minutes after the last explosion, waiting to make sure nothing else was going to blow.

Once again, we ventured out to survey the damage. The vehicles in the motor pool were in shambles. There were no identifiable pieces left of the two "deuce and a halves" containing the mortar rounds. Every vehicle was damaged beyond repair, with the exception of my jeep. Surprisingly, the only damage to it was a dent in the front wire catcher and a flat spare tire. The jeeps parked on either side were totally destroyed.

The rest of the day we worked trying to put some order back into the chaos the NVA had brought. After the twelve early morning rounds, nothing more was heard from the NVA mortars. We suspected they had fired and then run before we could zero in on them. They were probably back on some hill patting themselves on the back for the great job they had done. They had gotten our attention.

We spent much of the day filling sandbags to reinforce the bunker that had saved our lives. By the time we were through reinforcing it, that bunker would have taken a direct hit from a 500 pound bomb and held up. We were a nervous bunch of soldiers as night descended on us again. Chris Noel did not have us in her radio audience that night, we were hanging around the bunker keeping our eyes and ears alert to anything out of the ordinary.

Despite our tired and sleepy state, none of us made any attempt to go into our tents to sleep. All of us stayed close to the bunker and drifted in and out of an uneasy sleep lying around or in the bunker. The night passed slowly but uneventfully.

The next morning we received orders to move back to Artillery Hill near Pleiku. We made record time packing our equipment and belongings into borrowed trucks. We were extremely happy to see Plei Djereng disappear over our shoulder as we slowly wound our way back toward relative safety.

16 MAR 67 (CONT'D)

The trip was uneventful and we are now set up just north of Pleiku. We can sleep a lot better here than out at "3 Tango". Also, we have grass and very little dust. We will be here about a month before we make another move.

Alpha Company met their Waterloo again on the 14th. They were hit by another ambush out by the border and lost eighteen killed and twenty-nine wounded. Captain Keuker was wounded very seriously in the head. Once again bad luck is plaguing Alpha Company. They have now lost 50 killed and 150 wounded since we arrived in Vietnam. Their original strength was only 180 men.

Charlie Company had some contact yesterday and lost two killed and five wounded. Our company is still maintaining its luck and has not made any more contact. They are supposed to move the battalion fire base and companies back to this area tomorrow. It should be much calmer for the troops than out on the Cambodian border.

17 MAR 67

What seems to be the problem you can not write me any more? In the past ten days I have only gotten three letters... Maybe I am not being reasonable but I sure miss hearing from you, especially after all the crap that has happened the last few days...

18 MAR 67

... Please forgive me for the letter I wrote yesterday. Today I got three letters from you, a package of cookies, and penlight batteries. I guess the mail was just fouled up and there isn't a thing you can do about it...

They moved the battalion forward elements away from the Cambodian border today. The new fire base is southeast of "3 Tango" about six miles. They are going to work around that area for a week or two and see if they can find the people who mortared us. After they finish that, they are going to move up here northwest of Pleiku and clear the VC out of the villages in this area. It should be pretty good duty.

Tonight I am sitting here in my tent eating on a loaf of hot bread, drinking an RC Cola, and listening to "Grand Ole Opry" on Armed Forces Radio. It hardly seems like we were getting mortared only five days ago. This is a funny war...

19 Mar 67

... It rained for about an hour late this afternoon. It was needed and welcome but after the mortar attack our tents are not too waterproof with all the shrapnel holes in them...

28 Mar 67

Happy Birthday! I hope you enjoyed it. Next year I will be there to celebrate with you. We are finally starting to work in the area northwest of Pleiku trying to clear the villages of VC. It should be much better duty than any we have had since we left Tuy Hoa. Our company moved out last night to kick off the operation. We are going to encircle and search a village day after tomorrow to see what we can stir up...

You asked me what I think about the war. Any more I just quit thinking about it and accept it for the fouled up mess it is. Captain Ator is really good and so is our new S-3 (Operations Officer). But outside of that, things are pretty weak in the new officers we have received. They sure are not the team Rawhide built. So, I have just accepted it and try to keep ahead of the problem and take care of my own company.

In spite of everything that goes wrong, the job is still done. As long as you have a good company commander, the battalion can not foul us up. And our CO is #1.

As far as the Vietnamese people, I still have no respect for them. But, that, too, I have learned to ignore. Anymore I just say to hell with it, do my job and do not let anything bother me. My spirits are still good. It is easy to get in a rut and go stale around here...

2 Apr 67

Pay call was pretty exciting this month. I flew into what I thought was a secure LZ yesterday morning to pay the troops... (See story "April Fool's Day").

Aftermath of mortar attack on Plei Djereng

April Fool's Day, 1967

Every soldier wants to be paid on payday, whether he has a place to spend it or not. April 1, 1967 was no exception - it was the first day of the month, so payday it was.

The company had been operating for the past several days in an area northwest of Pleiku, a relative picnic compared to the jungles we had been working in since the 3rd of November. The terrain was fairly open, it was sprinkled with a series of Montagnard villages, and the only enemy seen were a few bands of Viet Cong.

It was a welcome relief to be out of the jungle, off the Ho Chi Minh trail, and fighting small VC groups instead of NVA regulars. Being payday, the company had not even sent patrols out. We were taking the opportunity to lay back, take it easy, and enjoy a well deserved break.

The sun was shining brightly and the countryside was beautiful as the helicopter I was on approached the landing zone beside the company defensive perimeter. The Montagnard villages dotting the area had always intrigued me. I was enjoying the view and the cool breeze blowing through the open doors as the pilot radioed Captain Ator.

"Oscar 6, this is Black Jack 33, mark your position, over." Harry Troutman, Captain Ator's radio operator responded back in his familiar southern drawl, "Black Jack, this is Oscar 6 Echo, our position is marked, over." "This is Black Jack 33, I see purple smoke, over." "This is 6 Echo, roger purple, bring it on in, out."

As the helicopter started its flare to hover onto the LZ, I grabbed my M16 and my brown briefcase full of MPC (military payment certificates) and prepared for a quick exit from the chopper - pilots don't like to stay on the ground in a potentially unsecured area. As I jumped to the ground, the pilot accelerated and headed back up into the sky as I casually started to walk toward the company.

The sound of gunfire punctuated the calm as bullets raked across the helicopter. The chopper lurched forward as the pilot lost control. The copilot reacted quickly, regained control, and nursed the crippled machine to a hard landing not too far from the LZ. At the sound of gunfire, I quickly sprinted to the safety of the company perimeter (it would have been interesting to have a stopwatch on me to see how fast I covered that ground).

Bravo Company reacted quickly to the gunfire. Before the rotors on the chopper had stopped spinning, a squad of men had formed a skirmish line and was moving across the landing zone to find the VC who had fired the shots. Another squad quickly grabbed their steel helmets and rifles and headed in the direction where the helicopter had gone down.

As I ran up to Buck Ator's command post, he was already on the radio alerting battalion headquarters. As I dropped down beside him, out of breath from my sprint, he asked me, "Did you see where they were firing from? Did anyone get hurt on the chopper?"

"Negative, I did not see anyone. Beats me if they hit anyone, I got the hell out of there as fast as I could."

Buck started issuing orders. "Harry," turning to Harry Troutman, "go check on the crew and see if they are okay and report back to me. Babcock, get some platoons sweeping the area and see what they can find. I am going to see if I can get one of those jets circling up there to drop his load for us."

As Buck started calling the Forward Air Controller to bring in an air strike, I called the three platoon leaders to alert them to get ready to move out. In less than five minutes, my old third platoon and the second platoon were started on a pincer movement around either side of the landing zone.

They headed down into a wood line that led to a creek where we suspected the shots had come from. It was a lot more fun being on the command side telling the platoons where to go. In the past, I had always been out there slogging through the woods.

It became a game of cat and mouse as the platoons radioed back they had found nothing. Since I had a good view of the terrain, I kept adjusting their movement to try to get them to spots which looked like good hiding places for the sniper.

In the meantime, Buck had been successful in getting a flight of F-4 Phantom jets to blast the downstream side of the valley to try to cut off that escape route. Four jets screamed in, one after the other, and dropped their loads of bombs and napalm. As usual, the display of firepower was awesome.

After about an hour of futile searching, we called the platoons back in to the perimeter. A medevac chopper had come in to take out the pilot who had been shot in the foot and the door gunner who had been clipped in the nose by a bullet. Another helicopter was on the way to lift the disabled chopper out.

I paid the troops, took notes on the pay and personnel problems I needed to work on, and spent the afternoon talking to the soldiers while waiting for the evening chow chopper to come in. Patrols were sent down into the valley before this chopper started the same approach we had taken that morning.

No shots were fired as it landed. As I climbed aboard for the return flight to base camp, I remained tense until we were well clear of the sniper area and had climbed out of range of small arms fire.

The next day, as the battalion commander and sergeant major were landing at Charlie Company's defensive perimeter, a single shot felled their helicopter as it was landing. Again, no one was seriously hurt but the repercussions were widely felt.

The order was given, "A company will secure an area 500 yards all around a landing zone before any helicopter will land." This was not just an empty order; the company commander had to personally tell the pilot he had secured the 500 yard area before calling the chopper in.

Trying to secure a 500 yard area on a parade ground or parking lot might have been easy, to do so in the terrain we were in was impossible. Regardless of how much the CO's argued, the order was not rescinded. They were told they would be relieved of their command if another helicopter was shot down. Each time a helicopter approached his area, the company commander would cringe and worry about his career until the chopper was safely gone. (What a helluva way to fight a war.)

Three days later, a helicopter was again fired on as it approached Charlie Company's landing zone. This time, a patrol was lying in ambush along the glide path. They opened fire on the Montagnard farmer as he fired, killing him instantly. His rifle was primitive but his aim was deadly. He had wreaked much havoc on our operations before we finally got him.

2 APR 67 (CONT'D)

I am really shocked to hear about your Uncle Lynn's death...

6 APR 67

The last two days have been uneventful ones in this "war-torn, jungled" country. Bravo Company has not even had any helicopters shot down in its area in the last few days.

8 APR 67

... Operation Sam Houston is now over. The mission is still the same for us but now they are calling it Operation Francis Marion...

12 APR 67

Well, we moved yesterday. We are now at the Oasis, southwest of Pleiku about twenty miles. I do not know how it got the name "Oasis" because the area is nothing but a big dust bowl like "3 Tango" was. Our battalion area is real small and we are crammed in like sardines. If you are getting the idea I do not like it here, you are absolutely right. I did not like it when we were here in January and I do not like it now. But, it appears we will be here until I rotate so I might as well learn to like it...

13 Apr 67

... As you can tell by looking at the paper I am writing on, we are still plagued with dust here like we were at "3 Tango". Right now I have given up on trying to stay clean, so I look like Pigpen in the "Peanuts" comic strips. I can slap my clothes and dust billows out of them...

I am getting more impatient to see you, 97 days seems like an eternity...

18 Apr 67

Would you believe it rained all night last night and most of the day today? It settled the dust real nicely, in fact, it is even a little muddy. I will not start complaining about mud, yet. It is nice not to have to breathe dust for a change...

21 Apr 67

... I have been back in base camp the last two days. We drove back there night before last and ran out of gas on the way in. When I tried to use the spare gas can to get us going, I found it was empty, too. Luckily, a gasoline tanker came by and filled us up just as it was starting to get dark. I must say I was rather uncomfortable being out there on the road with just Robinson, my driver, and me and no gas. We made it inside the main gate just a few minutes before curfew. You can bet that I got Robinson's attention after that fiasco and he won't let my jeep run out of gas again.

22 Apr 67

It is really pouring down rain here tonight. It has been coming down in buckets full for about an hour now. The patches on our tent are beginning to leak so I guess we will have to get out the repair kit again. I think the monsoons are coming back and we can quit worrying about the dust...

28 Apr 67

Greetings from "Jackson Hole" Vietnam. The battalion trains moved again today for about the twelfth time since we have been in country. When we get everything piled on our trucks, we look like a roving gypsy band...

1 MAY 67

Another month out of the way. April went by fast and was a pretty good month. Let's hope May passes just as fast and uneventful... Pay day went real smooth this time - no helicopter shot down when I went to pay the troops...

You've probably read about the contact that was made today by the 4th Division. The 3rd Battalion, 12th Infantry ran into an NVA company about six miles west of here this morning and lost three men KIA. They have counted 17 NVA bodies so far. South of the Oasis, the 2nd Battalion, 8th Infantry made contact and killed 51 and were still counting bodies. They have not lost any men killed so far. That is the kind of results I like to hear...

8 MAY 67

Tonight I am feeling low. I have not received any mail from you (or anyone else) in five days. It is hot and humid, I am getting bored out here in this place, I am listening to a Johnny Mathis record and I want to come home to you so bad I ache... Some of the men (who got 45 day drops in their tour length) now have less than a month before they go home. It sure makes me envious. I guess time will really start to drag when people start going home and part of us are still here.

11 MAY 67

... I flew out to the fire base today and then went to a Montagnard village where the company was working. They are going back to base camp on 14 May for a few days for rest and administrative details. I have to get everything organized before they come in. I will be going back to base camp on the 13th and be there until the 18th or 19th...

15 MAY 67

The company came into Camp Enari (the new name for the base camp) yesterday and is enjoying the first day off they have had since 3 January! I sure am glad they got to come in, they definitely deserve it. I do not think any other units operate constantly in the field like the 4th Infantry Division does... (See story on "The Naming of Camp Enari").

THE NAMING OF CAMP ENARI

As Colonel Jud Miller, commanding officer of the 2nd Brigade of the 4th Infantry Division, completed preparations in late June 1966 for leading his brigade from Fort Lewis, Washington to Vietnam, Major General Arthur Collins, Division Commander, called him to his headquarters to wish him luck and give him final instructions. Among other things, Colonel Miller was to establish the base camp which the division would occupy when they arrived later in the year.

"Jud, I want you to name the base camp after the first GI killed by hostile fire after you get to Vietnam. That would be a fitting tribute to a brave soldier", said General Collins in his parting instruction as Colonel Miller left in early July, 1966 to board the plane taking the advance party to the division's new home south of Pleiku, Vietnam.

On September 3, 1966, while operating on a search and destroy mission as a member of Charlie Company, 1st Battalion, 22nd Infantry Regiment, PFC Albert Collins became the first 4th Infantry Division soldier killed in action when he was cut down by heavy fire from a Vietcong unit.

Knowing General Collins would not want it to be perceived that the base camp was named after him, Colonel Miller sent a back channel message to General Collins at Fort Lewis explaining his proposed alternative plan for naming the base camp. "Since the first enlisted man killed in action was named

Collins, I recommend we name the base camp after the first officer killed in action." General Collins agreed with Colonel Miller's recommendation.

On November 5, 1966, while participating in Operation Paul Revere IV with Alpha Company, 1st Battalion, 22nd Infantry Regiment, Lieutenant Richard Collins, graduate of the West Point class of 1965, became the first 4th Infantry Division officer killed in Vietnam when he was shot by a dug in North Vietnamese force. By now, General Collins had arrived in Vietnam and discussed the dilemma with Colonel Miller. "We'll name the base camp after the first posthumous recipient of the Silver Star, regardless of his name or rank," was the agreed to plan.

Lieutenant Mark Enari had worked on the 2nd Brigade staff and was constantly prodding Colonel Miller to let him go to a line company to lead a rifle platoon. As a replacement was needed in the 1st Battalion, 12th Infantry Regiment, Lieutenant Enari received his wish and was sent to take over a rifle platoon. On December 2, 1966, Lieutenant Mark N. Enari earned the Silver Star while fighting the North Vietnamese regulars during Operation Paul Revere IV in the Central Highlands of Vietnam. Lieutenant Enari died as a result of the wounds he received during that battle.

Early in 1967, the 4th Infantry Division's base camp, sitting at the foot of Dragon Mountain in the Central Highlands of Vietnam, was named Camp Enari in honor of Lieutenant Mark Enari and retained that name as long as American forces were in Vietnam.

PFC Albert Collins' name is engraved on Panel 10E, line 66 on the Vietnam Memorial Wall in Washington, D.C., Lieutenant Richard G. Collins' name is engraved on Panel 12E, line 27 on the Wall, and Lieutenant Mark N. Enari's name is on Panel 13E, line 4 on the Wall.

19 MAY 67

... The company moved out today right after noon. The 1st Battalion, 8th Infantry had heavy contact out by the border yesterday and lost 30 killed and 30 wounded. They were sending our company out to help. By the time they got headed that way in Chinooks, all contact with the NVA had been broken and the 1st of the 8th had control of the situation. They diverted our people to Jackson's Hole where they are spending the night prior to moving out on their planned mission. I am going to catch a chopper out there later today. It still looks like we will be moving back to the Oasis in about a week or so...

We had a new platoon leader come in to the company today. He is a young guy who has only been out of OCS since October 1966. The battalion has really been getting some young second lieutenants in lately...

22 MAY 67

The battalion supply trains are now located at the Oasis (for the third time) instead of Jackson Hole. The battalion went back under control of the 2nd Brigade yesterday afternoon so we moved today. The move was uneventful - we went right back into the same place we left on 28 April. This should be our last move before I leave. Of course I said the same thing two moves ago.

Tonight I came on into base camp. We got 25 replacements in so I am trying to get them outfitted and ready to go to the field tomorrow. It sure is nice to see some new guys start coming in. I plan to go out with them and spend the night with the company tomorrow night. It will be a nice change of pace to be out in the field again...

25 MAY 67

... I really picked a good night to spend out in the field night before last. We got hit, first by mortars and then with small arms fire... (See story on "Buddha's Birthday").

BUDDAH'S BIRTHDAY

As had happened on Christmas, New Year's, and Tet, another cease fire had been called on Buddha's Birthday. Bravo Company was in a defensive position in the Ia Drang valley and was happy to have a day to sit around and rest rather than spend the day patrolling. Compared to some of the thick jungle terrain we had been in, we were in relatively open country. A tank from 1st Battalion, 69th Armor had joined us, one of the few times we had worked with a tank.

We had seen enough signs of the enemy in the previous few days to keep the company alert. Just that morning, a claymore mine had been stolen from outside the perimeter. It gave us all an uneasy feeling to know an NVA had come that close during the night without being detected.

After an uneventful, restful day, the company started preparing for the inevitable nightfall. When the claymores were put out, extra care was taken to insure trip flares were attached to each one. If an NVA wanted to mess with our claymores again, he was going to pay for it! A light rain started to fall as the company settled down for the night. Listening posts snaked out to assume their early warning positions. A general uneasiness gripped the company as darkness engulfed them and the long wait for morning began.

Cease fires were fine for politicians but were a mixed blessing for infantrymen. The day of no patrolling was nice but a cease fire also meant artillery fire and air strikes were not on immediate call. It took special permission from Corps headquarters to get artillery or air support during the hours of a cease fire. At midnight, the cease fire would be over and support would be back to normal.

The light rain continued to fall when, shortly before 11:00, without warning, an NVA B-40 rocket screamed into the perimeter hitting the tank with a loud explosion. Everyone jumped to full alert as each man scrambled into his bunker and scanned the terrain to his front. Two medics responded to the cries of, "Medic!" from the two tank crewmen and one rifleman who had been superficially wounded by the rocket explosion.

As the company waited, with hearts pounding, the NVA started peppering the area with 82mm mortar rounds. As soon as the rocket had hit the tank, Captain Ator had started calling for help.

"Redleg, this is Oscar 6, fire mission, over." The artillery unit accepted the information on the fire mission and Buck waited for the rounds to start hitting the NVA mortar position. As the NVA rounds continued to pound the area, he waited and no fire was heard from our artillery. He got back on the radio and called, "Redleg, fire your mission, we are under heavy attack, over!" The response infuriated him.

"We can not fire now. We are trying to get permission from higher up to fire for you. The cease fire is still on and we can not fire. We will keep you advised. Out." Buck immediately switched to the battalion frequency and called the battalion commander.

"Get those people off their duffs and give us some support! We are getting hit by mortar and rocket fire and my listening posts report movement in front of them! Get me some firepower! Over."

"Stay calm, we are trying to get permission to fire. We will get support to you as quickly as we can. Out."

It was obvious artillery support would not be coming in very soon. The enemy mortars were out of range of our own 81mm mortar platoon, so Buck could not order them to return fire. He knew he was on his own to fend off the attack he knew was imminent.

Specialist Charles Marrano, a grenadier in the third platoon (my old platoon), decided to take the matter into his own hands. He had tried firing counter mortar fire with his M79 grenade launcher but could not get a good angle through the trees from inside his bunker. Pulling his helmet down tight, he crawled out of his bunker, lay on top of it, and started using his M79 as an indirect fire weapon to fire on the enemy mortar position he could hear but not see.

Marrano had always been an uncanny shot with his M79, despite his thick glasses that resembled the bottoms of Coke bottles. He looked like anything but an expert marksman. But after a few minutes of Marrano's rapid and deadly fire, the mortar position abruptly went silent.

As the mortar fire ceased, the NVA began their attack. Under cover of the mortar fire, an NVA had crawled up close to the perimeter. As he attempted to turn a claymore mine around to face our perimeter, the trip flare went off, illuminating him and the entire surrounding area.

Ready for just such an attempt, the GI with the claymore charger handle squeezed it, killing the NVA instantly. At the same time, several other NVA headed toward the perimeter, firing as they ran. Bravo Company responded with intense machine gun, claymore, and rifle fire, stopping them in their tracks.

By 11:30, the night again fell silent. The listening posts, which had come in when the mortar attack started, again went out to provide early warning. About ten minutes before the official cease fire was over, Buck got a call from the artillery battery, "We are ready to fire the mission."

Fifty minutes after the initial attack and long after the immediate need had passed; they had finally gotten permission from Corps headquarters to fire. Rather than fire the mission he no longer needed, Buck redirected the fire to cover several of the likely routes of retreat. The rain tapered off, the moon briefly came out from behind the clouds, and Bravo Company waited through the remainder of the uneventful, but certainly not restful, night.

At first light, a patrol crept out to check the area. The NVA who had been blown up by the claymore was no longer there, he had been dragged away. Two dead NVA soldiers lay where they were shot, along with their

AK-47 assault rifles. The patrol probed further into the jungle and found the NVA mortar firing position. Green leaves on the ground, fresh scars in the surrounding trees, and traces of blood indicated Marrano had been deadly accurate with his M79 fire and could be given credit for silencing the weapon.

As a medevac chopper came in to take out the four slightly wounded men, First Sergeant MacDonald jumped on with them and took off, not telling anyone why he was leaving. After the helicopter cleared the ground, First Sergeant Mac directed the pilot to drop him off at the artillery fire base before taking the men to the hospital. As the chopper eased down on the landing pad, Mac bounded to the ground and headed straight for the battalion command post.

Our battalion commander and the artillery battalion commander were casually sitting, drinking coffee under a parachute rigged to provide shade from the morning sun. First Sergeant MacDonald bolted up to them, saluted smartly, and then let them have it.

"You stupid, no good, worthless sons of bitches, you could have gotten all of us killed last night. Why didn't you have the guts to do what was right and make a decision to fire support for us. If you ever screw up like that again, I am going to personally kick your asses."

With that, he turned and walked back to the helicopter landing pad, got on a chopper that was taking supplies out to the company, and flew back to join the unit. The two colonels sat dumbfounded under the parachute, trying to figure out what had just happened.

First Sergeant MacDonald got no repercussions for his outburst at the two colonels. Rather than lose respect, he gained more for having the guts to stand up for what he knew was right. That was the only incident all year when we did not get the artillery support we needed from 4-42 Field Artillery – they were always great support for us.

Specialist Marrano was awarded the Bronze Star for Valor in recognition of his bravery on Buddha's Birthday.

27 MAY 67

I sure wish I was at home with you. This is one of those days when nothing went to suit me. It rained most of the day and I got soaked riding back to base camp in an open jeep. I went on into Pleiku to the 18th Surgical Hospital to see our guys who were wounded the other night but they have all been evacuated to Qui Nhon.

We did stop by the Pleiku Air Force Base and bought some ice cream at their snack bar. The Air Force is really something else.

First, they would not let us in the front gate with hand grenades on us. They do not seem to know there is a war going on and we might need them. We drove back around a corner, out of sight, stuck the grenades under the seat and they waved us through. I do not know what they thought we did with them.

Second, an Air Force master sergeant was in line in front of us waiting to get an ice cream cone. All he did was complain he only had two wall lockers in his barracks room. Sort of a disgusting comment to hear when everything we have has to be carried on our back.

This is one of the days when the incompetence of our battalion really gets to me. Some of our officers are so fouled up it is pathetic. There is no doubt in my mind today I want to get out of the Army just as fast as I can.

Enough about my bad mood. The 173rd Airborne Brigade has been flying into this area the last couple of days and is just about ready for operation. They will be operating south of us down around the Ia Drang Valley. There are now three brigades operating in this area, which is just fine with me. The more the merrier. (See story on "The Crazed Sergeant").

THE CRAZED SERGEANT

The tent flap flew open and the obviously drunk sergeant burst through the opening. He pointed his loaded M-16 rifle at the company clerk, Sergeant George Wilhelm. In a surly voice he demanded, "Where's that no good son of a bitch Babcock?" Startled, George responded, "What do you want him for, Sergeant Smith?"

"I'm going to kill that son of a bitch! He got me busted and my wife is threatening to divorce me and I'm going to kill that worthless son of a bitch. Now where is he?!" He waved the M-16 menacingly in George's face. Specialist Lisui, the company clerk/typist, his eyes wide with fear, backed to the far corner of the tent, scanning the walls trying to find a way to get out of there. Sergeant Smith (not his real name, but used for this story) stood between him and the only way out.

"Now calm down just a goddamned minute, Sergeant Smith. Babcock wouldn't do something like that." George's face was ashen as he tried to calm Sergeant Smith. He slowly raised his arm and pushed the M-16 away from his face.

"Don't try to protect him! I'm going to kill him! Where is he?!" George stepped back to keep from further irritating the obviously irrational man. "He's not out here, he's back in base camp at Dragon Mountain." Specialist Lisui, unable to say anything, nodded in agreement as Sergeant Smith looked at him to verify what George had said.

Believing their story, Sergeant Smith turned and half walked, half staggered out of the tent, as George and Specialist Lisui exchanged looks of relief. George grabbed the field telephone and feverishly rang the switchboard.

"Get me the Bravo Company orderly room at Dragon Mountain (Camp Enari) and do it fast!" he barked at the switchboard operator. After a short wait that seemed to take forever, George got First Sergeant MacDonald on the phone and related the incident. "Keep an eye on him and let me know when he leaves to head back this way. I'll go find Lieutenant Babcock." At that, the First Sergeant sprinted out of the orderly room to find me.

As I drove into the company area, completely unaware of what had transpired earlier, First Sergeant MacDonald met me before I could get out of my jeep. "Sir, I need to talk to you. We've got some big trouble here." The look of concern on his face convinced me something was seriously wrong. I followed him into the orderly room.

My stomach knotted up as he related the incident. "High Noon in Vietnam," I thought. As I reached for the field telephone, he asked, "Who are you calling, Sir? I have already called the MP's."

"What did they say - are they going to arrest him?" I asked. "No sir, they said they need more proof. Before they can do anything, he has to make an actual attempt on your life, not just a threat." My heart thumped even harder as I heard those unwelcome words.

"Why in the world would Sergeant Smith want to kill me? I did not have anything to do with him losing a stripe, and I do not even know his wife." My brain whirled as I tried to piece together what could have ignited Sergeant Smith to such a drastic action.

I recalled an incident several weeks earlier, when Sergeant Smith had left the company in the jungle. He complained he had hurt his back but everyone thought he was just shirking his duty as a squad leader.

After the second week of watching him drinking every night and hanging around doing as little as possible each day, I had started pressuring him to get back out to the field with his squad.

I had not threatened him, just tried strongly to persuade him. "Your squad needs you. Get back out there and provide the leadership you are being paid for." He continued to complain and convinced the medics he could not carry a rucksack and, therefore, could not function in the field.

One night at the NCO club, he had gotten drunk, started a fight, and the MP's were called to break it up. The Sergeant Major hit the ceiling and brought charges against him. In the subsequent Article 15 (non-judicial punishment), he was reduced in rank from Staff Sergeant E6 to Sergeant E5.

A few days later, he had gotten a letter from his wife stating she was not going to be able to meet him in Hawaii on R&R as they had planned. He came to me, again in a semi-drunken state, and asked that his R&R orders be changed from Hawaii to Hong Kong. Since we had more requests for Hawaii than we had slots, I agreed and had his R&R orders changed.

The day he left for Hong Kong, we received a wire through the Red Cross. His wife's plans had changed and she was in Hawaii, eagerly awaiting his arrival. We called the R&R debarkation station at Cam Ranh Bay but found he was already on a plane bound for Hong Kong.

As I entered his tent upon his return from Hong Kong, he was telling a wild story about the prostitute he had spent the week with. He suddenly sobered up as he read the wire from his wife. He scrambled out of the tent and sprinted toward the Red Cross tent and the short wave radio station to try to call her and explain away his change in plans.

Evidently the call had not gone well. He continued to drink more and more. From a soldier with a fairly good military bearing, he deteriorated to looking like what he was, a drunk. I increased my pressure on him to cut out the drinking, get off his ass, and get back out to the field where he belonged.

First Sergeant MacDonald was not nearly as subtle in his pressure. Having just come in from the field himself, Mac had absolutely no patience for an NCO who did not do his job. He put him on more and more details, made him sergeant of the guard every other night, and generally made life as miserable as he could. Everyone, including the battalion surgeon, was convinced he was a malingerer.

But, he continued to complain about his bad back. Taking the cautious medical approach, the battalion surgeon would not order him back to the field. He did not fully understand the importance of having a squad leader in the field with his squad.

And that brought us to the present where I am supposed to get killed by this drunken sergeant. All I had done was to try to convince a soldier to shape up and do his job. Needless to say, I was more than a little concerned. "What you gonna do now, Lieutenant?" again came into my mind.

"What do you think I should do, First Sergeant?" His reply should have been obvious to me, "Carry a loaded .45 with you everywhere you go and shoot that son of a bitch if he makes one false move."

Unfortunately, I could not think of a better alternative. I always wore a .45 but division policy was to keep it unloaded in base camp. Disregarding that order, I slipped a magazine into it, chambered a bullet, and practiced a few quick draws. Even though I had never been a good shot with a .45, I figured if I could get it out of the holster fast enough and shoot, I could at least scare him away even if I did not hit him.

First Sergeant MacDonald came into my tent as I was practicing my fast draw routine. Under other circumstances, it would have been comical. But the First Sergeant understood the gravity of the situation and did not even crack a smile at my actions.

"George called in from the Oasis and said Sergeant Smith just left there in the last convoy of the afternoon. He should be back here around supper time. George said he seems to have sobered up."

Never had I been as concerned as when I saw the truck driving up to the company area with Sergeant Smith aboard. I did not want to be forced to kill the poor drunken fool, but he may leave me no choice. First Sergeant MacDonald met the truck and escorted him into his tent. I headed for the mess tent to eat, imagining the grief Mac was laying on Sergeant Smith.

I positioned myself in the rear of the tent, facing the entry door. From my spot, I could see everyone in the tent and had a good view of anyone coming in. Soon the First Sergeant came in and joined me. "He is sober and denies everything. I think you are okay for now but be alert." (That was a warning I did not need, I was probably never more alert, even on an ambush patrol).

The evening progressed and nothing happened. Sergeant Smith was sergeant of the guard and headed for the perimeter soon after dark. I finally lay down on my cot and tried to go to sleep. Knowing my potential killer was on guard did nothing to assist the sleep process.

Sleep would not come. At every sound, I reached under my pillow and fingered the trigger of the loaded .45. Finally, the strain of the day overcame me and I drifted off into a fitful sleep. Hearing a noise outside my tent, I awakened with a start, grabbed my pistol, rolled from the cot to the wooden floor, and drew a steady aim on the door flap. Seconds turned into minutes and nothing happened.

I got up, cautiously looked outside, found nothing, and went back to bed. The same sequence was repeated several times throughout the night. As daylight returned, I thanked God I had made it through the night. The perimeter guards and Sergeant Smith returned to the company area and headed for breakfast, then to their tents to catch some sleep. After breakfast, I got into my jeep and headed for the MP headquarters.

As I walked into the operations tent, the duty sergeant said, "Lieutenant, you have to take that magazine out of your pistol. That is not allowed in base camp." Feeling fairly safe in the MP compound, I took the magazine out as I asked to see the duty officer.

After explaining the situation, he reaffirmed what the MP's had told us the previous day. "We get a lot of threats over here. If we did something to everyone who got drunk and mouthed off, we would have the stockade full of people. Just try to forget it, you will probably never hear anything more from it." That was easy for him to say, it was impossible for me to do. I could not overlook the threat. As I climbed back into my jeep to return to the company, I slipped my magazine back into my pistol and chambered a round.

That afternoon, I left base camp and headed for the Oasis, the forward support area where I spent most of my time. The First Sergeant had alerted several men to keep an eye on Sergeant Smith and to call me immediately if they saw him leave the battalion area.

I slept an exhausted sleep that night but still stirred frequently and felt for the pistol under my pillow. For several days things went along normally. Sergeant Smith continued to complain of his bad back to stay in base camp and I remained at the Oasis.

But the first of the month came and I had to return to base camp to pick up the payroll. My stomach knotted again as I drove into the company area. I had ignored the warning of the MP at the main gate to take the magazine out of my pistol. If Sergeant Smith wanted me, I was going to be ready for him.

Two days later, after paying the troops in the field, the hospitals, and at base camp, I turned in the payroll. It was too late to drive back to the Oasis so I had to spend the night in base camp. Sergeant Smith had been drinking in the NCO club for several hours when he approached me as I sat outside the mess tent drinking a beer with some of the troops.

He sat down beside me and started a side conversation. "Lieutenant, you really screwed up when you gave me that Article 15 and cost me a stripe. Why do you have it in for me? I didn't do anything to deserve that." The conversation continued as I tried to stay calm and talk sensibly to him. The other troops sauntered off to their tents, leaving me alone with Sergeant Smith.

The more we talked, the more irrational he became. He talked in circles and tried to blame all his problems on me. He accused me of changing his R&R orders from Hawaii to Hong Kong against his will and because of that, his wife was threatening to divorce him.

He finally made the threat to my face, "You had better watch out because I'm going to kill you for doing that."

There were no witnesses so I knew I was on my own. My heart was pounding as I decided to call his bluff, "If you even come close to me with a weapon, I'll blow your f**king head off. Do you understand that, asshole?" He glared at me and the .45 hanging from my hip. With a few more profanities, he turned and headed for his tent.

Another sleepless night. Rather than stay in my tent, I went over and slept, or at least tried to sleep, in the tent with several of the Headquarters Company officers. Again I spent the night jumping at every sound. My hand never left the .45 under my pillow.

The next morning, I returned to the Oasis. It seemed strange to feel safer in the forward area than in base camp. Five days later, Sergeant Smith's tour of duty ended and he returned to the States. The next time I passed the MP post at the main gate, I gladly took the magazine out of my pistol when he told me to unload my weapons.

It had been the longest and most unsettling few weeks I had ever experienced. I am glad the real showdown between us never happened.

I have never seen nor heard from Sergeant Smith again (again, Smith is not his real name). I have frequently reflected on what might have been, if I had been at the Oasis the day he came to kill me.

1 Jun 67

Next month I will be home! It sure sounds good to say that. We are down under 50 days now, 48 to be exact. This time last year I was going on the brigade FTX at Fort Lewis getting ready for this year and now it is coming to an end.

It is still raining and mud is beginning to be a problem. Tonight I drove down to the shower point and we barely could make it back up the hill because it was so slick. I have also quit trying to walk around the mud; I just slosh on through it.

2 Jun 67

I flew out and paid the company today. They are wet and filthy but their spirits are still high. Of course everyone is counting the days until they go home. For about 65 of them, there are only eight more days in the field before they go in and start processing for a 20 June DEROS.

The company is really going to be hurting when all those men leave. I am sure we will get replacements but they will probably all be fresh recruits right out of Basic and AIT. We will really be short on experienced NCOs.

8 Jun 67

I no longer have a replacement. The guy who was going to replace me is going to brigade and take over as LRRP (Long Range Reconnaissance Patrol) platoon leader. I am sort of happy about the whole deal. Now I do not have to worry about being stuck in some sorry job while waiting to come home.

Also, the longer they go without replacing me, the more likely they will not assign me to another job when I do get replaced. It would be great if I got a replacement about 20 June, was declared excess, and then got a port call soon after that date...

I am sorry my letters have been so bad lately but I have had a lot on my mind. I guess one of the biggest problems was thinking about being moved out of Bravo Company to another job. Now, that is no longer imminent so I feel a lot better. (I never did tell her about Sergeant Smith's threat on my life).

I really feel like a part of this company and do not want to leave it except to come home. Right now I am the only officer who is still with the same company he trained with at Fort Lewis. If my luck holds, my entire Army career will have been spent with Bravo Company, 1st Battalion, 22nd Infantry Regiment of the 4th Infantry Division (and it was)...

12 Jun 67

I still do not know anything about when I will be leaving here. I checked today and my orders are supposed to be cut tomorrow. That will at least be a step in the right direction. Port calls can not come down until after you get your orders. So stay loose between the 1st and 20th of July. As I said before, you can bet I will be doing my best to get out of here as soon as possible after 1 July.

Yesterday we had an officer killed in the battalion. (See story on "The Montagnard Crossbow")...

THE MONTAGNARD CROSSBOW

In less than a month, my tour would be over and I would be returning to the States. For quite some time, I had had my eye on the crossbows the Montagnard natives made and hunted with. Many GIs had gone into their villages and traded C rations or other items for them. I had made up my mind I was going to do the same and take one home as a souvenir.

The opportunity presented itself while I was sitting around the battalion Officer's Club tent in base camp one night. I had been talking to Captain Castillo, the battalion civil affairs officer.

Several days each week, he went to the Montagnard village outside our base camp to give them food, soap, medical supplies, and other items which the U. S. Government donated in their efforts to try to make the natives friendly to us. I asked if I could ride along with him the next morning so I could pick up one of the crossbows. Always happy to have someone go with him on the routine missions, he invited me along.

As we turned in for the night, he told me he would wake me early so we could be on the road soon after daylight, finish what we had to do, and be back before noon. At the time, that sounded good since I had a lot of work that needed to get done the next day.

It was still dark outside when I sensed someone approaching my bunk. I groggily raised my head to see Captain Castillo standing there. "Time to get up, we've got to get on the road," he said. The Montagnard crossbow did not seem nearly as important to me at that early hour of the morning. "Go on without me, I am too sleepy." With that, I rolled over and went back to sleep.

Captain Castillo and his driver left the main gate of the base camp just as daylight was breaking. As they were approaching the Montagnard village they had visited without incident on so many mornings, they were ambushed.

A B-40 rocket smashed into the front of the jeep as they were swept by a hail of automatic weapons fire. Captain Castillo was killed instantly as the bullets raked through his body. The driver slumped over in his seat as a bullet penetrated his steel helmet. Miraculously, the bullet clung to its contour rather than going through his head. The blow from the bullet hitting his helmet stunned him, knocking him out.

Another jeep, following fifty yards behind, screeched to a halt as the VC turned their fire onto it. Raymond Carvalho, a machine gunner friend of Captain Castillo, who had also volunteered to go along on the mission, tumbled into the ditch and returned fire with his M16. Rapidly emptying his magazine, he reached for another one, only to find that all of his other ammo was still on the jeep, along with his machine gun.

Scampering across the road with bullets clipping at his heels, Carvalho dived behind the jeep, grabbed his machine gun and start returning deadly accurate fire on the ambush position. As two of the VC fell dead, the remaining force disappeared back into the underbrush to escape the withering fire. When the guards on the base camp perimeter heard the firing, the reaction force that always stood on alert was quickly dispatched to the scene. No further sign of the VC was found as they swept through the ambush area.

When I went into the mess hall for breakfast, a friend looked at me like he had seen a ghost. "How did you make it back?" he asked. "What are you talking about?" I replied. As he explained what had happened that morning, I suddenly lost my appetite. If I had not been such a sleepy head, I would have been sitting on the jeep radio behind Captain Castillo and would have been the most exposed target for the ambush to hit.

I came home without a Montagnard crossbow. After that incident, I no longer wanted a souvenir to remind me of what might have been.

Captain Castillo's name is engraved on panel 21E, line 86 on the Vietnam Memorial Wall in Washington, D.C. The driver escaped with only a headache and slight burn on his neck.

16 JUN 67

I came back out to the Oasis day before yesterday and went out to the fire base to spend some time with Captain Ator. He is in fine spirits. We got another new lieutenant into the company. He will go out and take Lieutenant Irizarry's platoon and Irizarry will leave the field in about a week or ten days and start working as XO in my place.

With this next guy we just got in, all three rifle platoon leaders have less than a month of experience in Vietnam. That is bad considering we are losing or have lost all of our NCOs through rotation back to the States. Luckily, the battalion is operating in an area where there is not much activity. They will get a little training time before they go back into NVA territory. And, Captain Ator will keep an eye on them and not let them screw up...

My orders finally made it out to me. Enclosed is a copy. If you will notice my DEROS date is 7 July instead of 20 July. This means I have a 13 day drop! Now we only have 20 days to go instead of 33!...

21 JUN 67

...Yesterday I spent most of the day out at the fire base. The company made a Combat Assault by helicopter to the new fire base location down in the Ia Drang valley. I helped Captain Ator coordinate the choppers and got the people loaded up. For twenty-five of our men, including all three platoon leaders, it was their first CA so it took a little supervision. Even though I do not like to volunteer for anything (especially when I am this close to coming home), I went along on the assault. We made the landing unopposed and I came back to the Oasis about 4:30.

Today we got thirteen more replacements. I had to get them outfitted and ready for the field. Right after noon we flew out to the new fire base and got them linked up with the company.

Tomorrow I am going to mail you a small package with our old company guidon (flag) in it. We got a new one the other day and Captain Ator presented the old one to me. I am the only officer who has spent an entire year with the company and he thinks I deserve to have it. I agree. I want to frame it and hang it in a place of honor in our home. (Even now, that guidon is hanging above my desk in my home office)...

22 JUN 67

... This morning I took our company safe over to the 704th Maintenance Battalion to have it "cracked". The combination lock broke yesterday when I locked it and I could not get it open again...

I just got a call from Sergeant Wilhelm in base camp that one of our men has died of malaria. It really was a shock to me. He left out here about three days ago and had a port call to go home yesterday. Sergeant Wilhelm said he got sick night before last and was taken to the hospital. He was a quiet, Puerto Rican kid who always did a real good job. It is really a shame... I have to stop and write a letter to his family. More later.

24 JUN 67

... One of the officers got a letter from Jay Vaughn (a West Point officer in our battalion) today. Jay got a 45 day drop and is at home now. He said the good old USA is just like it was when we left; the people do not give a damn about what is happening in Vietnam. He seemed disillusioned by the questions people asked him and the attitude they have about this place...

28 JUN 67

Still no word on a port call. They were supposed to be down yesterday or today but still have not been heard from. Now they tell us we should know tomorrow sometime. I am still hoping for the 7th...

Time is really starting to drag. Lieutenant Irizarry is taking over all my job responsibilities so I am just sort of "in the area" and marking time until the day I can get on that big bird and make the flight back across the big pond to the one I love.

29 Jun 67

Meet me in Kansas City! I got my port call orders today and I am getting out of here on 5 July, two days better than I had hoped for. This will be my last letter from Vietnam because I AM COMING HOME!!!... (See story on "Coming Home").

Thus ended the most significant and memorable year of my life. At the time, I did not realize how significant the year had been. The next two sections wrap up the experience and bring it to the current date.

Huey helicopters lifting off on one of many combat assaults

COMING HOME

The thought, the dream, the hope, the driving force that has kept soldiers going in all wars are those two magic words – "coming home". From the day you find out you are going to war, you start thinking about coming home. You think about the possibility of not making it, and try as you will, you can not totally drive those thoughts from the back of your mind. But most of all, you dream about how great it is going to be when you come home.

As a boy, I remembered looking at the old copies of Life, Colliers, Look, and Saturday Evening Post magazines and seeing the welcome home scenes from Times Square, from the ticker tape parades in New York, and the troop ships coming past the Statue of Liberty at the end of World War II.

I also remembered vividly from my boyhood the celebration, the parade, and the patriotic event held at the high school football field when John "Patch" Patton, a local high school football hero, was released from a prisoner of war camp at the end of the Korean War.

The whole town turned out to welcome him home. As a 5th grader, I was dressed as Uncle Sam and rode on a float with a girl dressed as the Statue of Liberty - everyone was singing and the band was playing, "When Johnny Comes Marching Home Again, Hurrah, Hurrah".

Dreams of events such as those danced in my head during those long nights when I fought sleep while peering into the dense jungle listening for approaching NVA troops. Later, while lying on my cot as executive officer listening to the H&I fires of the artillery, the dreams were just as vivid. Coming home was going to be great and I could not wait for it to happen.

My short timer's calendar kept ticking down until finally the orders came. I had orders to leave Vietnam on July 5, 1967, sixteen days short of one year since we had left Fort Lewis to begin our tour of duty.

After my close call experience a few days earlier with the Montagnard crossbow, I was hesitant about getting on a helicopter to fly out to the company, which was operating in the Ia Drang valley. But, I wanted to bid farewell to my friends that were still out there. I boarded the resupply chopper to spend one last day in the field.

As I sat around the company perimeter position talking to Captain Ator and my other friends who had not left the field yet, I was a little more apprehensive than usual. I certainly did not want to be one of those stories told about a soldier who was killed on his last days in country. When the final helicopter of the day came into the patrol base, I was more than happy to get on it and head back to base camp.

It was a feeling of mixed emotions as the helicopter lifted out of the jungle and climbed to a comfortable altitude, out of the range of small arms fire. I was happy to be getting out of there. I was a little ashamed I had been so afraid as I made this last trip into the jungle. I hated to leave Captain Ator and my friends there while I left. A myriad of other thoughts flew through my mind.

I was struck by the sheer beauty of the Ia Drang valley, the double waterfall that glistened in the sunlight, and thought of the major battle the First Cavalry Division had waged there just as I was getting out of AIRBORNE school. A friend I had gone through infantry school with had fought in that battle, only a few days after he left us at Fort Benning in the fall of 1965. Two months later, he was killed.

I also thought of the friends I had made in the past year. When we trained together at Fort Lewis, they had been troops entrusted to my care. Now they were real people, friends I shared a common bond and a lifetime of experiences with. Sergeant Roath was not just a crusty platoon sergeant; he was a guy who had helped me bring our entire platoon home alive. He would not have to make good on the threat he made to me that first day we met back at Fort Lewis.

Sergeants Benge, Muller, Cheatham, Burrell, and Baez had also become friends. As squad leaders they had not just done their job and what I told them to do, we had come together as a team. They did not hesitate to tell me if I was making a dumb decision - fortunately, I had the good sense to listen to them. They had all gone home, Muller and Cheatham after being wounded, the others when they got early outs to keep from replacing the entire company at once.

Stanley Cameron, George Wilhelm, Harry Troutman, Danny Schemp, Wilbur Miller, Sergeant Angulo, Robinson, Germek, Lisui, and a number of others either had already gone or were getting ready to leave - each to a different location and probably never to be seen by me again. But most of all, I was thinking about being a SHORT TIMER! - my day to go home to see Phyllis was almost here.

As the helicopter settled down into the base camp, I climbed off for the last time, headed for my tent and never looked back. That part of my life was behind me.

Out-processing was a breeze as I checked in my field gear, signed over all my duties as Executive Officer to Lieutenant Irizarry, and got ready to head out the next morning to catch the "freedom bird" out of Pleiku airfield.

There was one little glitch - Wayne Germek, the supply clerk, wanted me to check in my M16 rifle before he would sign my supply clearance form. I was scheduled to catch a truck at first light to make the trip from Camp Enari to the airfield in Pleiku.

In no uncertain terms, I explained to Germek I had only slept one night in Vietnam without my M16 being within arm's reach, and this night was not going to be my second. He could either get up with me long before daylight to check in my rifle or he could clear me now and pick up my rifle next to my cot when he got up. Either way, I was not going to give up my rifle until I left. It was bad enough to have to turn it in before I made the ten mile trip to Pleiku. He understood and decided he would trust me.

Another thing I left by my cot, and which I have regretted many times, was my jungle boots. I flew home in a khaki uniform with low quarter shoes and decided I would not need those beat up boots any more, I would buy some new ones when I got home. Those boots were the most comfortable things I ever wore, and they had the character to show what they had been through. The treads on the soles were worn thin, the leather spoke volumes of the tough terrain they had taken me through, and they had served me well over many miles of walking and could have told many stories. They would have made a nice memento - but I was not thinking about that then, all I was thinking about was catching that big bird to fly me back to the world and to Phyllis!

The time passed slowly until the C-141 appeared as a speck in the morning sky, glided down his final approach, and taxied to a stop in front of the Pleiku air terminal. We stood impatiently in line waiting for the incoming passengers to offload before we could get on our "freedom bird".

All of us did what troops before and since have done - we heckled the new, scared troops as they came down off the plane and into the heat of the central highlands ready to start their year in country. Our tanned, weather beaten faces and macho attitude was a marked contrast to the pale, apprehensive look of the replacements.

Since Pleiku airfield was within enemy mortar range, it took no time for the Air Force to load us aboard and head the plane back to Cam Ranh Bay for refueling prior to starting the long flight back across the Pacific Ocean. After the short refueling stop, a mighty roar went up from the troops as the plane again became airborne and crossed the coast of Vietnam, we were finally out of harm's way and on the way home!

It was a long flight home. Instead of a civilian airliner with pretty, round eyed stewardesses, we were on an Air Force plane with a lanky airman in charge of the passenger compartment. The seats were canvas and faced the rear. I guess the Air Force thought we had a better chance of survival sitting that way.

And, we did not get a hot meal on the plane. The airman came onto the PA system asking which officers wanted to eat on the way home. Naturally, we all raised our hands. He then informed us we were to go to the pay window when we landed in Guam, pay for the two box meals we would have en route, and get a receipt to verify it. We knew then that we were out of the combat zone and back into the military bureaucracy.

To further attest to being out of the combat zone, when we landed in Japan, we had to sit for eight hours while a crew was rested to take us the rest of the way across the Pacific. While waiting, several of us went to the officer's club. For the first time in almost a year, we saw real people leading real lives. Officers and their wives were having dinner at the Club, single officers were congregated around the bar, and those of us on the way home from Vietnam were ignored.

Another huge roar engulfed the plane as its wheels touched down at Travis Air Force Base outside of San Francisco. We had made it! The fear that came across me as we sailed past Seattle almost a year earlier was over. I had made it home alive!

Busses took us from Travis to the Oakland Army Terminal as the sun dropped down in the western sky. All that stood between me and the last leg of my trip was to get an Army physical, get paid, and finish my out-processing. Then, I would be on the way to Phyllis who would be waiting for me at the Kansas City airport.

Oakland Army Terminal was a bustle of activity as our busses pulled up and unloaded. By now, it had become the primary processing center for returning vets and operated around the clock - with one minor exception. Officers still on active duty just had to sign the register and were on their way. Enlisted men processing out of the Army or to other posts got into the appropriate line and were processed in sequence as they arrived.

But, officers who were processing out of the Army were handled only between the hours of 8:00AM and 5:00PM. I fell into the last category. It was now 8:00PM - another twelve hour wait before I could continue my journey toward home.

After paying for a room in the holding facility, I found the nearest pay phone and placed the long awaited call home. Phyllis was already in Kansas City. We had agreed I would let my parents, in Oklahoma, know when I would arrive. She would stay in touch with them to find out when to be at the airport (this was long before cell phones and the internet). Naturally, my parents were ecstatic to hear from me. Their prayers had been answered - I was home, safe and sound. It would be several days before they actually saw me but their worries were now behind them.

Finally, my processing was completed. I was a civilian again and boarded a cab to take me to the San Francisco airport. I drank in the sights as we crossed the Bay Bridge. I appreciated them much more than I had a year earlier.

My first dealings with civilians were at the San Francisco airport and on the plane flying to Kansas City. I was not spit on, heckled, called a baby killer or dope addict, or ridiculed. All of that came later in the war. Instead, I was ignored.

Although I proudly wore my Army uniform, Combat Infantryman's Badge, and appropriate ribbons, no one acknowledged me any more than they did a businessman traveling in his normal business day. I expected more than that and had a hollow feeling until we came into our final approach for Kansas City and my excitement overtook me. (*On an IBM business trip, when I was flying from Denver to Kansas City soon after our Army's excursion into Panama in 1990, I saw a young man no more than nineteen years old with a 7th Infantry Division patch and a Combat Infantryman's Badge preparing to board the plane. Knowing that he had just returned from Panama, I talked to the pilot of the Continental plane and convinced him to move him from the rear of the plane to sit next to me in first class - I wasn't going to ignore another American veteran like we Vietnam vets had been ignored*).

My greeting in Kansas City was much better - Phyllis was standing by the gate anxiously awaiting the moment she and I thought would never come. Everything was as I expected it would be as we ran to greet each other. We were in our own world as the other passengers deplaned and moved past us - either ignoring us or allowing us our moment together.

Three final things still stand out in my mind about my coming home experience.

First, after four days together in Kansas City in the July heat, I decided it was too hot to drive to Oklahoma in our Mustang with no air conditioning. The fact the Mustang was the soon to be classic 1965 model, that it only had 36,000 miles on it, and that it was almost paid for did not cross my mind. All I thought about was I had just spent twelve months in the heat of Vietnam and I was not going to put up with it any more.

So, we went to a local Chevrolet dealer, picked out the top of the line model sitting on the showroom floor, called the president of the bank where I had worked as a janitor all through high school (a close family friend), got his approval for a loan, paid for the car, and drove it off the lot.

Thus went the money we had saved over the past twelve months and began my life of having to work to make payments. I have often said there should be a law that did not allow soldiers to make major purchases until they had been home at least thirty days to get acclimated to reality again.

Second, as we listened to the radio while driving home from Kansas City, we heard stories of a major battle going on in the Central Highlands involving the 4th Infantry Division. Knowing my mother would be glued to the TV and getting all the details, my first question of her after our initial greetings was, "What is going on with the 4th Infantry Division?"

Her answer still bothers me today. "I don't know. I quit paying attention after you got back to San Francisco." To her, I was all that was important in Vietnam. To me, my friends were still fighting in a war I believed in. And, like most Americans, she went on with her life now that she did not have a direct involvement in the war.

The last thing that stands out in my mind is the reception I got in my home town. Having lived in the same small town of Heavener, Oklahoma all my life, I knew many of the people. As I walked down the streets and saw someone I knew, it was not uncommon for a conversation to go something like this – "I haven't seen you in a long time, Bob. Where have you been?"

When I responded I had just come back from Vietnam, I got an "Oh...", there was an awkward pause, and the subject was changed. To say the least, that hurt. My welcome was much different from the patriotic welcome I remembered the town giving "Patch" Patton upon his return from Korea. This is not to say everyone was that way. There were people who welcomed me, asked about my experiences, and made me feel good. Many of those people were veterans of World War II, my family, and my good friend, John Tatum, who had put me on the airplane in Oklahoma City a year earlier to start my experience. Those receptions were nice, and expected. The other ones still hurt.

I put off writing this chapter for three years. It has been the most difficult to write. It finally came to me sitting in church the weekend the troops started coming home from Operation Desert Storm in 1991.

The last thing I did prior to starting this chapter was watch the Desert Storm POW's return and be greeted by the Secretary of Defense, the Chairman of the Joint Chiefs of Staff, and a thankful crowd of thousands.

I shed a lot of tears watching that as well as the receptions the other returning troops got. I do not begrudge them a single bit of their welcome, they deserved it all. We deserved it, too. And it still hurts we did not get it. Thank God we are showing proper respect to today's Soldiers returning from service in the Global War on Terror.

LITTLE THINGS MEAN A LOT

Major events and happenings, such as the events that make up the chapters of this book, are easy to recall and write about. But to get a complete picture of my year in Vietnam, there are a number of little things that influenced me that are not significant enough for a complete chapter but need to be mentioned in some form. For instance:

Letters from Home

Probably the greatest single morale builder for any soldier in any war are the letters he gets from his loved ones at home. My mother committed to write me every day and she steadfastly stuck to that promise. However, her letters were always read second because on most days, I got a letter from Phyllis, and that always had top priority. Others wrote periodically and few mail calls found me without at least one letter from home.

A Letter from my Granddad

Letter writing was not one of my Granddad's favorite past times but I could count on a letter from him about every two or three months. His education had stopped at the fifth grade and his handwriting was a barely legible scrawl but the letters he wrote meant more to me than any I got - I could tell he was really proud of me.

Poncho Liner

When we first got to Vietnam, we slept on a canvas sleeping bag liner with a rubberized poncho hooch over us to keep out the rain and wetness. After about six weeks in country, we were issued poncho liners - silky feeling, fast drying nylon blankets that felt so much better to snuggle up under than the rough sleeping bag liner. Unless you were sleeping on the ground and in the elements all the time, it probably would not have made the impression it did on me. But, it gave a feeling of civilization to the rugged existence we found ourselves living in.

The Phases of the Moon

As a kid, I never had paid much attention to the moon except to notice when it was full. However, the phases of the moon took on a whole new meaning in Vietnam. A full moon and the few days before and after it meant there would be light to brighten up the dark jungle at night. The Vietnam War was fought long before the perfection of the night vision goggles used by our current military.

When there was a new moon, the darkness was so intense you could hardly see your hand in front of your face. And, it almost angered me to look up during the daylight hours and see the moon - that meant it would be down before the night was over and many of the long night hours would be lit only by the stars. Even today, I still appreciate the phases of the moon and think about how much a friend the moon is to an infantryman securing a defensive perimeter in the jungle, or on any hostile frontier.

A Supplement to C-Rations

C-Rations were a way of life to us - three meals a day. Unlike stateside duty where you knew you would be back to civilization within a few days, you learned to make the most of C-rations and learned how to mix and match the different meals to make them interesting and tasty.

However, it was always a great treat to have a box of warm sliced roast beef, fried chicken, or a box of fruit dropped down through the trees with our daily resupply of C-rations. We were like kids in an ice cream store when

Staff Sergeant Steve Angulo and his cooks went above and beyond the call of duty to give us some variety to add to our routine C-ration meals.

Coca-Cola and Schlitz

Troops in the rear seemed to always have Coca-Cola, Pepsi-Cola, Budweiser, and Schlitz but there never seemed to be enough to make it out to the Infantrymen in the jungles of the central highlands. We learned to like RC Cola and Ballentine beer and the other off brand soft drinks and beer that made it to us. When we occasionally got a Coke or a Schlitz, even without ice, it was like heaven.

Wet Toilet Paper, Warm Beer, and Wise Asses

I always said there were three things I can't stand - wet toilet paper, warm beer, and wise asses. Life as an Infantryman made me learn to tolerate the first two; I still do not like wise asses.

A Metal Mirror

Prior to leaving for Vietnam, I bought a metal shaving mirror in the Fort Lewis PX. It would not break, was excellent for shaving, and gave me another little benefit that showed how you grasp at anything in tough times. I always carried the mirror in my jungle fatigue shirt pocket, right over my heart.

My brain told me that, just maybe, if I got shot, the shaving mirror would deflect a bullet and not let it hit my heart. I am sure a bullet would have zipped right through it but I convinced myself it was a little added protection and I felt safer having it over my heart as I slogged through the jungle.

An Electric Razor

Shaving five to seven days beard off in cold water out of a helmet with a dull razor blade was a painful experience. In a care package, my wife sent me a battery operated electric razor. It was so handy - you did not need water and I found myself shaving every two or three days. It was a nice luxury that lasted until my rucksack was dropped fifty feet through the jungle from a helicopter and broke it - so much for luxury in the jungle.

My Camera

Prior to leaving Fort Lewis, I purchased a $12.95 Kodak Instamatic 104 camera with a cheap leather carrying case. I always kept it with me, carried in a third ammo pouch (two carried M16 ammo close at hand). Despite the times it got wet, it always took excellent pictures. As a result, I have a picture history of this very significant year of my life, some of those pictures are included in this book.

Letters and Kool-Aid from Mother

As mentioned above, my mother wrote me every day, without fail. In an early letter, I had mentioned the water tasted bad. From that day forward, she always included a package of presweetened Kool-Aid with my letter. After a while, I got used to the water and tired of the Kool-Aid but always found someone who was happy to have my mother's thoughtful addition to her daily letter. Mother, I really appreciated your letters and the Kool-Aid - little things mean a lot.

A Visit from the Chaplain

"There are no atheists in foxholes," is a famous quote from someone. God has always been important to me. In Vietnam, He became even more so. As His messenger, Chaplain Sauer was always a welcome sight. I do not recall ever missing a service either when he came out into the field or when I was in the relative safety of the rear.

In addition to his sermons, his portable altar, his tape recorder that played church music, and hymn books carried in an ammo can, I enjoyed the time he spent talking to my men and me. When I became Executive Officer, he and I became good friends. After having not seen nor heard from him in over 25 years, I finally located him in November of 1994. We have talked on the phone, traded letters, and a draft copy of this book, and visited with each other at a 4th Infantry Division reunion in 1996 and again in 2002.

Doughnut Dollies

Red Cross volunteers, round eyed American women in powder blue uniform dresses, silly games to entertain the troops, sincere caring about making the lives of the GIs a little better, a bright spot when they came around with stale doughnuts is another memory that sticks with me. I never learned any of their names, never talked to them one on one except to arrange for a meeting with some of my troops, but I knew they cared and were there to help take away some of the realities of the War - little things mean a lot.

Playboy

Even though it was usually very late, I eagerly anticipated the monthly issue of Playboy my wife sent me. (I am not sure she was as eager to buy it and send it as I was to receive it.) I guess it gave me another view of what we were fighting for. When I became XO, we maintained a bulletin board of centerfold beauties (which was quickly turned around to reveal the normal Army bulletin board items on the other side when Chaplain Sauer came around).

Jungle Boots and Jungle Fatigues

The most comfortable clothes I ever wore. After the first month of wearing leather jump boots and stateside fatigues, our newly issued jungle boots and fatigues were a Godsend. The boots dried out quickly, the fatigues were light weight, had pockets everywhere to store essentials, and also dried quickly after monsoon rains or wading through a jungle stream. I still have the two jungle fatigue shirts I wore in Vietnam - I still kick myself for leaving my jungle boots sitting by my cot the day I left for home.

The Ability to Read a Map

After struggling with map reading as a ROTC cadet at Fort Riley, Kansas, it suddenly clicked with me how to read terrain features on a map while I was in Infantry school at Fort Benning, Georgia. My great map reading ability served me well throughout my Army career.

I always knew where I was so could always accurately call in artillery or air strikes, find an objective, call for resupply or medevac, and generally make myself and my people feel like I knew what I was doing. Sandy Fiacco and I often debated about exactly where we were in the jungle and, more often than not, I was more accurate in my assessment than anyone.

Dust-off

Fortunately, we seldom had to use it, but it was a great comfort to know medical evacuation via helicopter was always on call. When the monsoon rains totally closed down flying, it significantly raised our concern factor, knowing we could not be evacuated if we got wounded. But most of the time, we could always count on a brave pilot and crew coming in to help us out when we needed it.

Running into Friends

The world is a small place and you can never totally get away from people you know. It was always a welcome sight to run into an old friend from my hometown, from college days, or from my earlier Army days. It made you feel not so alone in that far off place.

Excellent Leadership

As covered in the next section about "People Who Were Important to Me", I can not say enough about Sandy Fiacco and Buck Ator, my two excellent company commanders. But also, I worked with other excellent leaders both above and below them - Colonel "Rawhide" Morley, Colonel Jud Miller, First Sergeant Bob MacDonald, Platoon Sergeant Frank Roath, Squad Leaders Jim Benge, Doug Muller, Al Burrell, Willie Cheatham, Bill Bukovec, and Aubrey Thomas (to name only a few of the excellent leaders in Bravo Company).

Leadership was often cited as one of the serious flaws of the American military in Vietnam - that was not the case in my experience. I worked with, around, and for excellent leaders during most of my Vietnam experience. I did experience some leadership that, in my opinion, left quite a lot to be desired. But, there were always good leaders around to fill the holes left by the less than qualified leaders. If there is one thing that enabled so many of us in Bravo Company to come home alive, it was EXCELLENT LEADERSHIP - and that is a BIG thing that means a lot, not just a little thing.

A Wife to Dream About

Even though we have since divorced and gone our separate ways, the one constant dream that kept me going was knowing I had Phyllis at home waiting for me. Early in my tour, when I lost my billfold, I was more concerned about losing my pictures of her than about the money I had lost. I had carved her name on my rifle stock (which I often looked at as we slogged along on patrol). Dreaming about coming home to Phyllis let me focus on life in the world rather than always on what was happening in Vietnam.

DEROS

Date Estimated Return from Overseas - a date indelibly carved in the brain of every soldier in Vietnam. Rather than an assignment for the duration of the war as our counterparts in World War II had, we could start pointing toward our DEROS date as a known time we would be out of Vietnam.

It has been written that because of the DEROS system, we did not have a ten year war in Vietnam, we had a one year war ten times - and I can not disagree with that. About the time people got good at what they were doing, they went home and new, fresh people came in to make the same mistakes the old timers had learned to avoid.

The system also kept pressure off our Congressmen to put an end to the war - if a person were expected to stay for the duration, public opinion might have been much different - - and the outcome might also have been different. But, as a twenty three year old lieutenant, DEROS was one of those little things that meant a lot.

Chris Noel

The sultry voice of Armed Forces radio. There was something about her sultry, sexy voice as she opened her show with "Hi, Love" and closed it with "Bye, Love". Whenever possible, I was part of her nightly radio audience. And, I was more interested in the first and last minutes of the show than what was in between. She really knew how to make you think of home.

Short Round

Soldiers love dogs. Soon after we arrived in Vietnam, a small dog of obvious mixed breed was adopted by our company. I do not know who named him "Short Round", and I am sure they did not realize how we would learn to hate that reality of war. Wherever we went, Short Round went on our supply truck. He logged more than a few missions on airplanes and helicopters. He was a pet of the entire company and was loved by us all. It really hurt when he was hit and killed by a truck.

"combat loss"

Keeping track of every piece of government issued equipment was almost impossible. With people scattered across the jungles, the fire base, the forward base camp, and Camp Enari, not to mention the people in hospitals with malaria or wounds, we always had equipment missing.

One little rule made it bearable for those of us responsible for the inventory – "combat loss". Any time we were in direct combat, either a firefight or a mortar attack, we could claim equipment was lost in combat. It is amazing how much equipment we lost every time a shot was fired.

Without that safety valve, I would probably still be paying for equipment I was signed for. (It was embarrassing when a pistol showed up a few days after I had sworn it had taken a direct hit from a mortar round.)

The constellation Orion

In the southern sky is the constellation Orion. It is always there and is easy to pick out. On many a dark night in the jungle, I would look up and find "my" stars and feel a little better knowing a friend was there. I told Phyllis to locate Orion because I would be sending messages to her via those stars. I can't say why human nature clings to familiar things, but the constellation Orion always had a warming and calming effect on me when I saw it. Today, I still look up in the southern sky and remember the comfort Orion gave me so long ago.

Little things mean a lot.

SECTION SIX

People Who Were Important To Me

Sandy Fiacco
(A Born Leader)

"Extremely fortunate to have had him as my leader," is the best way I can describe my association with Sandy Fiacco, my company commander while training at Fort Lewis, and during my first six months in Vietnam. Few people have influenced me, taught me, and gained my admiration as much as Sandy did during that period from November, 1965 through December, 1966.

My initial introduction to Sandy, described in the chapter, "Training at Fort Lewis, Washington", was enough to make me wonder what kind of a man I would be working for. He was stern, unsmiling, and a stereotypical military taskmaster in all his dealings with me.

I decided early I did not want to get off on the wrong foot with him (and with my broken leg, it was going to be a tough challenge). Instead of blood, it seemed like military bearing coursed through his veins and muscle fibers.

Nothing happened in my first two months in the company to make me feel any more comfortable. The company manpower consisted of no more than forty of our authorized 180 men. With such a small force, it put more pressure on all of us to do more.

I was still very much a green rookie, trying to recover from my broken leg. Sandy continued to be very tough, almost a perfectionist, and did not give any slack to anyone in the company (himself, least of all).

By the start of my second month at Fort Lewis, we found out we would be receiving new troops, fresh out of basic training, before the month was over. Our mission was to give them Advanced Individual Training (AIT) and then retain them in the unit to bring us up to combat strength.

We had not received the word yet, but we were all certain we would be going to Vietnam with the troops we were getting ready to train and retain. The pressure continued to mount on the small cadre of people in the company as we prepared for this massive influx of troops and enormous training mission.

Sandy continued as a stern, no nonsense, demanding taskmaster as we worked long, six day weeks preparing for our new troops. Daily staff meetings with the platoon leaders and key NCOs mapped out the eight week training schedule down to the last finite detail. Sandy set high standards and expected us to meet them.

It was in these meetings his message began to come through loud and clear. "Men, we are going to take these troops into combat, and it is our responsibility to do every mission we are assigned, and bring back all of our men alive. Do any of you not understand this?"

Of course we all understood what he wanted, but we were not really sure what all we had to do to make it happen. We had gained a strong belief in his strength as a leader, and redoubled our efforts to get ready for our troops. We did whatever he directed us to do in the best way we knew how.

It was not an easy task. The work never seemed to get done. There always seemed to be another, higher, level of quality Sandy expected. He was not satisfied when we brought him a training schedule or lesson plan. He quizzed us on the content to make sure we fully understood what we would be teaching. If we could not answer the questions to his satisfaction, he sent us back to study more before we got another verbal quiz.

Preparing lesson plans and training schedules was not all he expected. Daily, he led us through rigorous physical training in the cold, rainy Puget

Sound weather to make sure we were in top condition when our troops arrived. He required us to practice marching troops so we would be sharp when we had to lead our troops in close order drills. As we were going through such intense preparation, the officers and NCOs from the other companies in the battalion looked at us in amusement.

They were getting ready for the new troops but were not working nearly as hard as we were. We ignored their remarks about how tough Sandy was because we were convinced Sandy's (and now our) approach to training was the right way and they were not working hard enough.

Troops finally arrived at the end of January, 1966. My platoon grew from eight to fifty men almost overnight. The company strength topped out at over two hundred men. The previous month had been a cakewalk, in comparison, as we started molding these new soldiers into Infantrymen.

Now I was responsible for fifty individuals, from all walks of life, with an average age of nineteen, who had been in the Army less than three months. Every day was filled with responsibility, from the time I got out of bed and drove to reveille, well before daylight each morning, until we finally finished the training day, usually long after dark. Sandy did not let up on any of his intensity and standards as we worked to get the most out of our new troops.

It seemed he called me into his office every day and pointed out one of my men had not saluted him, that two of my men needed haircuts, that he had found a cigarette butt in my platoon area, that he had seen one of my men not double timing in the company area, etc. It was my responsibility to fix all of those things.

Every night I went home exhausted both physically and mentally. I could not relax because I could not understand why Sandy was being so tough on me. I was working as hard and as smart as I knew how. I always tried to anticipate what he wanted and was always extremely demanding of my troops. Seldom had an hour of training time gone by when I was not with my men. I taught more than my fair share of the classes yet I never seemed to measure up to what he expected. I lay awake long into the night, unable to go to sleep, as I tried to figure out what I could do to please him. Finally, Phyllis suggested a solution.

"Rather than lay awake worrying about it, why don't you go ask him what you are doing wrong," was her suggestion. I had been so close to the problem I had overlooked the obvious.

The next day, after our daily debriefing, I asked him if he would see me in private for a few minutes. "Lieutenant Fiacco, I am busting my butt as hard as I know how every day. My men are doing well in all their training. But regardless of what I do, it never seems to be good enough. What am I doing wrong? How can I do my job better?"

He was astonished at my concern. His reply is as clear in my mind today as it was the day he said it. "Babcock, you are doing an outstanding job. If you were not doing a good job, I would have gotten rid of you a long time ago. My job is not to pat you on the back; it is to make you a better leader so you can lead your men better in combat."

I felt the weight of the world lift off my shoulders as I listened to him. From that moment, I knew I had a supporter I could count on. He would continue to drive me as hard as he could. But it was not because he was unhappy with me; it was because he expected me to accomplish every mission assigned to me and to bring back all my men alive. That night I went home and slept like a baby.

Our training continued without letup. Unlike most of the company commanders, Sandy spent most of his time in the field and in the classrooms with the troops. He was a highly visible commander, always demanding, always fair. The troops began to develop the same loyalty to him the officers and NCOs had. They knew they were being worked harder than their friends in the other companies but they knew "we" (the leaders) were sticking with "them" (the soldiers). They began to develop an 'esprit de corps' that is so essential to any organization, especially an Infantry rifle company.

After I understood where I stood with Sandy, I felt comfortable to stand toe to toe with him on issues or concerns where we did not totally agree. He always gave me a fair hearing and was not hesitant to go along with me if he thought my ideas had merit. He was also quick to stand firm when he disagreed with my point of view. There was never any question he was the boss, would always be decisive, and that all his decisions would be based on his firm commitment to accomplish every mission given to him and to bring back all of his men alive.

After the eight weeks of AIT, we started immediately into squad, platoon, and company training. Most of this training required three or four nights per week out in the field. As in AIT, Sandy stayed with the troops and pushed us hard. When the other companies were taking breaks before evening chow and night training, Sandy led us in five mile runs around the training area. It was tough but he never asked us to run unless he was running with us.

By this time, we had gotten our orders and knew we were headed for Vietnam. The entire company was convinced Sandy was the man we wanted to lead us into combat and if he wanted to run, we would run and not complain (too loudly) about it. Again, the other companies lounged around and laughed at that crazy bunch of 'gung ho' guys from Bravo Company.

Two things happened before we left Fort Lewis that made us think Sandy might not lead us in Vietnam. The first problem happened in AIT, on the hand grenade range. After completing the live grenade throwing exercises, a number of grenades were left. Sandy kept all the officers on the range when the troops went to the break area for noon chow. He wanted to make sure we were all totally comfortable working with live grenades - just another example of his total dedication to training on even the smallest, yet important, details.

Like a bunch of kids at a fraternity party, we took turns seeing how far we could throw the grenades and watched them explode. We quickly tired of that and decided to see if we could get air bursts. We would pull the pin, flip off the safety lever, count to two, heave it high into the air, and as far down range as we could. Most of the grenades hit the ground before the five second fuse had burned down.

Sandy was the one guy who consistently got an air burst. He could throw higher and farther than any of us. When we got down to the last grenade, Sandy pulled the pin, counted to three, and threw it high and far down range. We had already started walking away from the protective concrete bunkers toward the chow line when the grenade exploded. Almost immediately,

Sandy grunted and grabbed his leg. Blood oozed from a small hole in his fatigue pants. A fragment from the grenade had flown across the impact area and found Sandy's leg. The wound did not appear too serious but it caused us a lot of concern. There is not much demand for an Infantry company commander who can not walk.

The medics rushed him to the hospital. The doctor assured us it would not slow him down except for a few days. He did not even bother to take the piece of shrapnel from his leg. "You can now walk around like a lot of World War II and Korean War veterans," was the doctor's comment.

The second and most serious concern occurred while we were on the Brigade Field Training Exercise (FTX) which wrapped up our training. Colonel Morley had chosen Lieutenant Fiacco and Bravo Company to go on an all night forced march around the artillery impact area (a distance of twenty-two miles) to be in position to spring a surprise attack on the aggressors at first light the next morning.

True to his belief we could and would accomplish any mission, Sandy led our company, worn out from eight days of constant day and night exercises, on the trek around the impact area. After leading and prodding the company along through the dark for fifteen grueling miles, Sandy stepped in a hole and twisted his knee. He hobbled along for another three miles but finally had to succumb to the intense swelling and pain that coursed through his knee.

We all thought this was going to be the final thing that would take our commander away from us. Great concern swept us as we completed the all night movement and effectively surprised and overran the aggressor force as they were eating breakfast. Our mission had been a success but we had lost our leader. For two weeks we sweated out Sandy's knee until the doctors finally gave him a green light to continue as our company commander.

All of our training at Fort Lewis had built a camaraderie among Sandy and his four platoon leaders that was unique. We all totally respected him and his abilities. He drove us hard but supported us with the same passion for fairness and excellence. And, we became good friends in the process.

When we boarded the USNS Nelson M. Walker to take our sixteen day boat trip to Vietnam, it did not surprise us at all that he moved into our cabin rather than staying in the nicer cabins with the other company commanders. Staying true to form on the boat trip, Sandy insisted we have regular platoon meetings and physical training. He made himself available to the troops every day. He wanted to be close by to help alleviate their concerns as we got closer and closer to Vietnam.

The closer we got to Vietnam, the more he talked to us about his beliefs. We were to accomplish every mission given us and we were going to bring back all of our men alive.

He was a leader who truly cared about the welfare of everyone that worked for him. It was on this subject that he got into a heated argument one night with Major High, our battalion executive officer and a highly decorated veteran of the Korean War. Major High got tired of listening to Sandy's idealistic talk about not losing any men in Vietnam. Major High had fought through a number of the bloody campaigns in Korea and had seen a large number of men die as they accomplished their missions. (Some of Major High's Korean War experiences are chronicled in the book, "Heartbreak Ridge" by Arned Hinshaw.)

Sandy argued that good training and good leadership could prevail and his belief he could bring everyone home alive was clearly visible in his face as he argued. When Major High finally tired of the argument and left the room, Sandy turned to me, visibly shaken, and said, "Bob, don't you believe him. We are going to bring all our men home alive." And, I believed him.

As a combat leader, Sandy was everything we had expected and more. He maintained his high standards, drove his leaders and men hard but fair, reacted quickly and correctly in combat situations, listened to the opinions of others (if time permitted) before he made his decisions, fought the system when it was being unfair to his people, and never was given a mission he did not accomplish in a first class manner. When tough or unique missions came to the battalion, the odds were usually pretty good Colonel Morley would call on Sandy and Bravo Company to take it.

During our first three months in Vietnam, we operated primarily in squad and platoon size units with an occasional company size operation. That all changed on November 3, 1966 when we started Operation Paul Revere IV in the jungles of the Central Highlands along the Cambodian border. It was during that operation, where we operated almost exclusively as a company sized unit, that Sandy Fiacco proved time and time again, with his actions and decisions, how unique a leader he was.

First, Sandy trusted his platoon leaders' decisions. Even though he required us to defend our decisions, he seldom overrode a decision we made. He knew the man on the spot was better qualified to assess the situation and make a decision than he was from his position farther back in the company's line of movement. When he did get impatient with us and tried to override our decisions (as described in the chapter on "Trust the Dog"), he always made it a point to reassure us after the fact and eliminate any doubt from our mind about his support of us.

Second, he was not afraid to use common sense and good judgment, even when it was in direct conflict with the orders that came to us from "Rawhide" or the battalion operations officer. From the very first day of the operation, he made the decision to always stop early enough in the afternoon to scout the area where we would be setting up our nightly defensive position. This allowed us time to dig good bunkers and clear adequate fields of fire before dark.

Around 3:00 on the third day of the operation, he radioed in to battalion headquarters that we were stopping and preparing our defensive position for the night. The order came back, "Do not stop. Keep moving for at least two more hours." Less qualified commanders would have listened to that order, kept moving, and set their unit up for the night in a poorly prepared position (it got dark around 6:00 each evening).

More than once during the course of Operation Paul Revere IV (and other operations throughout the war), units that moved too late in the afternoon and did not prepare strong nightly defensive positions were hit with intense NVA human wave attacks. Being a commander with good common sense and judgment, Sandy radioed back to the battalion that we were still moving but were in real thick terrain and were not making much progress. In reality, we had stopped for the night and were preparing our normal strong defensive position.

Around 5:00, Sandy radioed back to battalion, told them we were stopping and where we were located. In the future, we stopped when we found the position we wanted to defend and did not tell battalion we had stopped until late in the afternoon. Some might question such apparent disregard for orders. In reality, we covered more terrain than the other companies each day and did not suffer the casualties they suffered.

Higher commands (i.e. battalion, brigade, or division) have an ultimate strategic or tactical goal in mind when issuing orders. Commanders at those higher levels only hope they have subordinate commanders (like Sandy) with intelligence and courage enough to achieve the objective and have a strong sense of responsibility for their troops. Orders are given to accomplish a mission, not to be followed to the letter.

After the first night attack on the battalion, orders were given to all companies to stop earlier in the day and prepare good defensive positions. It took others a loss of life to learn the lesson Sandy knew from common sense and instinct. Sandy trusted his own judgment more than he did the orders of those people safely removed from the situation.

Third, Sandy never allowed the troops to let their guard down. It was very difficult to keep everyone alert when we were all exhausted and had gone several days without seeing any signs of the enemy. Human nature made you want to relax and not take the extra security precautions that often could mean the difference between life and death. All the platoon leaders and NCOs believed as Sandy did. We consistently followed up on the security traits he had taught us at Fort Lewis, and after our arrival in Vietnam.

As a result, we never were caught by surprise by the NVA. We were always the ones who surprised them. Our success with security can be directly attributed to the constant attention Sandy paid to this seemingly small and obvious detail. The old adage, "People do well those things the boss checks," proved to be true once again.

One of our sister companies, who did not have this type of discipline, lost several men to an NVA ambush one afternoon as they were playing cards along the trail. They had taken a break and neglected to post security.

Fourth, Sandy was one of the early advocates of "managing by wandering around", long before it was recognized as a management technique in the 1980's book, "In Search of Excellence" by Tom Peters. Daily, he made it a point to talk to some of the men in each platoon. He learned what was on their minds, checked on the ones who were sick or hurt, joked with them, answered their questions, and generally reinforced the trust and confidence the entire company had in him.

Many other company commanders kept themselves aloof from their people. When critical times came, they did not understand the capabilities of their people and did not have the unwavering loyalty Sandy had from his troops.

Fifth, he was a strong advocate of using firepower. Each night Sandy made certain def-cons (defensive concentrations of artillery) were fired to insure we had a steel curtain of firepower pre-registered to call around our position if we needed it. As we moved during the day, he made sure we always knew where we were on the map. If there was any question, he fired artillery spotting rounds to insure we knew our exact location and that the artillery knew where we were.

Too frequently, units did not get fast artillery support because they did not know exactly where they were on the map sheet. (And it was very easy to get lost in that trackless jungle!) Sandy knew how to read terrain features and translate them into grid coordinates on a map. When we made contact with the enemy, or when we found fresh signs of them in the area, we used liberal amounts of mortar and artillery fire to soften the area before we moved into it. Artillery fire is cheap, American lives are priceless.

Sixth, he made the right decisions, even when they were tough ones. He was absolutely dedicated to our mission of searching for and destroying the enemy. However, when we captured a prisoner, he insured they were treated with compassion. Throughout the war, commanders like Captain Medina and Lieutenant Calley at My Lai, made bad decisions and let emotion take over when they allowed their people to slaughter civilians. Most commanders did like Sandy, when we found the old Montagnard man and woman in the jungle (described in detail in the chapter "The Old Man and Old Woman"). He would never sway from his basic beliefs as a caring human being.

As is very obvious by now, I am a real fan of Sandy Fiacco. It was not luck or coincidence that Alpha and Charlie companies of our battalion suffered heavy casualties during Operation Paul Revere IV while Bravo Company operated in the same area without suffering any casualties inflicted by the enemy. Our good fortune can primarily be attributed to the strong leadership skills exhibited day in and day out by Captain Sandy Fiacco. And, yes, we did do what he set out to do - we accomplished every mission given to us and brought back all of our men alive.

The only man killed while Sandy was in command of our company, David Mendez, was killed in an unfortunate accident no one in our company could have avoided. (See story "November 20, 1966").

We officers and men of Bravo company were extremely fortunate to have had Sandy Fiacco as our leader - we all learned from him. And we all thank and salute him for being such an outstanding leader of men and bringing us home alive.

Sandy Fiacco is out of the Army, and lives in the Seattle, Washington area.

Sandy Fiacco – in white tee shirt, on troop ship with Ron Marksity (left), Walt Ferguson (back), and Doc Maurer

BUCK ATOR

After Sandy Fiacco was promoted from company commander to Commandant of the 4th Infantry Division NCO Academy and Replacement Orientation School, we felt we would never get another CO as good as he had been. How wrong we were! The luck of Bravo Company held and Captain Buck Ator, though operating in a totally different style, proved to be more than competent to fill Sandy's boots.

Richard D. "Buck" Ator had been the aide to General Collins, the commander of the 4th Infantry Division, before taking command of our company. As the general's aide, he had his choice of companies and chose Bravo Company, 1st Battalion, 22nd Infantry Regiment. While at Fort Lewis, he had served as a staff officer in our battalion prior to his move to general's aide. Several of the old timers knew Buck but to most of us, he was a totally unknown commander.

Everything we heard about him was positive. In fact, those who knew him could not say enough good things about him. I hated to lose Sandy but was happy to be getting a commander who came so highly recommended. Buck was calm, professional, and much more laid back than Sandy. He was good with the people but did not have the personal involvement and intense personal interest in them that Sandy had. He worked through his officers and NCOs, letting them take care of the day to day needs of the men in the company.

I had just taken over as Executive Officer (XO) when Buck came in. From the very first day, he told me it was my job to run the company in the rear, providing logistical and personnel support to him and the troops in the jungle. If I had any problems, I was to let him know. If I could handle it, I was to do so, with his full support. It was a good feeling to start out with such a vote of confidence.

As the company moved back into the jungle on Operation Sam Houston, Buck showed he had many of the same traits we had admired and appreciated so much while working under Sandy. Buck had common sense and used good judgment in his decision making. He listened to the experiences our company had gone through in our first six months and elected to build on that base rather than trying to change our proven routine. Many commanders did not have the self confidence to listen to others. They felt they had to make their mark by making sweeping changes, whether they were needed or not. Buck did not suffer from that problem. He worked under the assumption, "if it's not broken, don't fix it".

Even though the fighting was intensifying in January and February of 1967, Buck stuck to the same methods that had proven to be effective during Operation Paul Revere IV. While other companies were regularly suffering substantial casualties, Bravo Company sustained its incredible record of not losing any men to the enemy. The company continued to stay out in the field more than the other companies, continued to cover more ground, and uncover more enemy activity than the others. Buck insured all our standards were maintained. The men quickly learned to trust and respect him.

We had gotten a new battalion commander soon after Buck took over the company. The new commander could best be described as an egotistical "wild man". He was interested in personal glory and gave little thought to the welfare of his men. This was in marked contrast to the style we had learned to expect and respect from "Rawhide" Morley when he was the battalion commander. Buck's strength as a commander was frequently tested by this man. But, unlike another new company commander who had listened to the ravings of this wild man and gotten killed by the NVA, Buck had the courage to say, "No!" to stupid orders.

A classic case of the grief Buck had to put up with happened after the company came down from a ridgeline they had been working on for five days. There was no water there and no LZ's for helicopters. Each day, drinking water was dropped from hovering helicopters. Many of the containers burst when they hit the ground, so the water problem was acute. It was a bedraggled company of troops that entered the fire base after that mission.

When the colonel saw Buck, he exploded. "Why haven't you shaved? Any officer in my battalion who does not shave should be relieved of his command!" "But, sir," Buck exclaimed, "my company did not have enough water to drink, let alone for me to shave." The response only infuriated the colonel more. "I do not want excuses! You will report to my command post and I will deal with you!" Fortunately, the colonel was wounded before he could act on his threat, shot by one of his own men (an accident). Buck never had to deal with the "wild man" again. The new commander was the type of officer we expected a battalion commander to be, not as good as "Rawhide", but at least reasonable.

In mid March, Bravo Company suffered our first casualties from the enemy. Throughout the fire fights and mortar attacks which lasted on and off for three days, Buck reacted as a true professional. He assessed the situation as it constantly changed. He made smart decisions which kept the casualties to a minimum while inflicting heavy casualties on the NVA. He kept artillery barrages and air strikes saturating the area to help neutralize the enemy while maneuvering his company to engage them. Four men in my former platoon were seriously wounded and evacuated. All four survived. Our record of no men killed in action by the enemy remained intact, due in no small part to Buck's outstanding command capabilities.

Soon after that action, I had the privilege of announcing to Buck the birth of his son, Steven. We were waiting daily to get the notification from the Red Cross that his wife, Joanne, had delivered their baby. When the message came to me at Plei Djereng, I lost no time in radioing the good news to Buck as he trudged through the jungle. That night, I flew out and spent the night in the jungle with him. We did not know many of the details of the birth but we had become friends and it was a time he wanted to talk. I was glad to be able to share that time with him.

As the end of our tour of duty neared, replacements started coming in to take the place of the men who had been there for nearly a year. Buck managed the transition of personnel and maintained a set of standards for Bravo Company that held until he returned to the States two months later, after most of us had already returned.

He maintained our record of losing no men killed by the enemy. As had happened when Sandy Fiacco was in command, we lost one more man, James Hubbard, killed by an unavoidable, unfortunate accident. (See story "Friendly Fire on Hubbard: A Tough Mission").

Why our company had been so fortunate is still a mystery to me. Of the 180 men who went to Vietnam with us, only three did not return home alive. Two were killed in separate, unavoidable accidents where "friendly" artillery and mortar fire had fallen on us. One died because he left a hospital where he was confined with malaria and, delirious with fever, had tried to catch the plane he was scheduled to go home on. I do attribute part of it to luck. But I attribute the largest portion of our phenomenal record to the outstanding leadership we had - Buck Ator and Sandy Fiacco were both outstanding leaders. I am proud to have served in their commands.

Buck Ator was killed in action on March 5, 1970 on his second tour in Vietnam. He earned the Silver Star while running through mortar and small arms fire to resupply the South Vietnamese unit he was serving as an advisor. His name is engraved on panel 13W, line 84 on the Vietnam Memorial Wall in Washington, D.C.

CPT Richard D. "Buck" Ator

STANLEY CAMERON

Stanley Cameron made an impression on me from the first week he joined our company at Fort Lewis. His appearance was much the same as many of the new people who came to us for Advanced Individual Training (AIT) - slim, wiry, and much younger looking than his nineteen years. He was different because he was not afraid to talk to officers. He was very comfortable asking questions, answering questions, and generally showed an ease about him that many of the new people did not have. Also, he was one of only two men who were married and had their wives with them.

I had to pick a radio-telephone operator (RTO) from our group of new people. It was an easy choice since he seemed comfortable with me and appeared to have the makings of a good soldier. He was eager to learn and it quickly became apparent my choice had been a good one. He seemed happy with the additional responsibility of being my RTO as well as going through the normal training and trying to find time occasionally to spend with his wife, Laura.

Stanley did extremely well in all our marksmanship training. It was obvious he had grown up with a rifle in his hands and had a lifetime of hunting experience. After he qualified as the best shot in the company with the automatic rifle, I went along with his request to transfer from RTO to automatic rifleman in one of my squads. It seemed like a waste to have a man with that uncanny shooting ability carrying a radio. He finished the rest of AIT and our unit training as an automatic rifleman in my first squad, and was an exemplary soldier.

My first indication of a problem was when we returned to Fort Lewis from leave and were preparing to board the ship for Vietnam. He came to me with a simple statement, "Sir, I am not going to Vietnam because I am a conscientious objector."

I was dumbfounded by the statement. My response was, "Stanley, you do not have a choice. You are not a conscientious objector. If you wanted to declare that, you should have done it when you first entered the Army, not now. You have been talking to your Mother too much. We are all scared but we are all going to Vietnam. Including you. Now cut out that foolishness and get back to work."

The problem was not going to be solved that easily. He told his squad leader, the platoon sergeant, the first sergeant and kept repeating it to me. He was a conscientious objector and was not going to Vietnam. I talked to Lieutenant Fiacco. He agreed Stanley was just scared and would get over it. My job was to get him on the ship with the rest of the people.

On the morning we were to board the ship, we went to the arms room to be issued our rifles. As the troops filed by to get their M16's, Cameron refused to take his. I signed for it, gave it to another soldier to carry, and once again told him he was going. He again told me he was not. At that point, I assigned a guard to him. I did not think he would run off, he was too level-headed to do something like that, but I wanted to be sure.

As we got to the dock and prepared to board the ship, he told me again he was not going. At that point, I decided to personally stick with him to make sure he got aboard. As we approached the gangplank, he turned to me and said, "Sir, I refuse to board this ship on grounds I am a conscientious objector." Through gritted teeth, I growled at him, "Cameron, get your ass on that boat!" Without further incident, he followed my order and walked up the gangplank.

I felt sorry for him on the sixteen day trip to Vietnam. The other men in the platoon avoided him like he had the plague. They were all convinced he was a coward. Only one man, Bill Bukovec, the other married man in the platoon, would even talk to him. Bill tried at great length to talk him out of his foolishness, but to no avail. Sergeant Roath and I both tried to talk some sense into him but we did not have any luck, either. But, we were both convinced that when we got to Vietnam where they were shooting real bullets, he would pick up a rifle.

As we got to our new base camp on our first day in country, Sergeant Baez, the first squad leader, approached me. "Sir, what are you going to do with Cameron?" My response was simple, "Sergeant Baez, he is an automatic rifleman in your squad. Put him on the perimeter with everyone else."

"But, sir, that isn't fair to the other people. They can't count on him." "I bet he will have a rifle in his hand before the night is over. Let's keep the pressure on him." With reluctance, Sergeant Baez returned to his squad. Rather than put him with two other men, Sergeant Baez did the right thing and put him in his bunker so he could keep an eye on him and not burden the others.

Several days passed and Cameron still had not wavered from his absolute refusal to pick up a weapon. He did everything he was told but steadfastly refused to carry a rifle. As we prepared for our first patrol, Sergeant Baez approached me again. "You're going to leave Cameron here, aren't you?"

"Absolutely not. He is going with you, that is his job. Get your men ready and let's go." "Sir, I do not like having the responsibility for a man without a weapon. Can't you transfer him to some other job?" I replied, "He will come around. Saddle up and let's go."

As we moved through the countryside on our patrol, it amazed me to look up and see Cameron walking along with his squad, like he was on a Sunday stroll. I am sure his gut was churning but he kept it well hidden. I kept hoping for some shots to be fired to see how he would react but we worked the whole day without finding the VC.

Cameron continued to refuse to carry a rifle. Sergeant Baez kept trying to convince me to transfer him to some other job. I could see it was causing a morale problem in the first squad so I knew I had to do something different. On our first patrol after we got to Tuy Hoa, Sergeant Roath needed a radio operator. Since Cameron had been a good RTO, Sergeant Roath suggested he use him to carry the radio. When we called Cameron over and told him what he was going to do, his response to Sergeant Roath was, "I may forget how to use this thing." Sergeant Roath's response was classic, "And if you get wounded, I may forget how to do first aid." We did not have any problems with Cameron handling the radio.

The man who had been my RTO was not doing a good job. I decided to solve everyone's problem and bring Cameron back to being my full time RTO. As we talked, it was obvious he was relieved to get away from the automatic rifleman's job, but he did have some concerns. "Sir, I can not call artillery fire in on the enemy. I do not believe in killing anyone." "Cameron, don't you worry about that. It is my job to call in artillery, all you have to do is have the radio there for me to use whenever I need it."

Things worked out well. For the first time since Cameron had left the RTO job in the States, I could count on reaching behind me and having the radio handset thrust into my hand. He stuck with me wherever I went and did a good job of helping me do my job. The RTO job was one of the most dangerous jobs in the unit but he handled it like a pro.

One day, while we were patrolling in the hills above Mosquito Valley south of Tuy Hoa, sniper fire broke the calm as bullets ricocheted off a large boulder behind us. We all jumped for cover. I got behind one big rock and Cameron got behind another one, about ten yards away. I shouted at him the normal command under such a situation, "Cameron, fire mission!"

Normally, he would be right there to hand me the handset so I could call in the mission. But this time there were ten yards of open ground between us - and the sniper had us in his sights. Using the good common sense he had been born with, Cameron stayed behind his rock, keyed the handset and relayed to the artillery fire base the fire mission I shouted to him. From that day forward, I still called most of the fire missions. But if the situation warranted, Stanley relayed my orders without hesitation.

We became more and more comfortable working with each other. It was very obvious Stanley had spent his life in the woods of his upstate New York homeland. He was observant, sure footed, and consistently brought things to my attention that others had passed without noticing. (See story on "The Boa Constrictor")

One day when we were deep in the jungles, bringing up the rear of the company movement, he found a cache of NVA 82mm mortar rounds off to the side of the trail. The entire company had passed by without seeing them. Because of his keen senses, those rounds were not used to kill Americans.

Stanley made his way through the jungle like a deer. He had the weight of the radio on his back, in addition to the normal pack we all carried, but never seemed to stumble. Seldom a day went by without most of us getting hung up in a vine or falling down a hill or over a rock. It became a running challenge for me to try to go a day without falling just to show him I was not clumsy. (I was not really clumsy, he was just unusually agile.) I can not recall a time I had to help him after he fell, but he helped me frequently.

We spent many nights together laying under the stars and talking about anything and everything. Stanley, Sergeant Roath, and I became close friends and learned to anticipate each other very well. Each afternoon when we stopped, we shared the daily responsibilities of digging our bunker and getting set up for the night. Stanley built our sleeping hootch and consistently built it to withstand any wind or rain that might come our way. During a late night rainstorm, it was not unusual to hear troops cursing as their hootch collapsed or leaked. We always stayed dry in the hootch Stanley built.

It was no longer an issue that Stanley did not carry a rifle. He was always there with the radio when I needed him. Captain Fiacco learned to trust and respect him and frequently passed detailed instructions to him when I was not close to the radio. He knew Stanley would be sure I got them accurately.

When I moved to executive officer from my platoon leader job, it was an easy sell to get Lieutenant Dean, my replacement, to keep Stanley as his radio operator. Stanley continued to do an outstanding job. Fortunately, Roy Dean recognized a good thing when he saw it and did not let the absence of a rifle get in the way of good judgment.

On March 3, 1967, Stanley showed how smart we had all been in overlooking his unwillingness to carry a rifle. The company had come under heavy small arms and mortar fire by a dug in NVA force. Lieutenant Dean was seriously wounded by a mortar round. Intense small arms fire pinned the platoon down. Though shaken by the impact of the mortar round, Stanley coolly and calmly took charge of the situation. He radioed the status back to Captain Ator, supervised the evacuation of Lieutenant Dean, relayed orders from Captain Ator, and controlled the platoon until the platoon sergeant could work his way to the front to assume command. For his reaction under fire, Stanley Cameron was later awarded the Bronze Star for Valor by General William Peers.

When I heard about the fire fight, I flew to the artillery fire base to meet my platoon when they came in from the jungle, knowing I could have a calming effect on them. As they filed into the fire base, Stanley came over and handed me Roy Dean's rifle. "Here, Sir, I don't need this." I have often wondered if Stanley would have used that rifle if they had been hit again as they moved back toward the fire base. My guess is he would not have. I learned he was very sincere in his religious beliefs and did not have a touch of cowardice in his body. Conversely, he had the courage to stand up for his beliefs when he was getting heavy pressure from his peers, as well as the authorities above him.

Stanley Cameron died suddenly of a brain aneurism on October 12, 1982. I have talked with his wife, his brother, and his three children (now adults) and relayed to them the respect I had for him as a soldier and as a person.

Stan Cameron, always right behind me as we moved
(this was the day I burned my face – thus the reason I am not wearing my helmet)

FRANK ROATH

May 16, 1951. The seventeen year old Army private huddled in his foxhole outside the bombed out South Korean village of Hangye. His ears pounded at the incessant noise of American artillery throwing round after round of destruction into the Chinese Communist army attacking the defensive lines several miles to the north. The rainy, overcast weather held the smoke and gunpowder from the thousands of rounds of artillery close to the ground, making a desolate, damp evening seem even more so. ....

Rather than curse the rain, the soldier only felt thankful that Item Company, Third Battalion, 23rd Infantry Regiment of the Second Infantry Division was part of X Corps reserve. If not here, they would be on the line facing the fanatical Chinese swarming against the United Nations forces fighting desperately to hold onto their defensive positions.

By daylight the next morning, word had filtered down to his position to start getting ready to move forward. The South Korean Divisions securing the right flank of the line had "bugged out" soon after the assault had started. The entire Corps defensive position was at risk as the Chinese poured through the exposed right flank. It would be the job of the 23rd Infantry Regiment to move forward and help shore up the holes that had been created in the line during the night.

As he picked up his heavy M-1 rifle and moved forward, Frank Roath wondered why he had lied about his age to get into the Army. Seventeen year old kids were not supposed to be put into situations like this. But, like the soldier he was, he shouldered his rifle and moved toward the battle.

Throughout the day and night of May 17-18, the Chinese continued their incessant pounding of the American positions. Over 40,000 rounds of artillery and frequent bombing runs by Allied planes helped to keep the Chinese from breaking through the lines. Frank Roath and his buddies continued to slug away at the wave of humanity that was thrust at them. They were determined not to let the little slant eyed bastards get the best of them. However, by morning of the 18th, it became obvious the 2nd Infantry Division would have to withdraw from the 'No Name Line' and establish another defensive line closer to Hangye.

In a total reversal of their fortunes of May 16, the 3rd Battalion, 23rd Infantry Regiment found themselves as the last remaining unit on the line. Their job was to fight a rearguard action as the remainder of the Division fought through the Chinese who had worked in behind them and withdrew to Hangye. Continuing to work as a cohesive team, the men of Item Company held intact and covered for each other as they withdrew without panic. Fighting against enormously unfavorable odds, the 23rd Infantry escaped disaster and consolidated onto the new positions that had been established around Hangye.

However, the final casualty figure was high. Over 400 Infantrymen from the 23rd Infantry Regiment were declared "missing" and presumed to be captured. Among the missing and captured was Frank Roath.

Twenty-seven months later, at the Korean village of Panmunjom, nineteen year old Frank Roath was among the 3,500 American prisoners of war who were returned to American control. As he crossed into freedom, he still wore the soft green patrolling cap he had worn throughout his grueling months as a POW. After the boat trip across the Pacific Ocean, he finally boarded a train in California to head back to his home state of Nebraska. When he ordered a beer in the bar car, his young looking face betrayed him and the porter asked for identification. "No, you can not buy a beer, you are under age," was the reply. Old enough to fight, not old enough to drink. (Rules were bent once Frank explained where he had spent the past twenty-seven months - he had all the beer he wanted as the train crossed the western states en route to Nebraska.)

Twelve years later, in November 1965, Staff Sergeant Frank Roath introduced himself to a green lieutenant with a broken leg and warned him, "Sir, if you get any of my men killed in combat, I will kill you." The unit this time was Bravo Company, 1st Battalion, 22nd Infantry Regiment, of the 4th Infantry Division and the mission was to train troops for battle in another oriental country.

From that unusual beginning, Frank Roath and I worked together to mold a platoon of raw recruits into a well trained fighting force who would spend a year as Infantrymen in the jungles of Vietnam and - we all came home alive.

Why we worked so well together is anyone's guess. Despite our differences, we seemed to complement each other and learned to respect each other's strengths early on. He was not intimidated by officers and constantly needled all the company officers with subtle reminders that we were green and dumb and he was seasoned and smart. Other lieutenants were offended by him but I learned to live with it and even enjoyed his style. One of his favorite comments was, "Don't forget, Sir, there is a reason they call me a 'senior' NCO and you a 'junior' officer. Keep your eyes and ears open and learn from me." And I did.

As we completed our training at Fort Lewis and the reality of going to Vietnam came closer to us, Sergeant Roath found out he did not have to go - since he had been a prisoner of war in an oriental country, he would not be sent to another one unless he volunteered. My heart sank as I thought about deploying without my platoon sergeant.

For several weeks he needled me about not going before he finally signed the papers to waive his right to stay home - he was a soldier and was going with his unit where he was needed. I breathed a huge sigh of relief when he flashed his grin and told me, "I can't let you go alone, you couldn't get along without me." Modesty was not one of his strengths.

As with my company commanders and radio operator, I consider myself blessed to have had Frank Roath as my platoon sergeant. Several memories are indelibly etched in my mind as I think about Sergeant Roath. Despite his gruff outside, he was a leader who cared deeply about his men. When Stanley Cameron declared his conscientious objector status and was ostracized by the members of the platoon, Frank spent hours on the boat trip to Vietnam helping Stan work through his challenges. It would have been both easy and acceptable for Frank to have written him off as a coward, but he did not.

Throughout our time in Vietnam, Frank constantly talked to the men and understood what was on their minds. He knew who had not received any mail from home, who had just gotten a 'Dear John' letter, who was sick and kept on working, who acted sick and tried to get out of the field - and he handled each situation with care and understanding (except for anyone who tried to be a malingerer). The men respected him and looked up to him as a good, caring leader.

Because of his closeness to the men, he was able to help me select our squad leaders and fire team leaders. As covered in the chapter "Training at Fort Lewis", we did not have many experienced NCOs. We had to pick leaders from the ranks of the recruits. Together, Frank and I selected some great small unit leaders - Aubrey Thomas, Doug Muller, Willie Cheatham, Bill Bukovec, and others.

Frank, Stanley Cameron, Sergeant Quann (our Vietnamese interpreter), and I always shared a bunker and hootch when we stopped in the jungle at night. Even though he and I both had to make sure our platoon's positions were set properly and bunkers and fields of fire were prepared, he always took his turn, along with Cameron and me, in digging our foxhole and cutting down trees to build overhead cover.

When Sergeant Quann would try to avoid his turn at digging, Frank would give him a tongue lashing and threaten him until he got off his duff and took his turn with the entrenching tool. It was always comical to me that First Sergeant MacDonald had assigned the only interpreter in the company to Sergeant Roath to look after - Mac knew about Frank's unpleasant experiences in Korea and his dislike of all Orientals.

Almost every afternoon when we were preparing our night position, I would look for Frank and find him missing. I soon learned he always conducted a one man patrol in front of our platoon position to see if there was anything out front we should know about, to check our noise discipline and security while digging in, and, most importantly, to study our position from the eyes of our enemy. It was not uncommon for him to come back from one of his patrols and recommend I shift a bunker or machine gun position to better cover a likely avenue of attack. I always went along with his recommendations.

It was Frank's responsibility as platoon sergeant to handle the logistics for the platoon - ammunition re-supply, C ration distribution, mail call, etc. He handled these jobs flawlessly. He always made sure every man had enough ammunition for his basic weapon and made sure to know when claymore mines, hand grenades, smoke grenades, sand bags, LAW's (Light Antitank Weapons or portable, throwaway bazookas), and other combat essentials needed replacement because of damage.

He showed no favoritism in re-supply, even to me. One case of C rations was a day's rations for the four men in our headquarters group. Frank had a system where he rotated giving each of us the best meals (yes, there were good meals in C rations) and we each had our turn at 'ham and eggs, chopped' and 'ham and lima beans' - the worst meals ever invented by some sadistic Army dietician. Try as I would, he would not let me trade 'ham and eggs, chopped' for anything else. So, for one meal every four days, I jammed my bayonet or entrenching tool through the offensive meal and buried it - no one would ever trade for 'ham and eggs, chopped', they were terrible. (I finally learned to like 'ham and lima beans'). He did humor me at mail call. He recognized my wife's handwriting and would hand me my letters as he came to them as he sorted the platoon's mail. And he knew I would be in a sour mood when I did not get a letter from Phyllis.

Another of Frank's daily jobs was to insure we each took our daily malaria pill, dapsone. Soon after daylight each morning, Frank would wake up, go through a coughing fit, stick a cigarette in his mouth, and turn to me and say "open your mouth". He dropped a malaria pill in and then started making his rounds of the platoon, personally putting a malaria pill in each man's mouth. Once a week, he added the large, yellow malaria pill to his ritual. No one ever seemed to mind his dirty hands, ours were not any cleaner.

After the Christmas stand down and I had moved out of the platoon, Captain Ator and First Sergeant MacDonald decided to move Frank to the second platoon – they had a new platoon leader and their platoon sergeant had moved to another unit. Frank did a great job running that platoon just as he had in running our third platoon.

When Roy Dean, the platoon leader who replaced me, was wounded, Frank requested to move back to the third platoon. I could see the look of relief on our men's faces when they got Frank back. For a few weeks he ran the platoon alone before a new, green second lieutenant came into the unit. For the remainder of his tour, he took on the responsibility of training the rookie lieutenant to get him prepared for the rest of the veterans leaving at the end of their year. His style of looking down his nose at lieutenants did not change, I smiled as I watched Frank train this new man as he had trained me. When the lieutenant came to me to complain about Frank's style, I told him, "Appreciate what you have, he will be gone before long and you will be on your own - you will not get anyone nearly as good as him as a replacement."

Frank Roath was truly an outstanding NCO. He moved up the ranks, served another tour in Vietnam as an advisor to a South Vietnamese unit, and retired as a Command Sergeant Major. As he moved up in rank, I feel certain he included captains (and maybe even majors) in his speech when he pointed out, "There's a reason they call me a 'senior' NCO and you a 'junior' officer..."

One last story about my experience with Frank Roath. I mentioned his soft green patrolling cap he wore throughout his time as a POW in Korea. That same hat was on his head every day from the time we stopped to dig in for the night until he put his helmet on to move out the next morning.

In the spring of 1967, Frank got a case of malaria (despite the pills he so religiously took) and spent time in a hospital. When he came back to the unit and got his equipment from the supply tent, he could not find his soft green patrolling cap. Knowing how much the cap meant to him, I turned the supply tent upside down trying to find it but to no avail (we had made several moves during his absence). As company executive officer, it was my responsibility to keep track of all the company's supplies and personal gear. That loss gnawed at me for over twenty years when I thought of Frank.

After losing track of him for a long time, I located him and visited with him in May of 1991. As our reunion day wore on, I apologized again for having lost the cap that had served him so well in two wars. "Sir, I found the cap the day after I reported it lost – that's the cap I wear now when I mow my lawn." I can not recall when such a little thing as knowing his cap had been found made me so happy.

Frank Roath is retired from the Army and owns a small engine repair shop in Idaho.

OTHER KEY PEOPLE

This is a tough chapter to write because, in all probability, I will leave out someone I should have included. The realization will come to me after the book is finished, published, and it's too late to go back and change. So, understanding my list probably will not be complete, here goes with some thumbnail sketches of key people from my days as a soldier.

First Sergeant Bob MacDonald - It would be easy to write a separate chapter on First Sergeant MacDonald in addition to the one I have written entitled "First Sergeant MacDonald's Bronze Star". Bob MacDonald was as good a First Sergeant as there ever was in the Army. Like Frank Roath, he was a combat veteran of the Korean War. He landed on July 18, 1950 as a twenty-one year old platoon sergeant with the 1st Squadron, 8th Cavalry as part of the 1st Cavalry Division.

Seriously wounded on July 31, 1950, he volunteered to return to his unit in early November 1950 and fought through the winter, spring, and summer campaigns of 1951. Also, like Frank, he was a prisoner of war in Korea, but only for a short time. He escaped after a few days and worked his way back to American lines to continue to fight with his unit.

He was tough, gruff, and earned the respect of everyone who worked with or around him. While training at Fort Lewis, he intimidated me. After we got to Vietnam, I learned to rely on him and him on me. He was a field soldier, unlike the other First Sergeants in our battalion. All of his time was spent humping the jungles with the company. Even in the jungle, with several days' growth of beard, he was meticulously neat and looked the part of a "top kick" (Army jargon for any First Sergeant).

There was an air of authority and assurance about him that made all of us feel better when he was around. He was not afraid to tackle the system and would take on any comers to make sure his company was taken care of and not taken advantage of (see chapter entitled "Buddha's Birthday"). He led by example and would not ask anyone to do anything he would not do himself.

First Sergeant Bob MacDonald influenced everyone he came in contact with. He rightfully shares with Sandy Fiacco and Buck Ator in the excellent record our unit earned in 1966 and 1967.

After losing track of Bob for many years, and even hearing he had died, I located him in April 1991. Since then, we have stayed in close contact and have developed an even better friendship. Seldom a Christmas, Memorial Day, or Veteran's Day goes by without us talking to each other. I feel even stronger about the strength and character of this fine veteran of two of our wars.

Colonel Len "Rawhide" Morley - Our battalion commander while we trained the troops at Fort Lewis and during the first six months of our tour in Vietnam. Len had fought through Europe in World War II with the 42nd Infantry Division, earning a battlefield commission. His platoon had taken part in the liberation of the Dachau death camp.

He took a personal interest in all his officers and men. His wife, Chartley, took the officers' wives under her wing as we went through the grueling training days at Fort Lewis. Just as "Rawhide" taught us to be good Army officers, Chartley taught our wives how to be good Army wives.

As a combat leader, he did an excellent job in motivating us and insuring our missions were accomplished while letting the company commanders run their units with minimal interference. Older than most battalion commanders in Vietnam, he had the stamina and drive to outlast men many years his junior.

He took on the radio call sign "Rawhide" while our battalion was attached to the 101st Airborne brigade early in our tour. To this day, he is still affectionately known to all of us as "Rawhide". He and Chartley have been my strong supporters in all my veterans' activities. Chartley died in September 2004.

Our Company Officers - In addition to Sandy Fiacco, we arrived in Vietnam with an unusually close knit and competent group of officers in our company. From the day we first came together at Fort Lewis, we developed a mutual respect, loyalty, and friendship.

Russ Zink, the executive officer, joined us at Fort Lewis from the California National Guard. As ranking lieutenant, he was second in command of the company. He led our advance party to Vietnam and was responsible for the myriad of logistical support requirements associated with our movement. He provided excellent support for us until he moved on and became Headquarters company commander.

Ron Marksity, our weapons platoon leader, was the officer I was closest friends with in the company. Although our approach to our jobs was totally different, we and our wives were inseparable after duty hours. He worked his mortar section into a precision unit who could provide pinpoint fire support whenever we needed it, night or day. Ron was selected as aide to our assistant division commander and left our company after three months.

Walt Ferguson, our second platoon leader, could always be counted on for challenging missions. Sandy regularly split the tough missions between Walt's platoon and my platoon. Walt's first son was born while we were in Vietnam. He was wounded in the knee on November 20, 1966 and spent the remainder of his tour training replacements and NCOs before they went to their units.

Lou Dinetz, our first platoon leader, was a born comedian and strong leader. His sense of humor was a constant source of entertainment for us. His Jonathan Winters and Jose Jiminez routines kept us laughing. Lou had the distinction of being the first 4th Infantry Division man to come under fire in Vietnam. He also stayed in the field longer as a rifle platoon leader than any of the rest of us. In early February, Lou moved to Camp Holloway to command their security platoon.

Lou, Walt, and Russ all served a second tour in Vietnam. Walt and Russ have both retired after careers in the Army. Walt was killed in an automobile accident in 2000.

My Squad Leaders and Fire Team Leaders - A platoon leader can not ask for anything more than to be surrounded by good small unit leaders. I was fortunate to have excellent leaders in Sergeants Jim Benge, Al Burruel, Doug Muller, Aubrey Thomas, Willie Cheatham, Bill Bukovec, and Raul Baez to name a few of our leaders. (Thomas, Muller, and Cheatham were all wounded in action during the course of the year - leadership has a price).

As our training progressed, we developed excellent fire team leaders to help the squad leaders. By the time we arrived in Vietnam, we worked like a well-oiled team.

Almost every evening, I sat down with my squad leaders and discussed the day we had just lived through and what we should do better to be sure to live through many more days. If I was going off in the wrong direction with my thinking, they did not hesitate to suggest a better way to accomplish what we were trying to do. Each of them took good care of their men and kept Sergeant Roath and I informed on everything that needed our attention.

George Wilhelm - While serving as company executive officer, George was my right hand man. A draftee who could not wait to get out of the Army, George consistently did a great job and performed far above what was expected. His New York City accent and attitude were different from my Oklahoma twang and style but we worked very well together. We shared a tent and he ably handled both my responsibilities and First Sergeant MacDonald's responsibilities when we were away from the company rear area. Recently, I found out George died in the early 1980's. I never saw or talked to him after we returned from Vietnam.

Harry Troutman - The company commander's radio operator. Harry was unmistakable when you heard his North Carolina drawl come over the radio. Always cool under any conditions, he served both Sandy Fiacco and Buck Ator well. Whether driving a jeep or humping through the jungle with the CO's radio on his back, Harry was always an extension of the CO. He could always be depended on and was well thought of by officers, NCOs, and soldiers alike. When you passed something over the radio to Harry, you knew he would make sure it was handled properly. One of the last of the original company to go home, he left the jungle and his radio less than 24 hours before flying home. His were tough boots to fill. (I have recently located Harry in his native North Carolina).

Steve Angulo - Our mess sergeant. Sergeant Angulo took a fierce pride in taking care of the men he fed. It upset him greatly when the troops inevitably complained about the Army chow. When complete meals could not be gotten to the troops, he became creative and cooked hot meat supplements which helicopters dropped to us in the jungle in C ration cases. It was not unusual to have warm roast beef or fried chicken or fresh fruit to eat with our C rations. Unlike many mess sergeants, Sergeant Angulo liked to get into the field and always seemed to be spoiling for an opportunity to mix it up with the NVA or VC. After many years of looking for him, I am now again in contact with him – a retired First Sergeant living in California.

Chaplain Walt Sauer – God's man with our battalion. He did a great job of tending to the religious needs of our troops. I am sure circumstances played a role in it but some of the most memorable church services I ever attended were conducted by Chaplain Sauer. He conducted services on the ship going to Vietnam, in the jungles, in a fire base, or in the base camp - and it was as likely to be on any day of the week as it was on Sunday. In addition to church services, he regularly visited with the troops and was always there when casualties came in.

The Individual Soldier in Bravo Company - He has many names and knows who he is. He might have been a rifleman, a grenadier, a machine gunner, a radio operator, part of a machine gun crew, a fire team leader, or a squad leader. His daily mission was like all Infantrymen who came before or after him – "to close with and kill or capture the enemy through firepower and maneuver." He was well trained, well motivated, and always did an excellent job. He knew he would not be rotated out of his front line Infantry job - that he had twelve months to work in the field seeking out the elusive enemy, hoping he would not be killed or wounded. He had two opportunities to leave the field - R&R and end of tour. Any other time he left, it was because of sickness, injury, or wounds.

He spent his year living the most primitive of existence. He always wore his steel helmet, web gear, and carried his weapon. He also carried a rucksack weighing well over sixty pounds in which he carried his essentials - ammo for his basic weapon, claymore mines, hand grenades, C rations, bed roll, entrenching tool, machete, sand bags, writing paper, basic toilet articles, dry socks, and any other personal item he was willing to trudge through the jungle with. Most men eliminated all but the barest essentials - air mattresses and a change of clothes were among the first things to go. Cigarettes, writing paper, the latest letter from home were the most cherished personal items. Sometimes, he was weighted down even further with extra machine gun ammunition or a mortar round.

Shaving and taking a bath in a stream or bomb crater were luxuries that happened maybe once every week or two. Leeches, mosquitoes, and bugs were as commonplace as the smell of sweat and body odor that permeated each man. He seldom knew where he was, and hardly ever looked at a map, compass, or talked on a radio. He depended on the leaders above him to tell him what to do. It was his job to do what he was told and to do it to the best of his ability. All too frequently, he was called on to sit with another man or two in an all night listening post outside the company perimeter. The nights seemed to last forever as he lay motionless, listening for the slightest sound of an approaching enemy. Another day, he would walk point and lead the company through the dense jungle.

Constantly, the fear of running into the enemy was in the front of his mind. Caution and alertness became second nature to him. He learned to observe and react to his surroundings more than ever before in his life. All his senses were honed to a fine edge. He learned what trusting your buddy is all about. He also forged friendships that he would never forget. White men, black men, Hispanics, and Orientals became closer to and depended more on a man of a different race than he had ever dreamed possible.

These men were too busy to use drugs or to dislike someone who was different. He was the Infantryman and he did his job, day in and day out, as Infantrymen before and after him have done. And only he can truly appreciate and understand this:

When you stare Death in the face
in a foxhole with other guys,
you form a strong bond of friendship.
Those friendships are the kind that go on forever.

George H. Morgan 1915-1988
Technician Fifth Grade - 22nd Infantry
World War II

Our Support Troops - All troops' jobs, ultimately, are to support the Infantryman doing his job. It might have been an artilleryman, a forward observer, a medic, a scout dog handler, a mortar man, a combat engineer, a helicopter crewman, a cook, a supply clerk, a chaplain's assistant, a pilot, a construction engineer, a truck driver, or any of hundreds of other military specialists who supported us. Without all of their help, we would not have been able to do our job. Some of them lived the same primitive existence as the Infantryman; others lived less Spartan lives, some in relative comfort. Each of them had an important job to do, and, during the time I was in Vietnam, we almost never had to worry about their being ready, willing and able to do whatever job was required to support us.

SSG Jim Benge (with bananas on rucksack) and PSG Frank Roath

SECTION SEVEN

My Experiences Since I Returned from Vietnam

My Experiences Since I Returned from Vietnam

In late August, 1967, scarcely more than a month after my return from Vietnam, I started work for Phillips Petroleum Company. While in a training program in Kansas City, I started waking up in the middle of the night with chills, fever, and sweats. After several weeks, I went to the Veterans Hospital and was diagnosed with Falcipirum and Vivax malaria. I watched the 1967 World Series from a hospital bed in the Veterans Hospital. Malaria was such a rare disease in America at that time, I agreed to volunteer to talk to and be examined by a class of medical students at the University of Kansas Medical Center. Before long, the treatment eliminated my symptoms and I continued at my new job.

In November, 1967, I transferred to Chicago with Phillips Petroleum and officially started my business career. I watched the battle of Dak To and the Tet offensive on television along with the rest of America. I watched closely for any mention of the 4th Infantry Division. Few of my friends or acquaintances ever asked me about my Vietnam experiences.

By March, 1968, my malaria symptoms began to return. Two weeks were spent in the Chicago VA hospital. This included the time when Martin Luther King, Jr. was killed and the cities were struck with burning and rioting. I felt helpless and more than a little concerned as I looked out my hospital window and saw the smoke rise from a burning Chicago. Phyllis found it very unnerving to pass National Guard outposts along the highway when she came to visit me each day.

The hospital rest eliminated my malaria (I've never had any further problems with it) and I returned to work. In April, 1968, I learned my boyhood friend, Fred Sonaggera, had been killed in Vietnam while leading a long range patrol.

In August, 1968, I again sat in front of my television like most Americans and watched the rioting associated with the Democratic National Convention in Chicago. Unlike many Americans, I did not agree with the war protesting. Instead, I felt a hollow, sick feeling as I thought of the men still fighting in Vietnam. What were the men in Bravo Company, 1st Battalion, 22nd Infantry Regiment, of the 4th Infantry Division doing? Had they been as fortunate as we had been in avoiding casualties? What did they think about what was going on in the country that had sent them to that far away place to fight?

In September, 1968, I started work as a salesman for IBM in Kansas City. My business career began to progress and the Vietnam war continued to wear on. I continued to watch it on television and wonder about my unit and many of my friends who had doubtless returned for a second tour. In 1970, I got a call from "Rawhide" informing me Buck Ator had been killed while serving as an advisor to the South Vietnamese.

The only outward sign I showed of my Vietnam experience was the POW bracelet I wore with the name of an Air Force pilot, Captain Ronald Mastin, engraved on it, along with the date he had been captured, January 16, 1967. I had intentionally picked the name of a pilot who had been shot down during my time in Vietnam.

Time moved on and American troops began their withdrawal from Vietnam. When the Prisoners of War were returned from Hanoi, I sat up far into the night in front of my TV set watching them come off the airplane and stepping into freedom. When Captain (by then Major) Ronald Mastin stepped off the plane, tears streamed down my face and my emotions raced. But it was late at night, no one else was awake, and I kept it all to myself.

A few weeks later, I attended a welcome home ceremony for Major Ron Mastin as he returned home to his native Kansas. I waited impatiently with a throng of people for his plane to arrive at Richards Gabaeur Air Force Base outside Kansas City. Pushing forward with the crush of well wishers, I shook his hand and welcomed him home. I did not give him the POW bracelet I had been wearing for many months. I wanted to keep it as a remembrance of what he and others like him had done in the name of Freedom. He went to Vietnam at the same time I did. I had returned home, started a career, and had a child. He had languished for month after month - for over six years - in a small, dark cell in Hanoi. (To show how small this world is, I located Ron Mastin a few years ago - he is a member of my church in Marietta, GA and I shake his hand every Sunday morning - but that is another story...).

My career took me to Atlanta in early 1975. In April that year, I watched on television as Saigon fell. Why did it happen? Why were we Vietnam vets looked at with such disdain or disinterest by the American public? We were not responsible; we were just doing what our government told us to do.

All my attention and energy was focused on my career by the late 1970's and I had moved to Evansville, Indiana. After a divorce and remarriage, I moved back to Kansas City in 1982. Nothing of significance was done about my Vietnam feelings and experiences until January 1983 when I met Hal Reynolds at an IBM meeting - that story is covered in the first chapter of this book.

The remainder of this book focuses on what has happened since then.

My Speech at the Moving
Wall, April 1986

In March of 1986, I was asked by Lily Adams, a former Army nurse in Vietnam and a fellow member of Vietnam Veterans of America, to speak about my Vietnam experiences at an exhibit of the Moving Wall when it came to Atlanta in April. The Moving Wall is a half size replica of the Vietnam Memorial Wall in Washington, DC and has been moved around the country to bring the experience of the Wall to those who can't make the trip to Washington. (I visited the Moving Wall again in August 2005).

After considerable soul searching, hesitation, and a lot of encouragement from Lily Adams, I agreed to share my experiences about six of my friends who were killed in Vietnam and whose names are on the Wall. My wife, Jan, and Rob, my son, accompanied me to the sunset ceremony at a park in downtown Atlanta.

While at the ceremony, I talked to Chris Noel, the voice of Armed Forces Radio I had listened to in Vietnam, a weekend house guest of Lily and Jim Adams. I also was privileged to talk to two wives whose husbands are pilots that are still listed as missing in action while flying missions over North Vietnam. Both men had been missing for nearly twenty years at that time.

Finally, I talked to Colonel Ben Purcell, the highest ranking Army officer held prisoner by the Viet Cong. He was a prisoner of the VC for five and a half years before his release. Colonel Purcell now runs a Christmas tree farm north of Atlanta.

The ceremony and discussions with the above mentioned people and other veterans, as well as once again experiencing the Wall, were very touching to me. Jan and Rob also got a little better feeling of Vietnam as a result of this experience. The following is the speech I gave that night:

This is one of the greatest honors of my life - to share the stage with Ben Purcell who spent five years as a Prisoner of War in Vietnam, with Chris Noel who was the voice from home that most of us in Vietnam remember as a highlight of the Armed Forces Radio Network. With the Gold Star Mothers and Wives who lost loved ones in the war. With the members of the POW/MIA League of Families, and with the over 58,000 comrades in arms who went to Vietnam and paid the ultimate price in service to our country.

Many of us here tonight have friends and loved ones whose names are on the Wall. Many of us have brought our children to let them try to get a glimpse of what we as individuals and we as a country experienced in Vietnam.

Behind each of the names on the Wall, there are stories - hopes and dreams, personalities, and pleasant things that are remembered by those of us who knew them.

Tonight, I want to share with you the stories of six of my friends and fellow soldiers whose names are on the Wall.

Like most of us who served in Vietnam, four of them were civilians who answered their country's call to serve, two were career soldiers. They were from Tennessee, the West Coast, New York City, Puerto Rico, and my home state of Oklahoma. All of them were genuinely good people.

My company commander's name is on the Wall. He was a great soldier from whom I learned a lot of leadership traits. He always accomplished the mission, but never forgot to take care of the men who served under him. It was a rare privilege of mine to relay a radio message from the Red Cross to him announcing the birth of his son. Buck Ator made it home to see that son, who will be 19 years old this month, but was killed three years later while serving his second tour in Vietnam.

Two of our radio operator's names are on the Wall. As a platoon leader, I worked closely with both of them. One was from Tennessee, the other from New York City. They shared the trait of always having a positive attitude, of doing their job in a superior manner, and they were both killed, three months apart, by friendly fire. Neither one ever knew what hit him.

One of many of the West Point class of '65 whose names are on the Wall was a friend and comrade of mine. He was married during June Week at West Point and had a baby born just before we left for Vietnam. We were friendly competitors as platoon leaders and soon became good friends. The one night I spent in Saigon was with Dick Collins - six weeks later he was killed while working with a scout dog team - the same dog team I had been working with only two days earlier.

One of my friends made it through the year, was out of the field for good, and couldn't wait to get home. He was so anxious; he wouldn't go on sick call when he started running a high fever. He was afraid he would miss his port call. During the night, two days before he was to return home, his fever overtook him and he died of malaria.

Finally, my best boyhood friend's name is on the Wall. When we were the age of my twelve year old son, who is here tonight, we were inseparable. Fred's house was where my mother always called when she didn't know where I was. Fred was very mild mannered and much less aggressive than I. As a teammate playing football, he had severely injured his knee. Yet, after completing college, he volunteered for service in the Army.

He went to Officer's Candidate School and went to Vietnam as an Infantry lieutenant. He always wanted to prove himself so he volunteered as a long range reconnaissance patrol leader. He lost his life while shielding one of his men from an enemy grenade blast. For this act of heroism and sacrifice, he was posthumously awarded the Silver Star, our nation's third highest decoration for valor.

As I wrote to Fred Sonaggera's mother, and is true of all the men and women whose names are on the Wall – "I feel that Fred gave his life in service to his country. The job that he did was every bit as important and noble as the troops who fought with George Washington or in any of the other wars where our Country has called on its citizens to fight for it."

Vietnam was a war run by politicians - but to those of us who served there, it was a very personal war. There are over 58,000 other stories to be told about the names on the Wall. Tonight I tried to reflect back on six of those stories.

Locations of names on Vietnam Memorial Wall in Washington, DC:

Richard D. Ator	*Panel 13W, Line 84*
David Mendez	*Panel 12E, Line 96*
James R. Hubbard	*Panel 15E, Line 105*
Richard G. Collins	*Panel 12E, Line 27*
Francisco Marin	*Panel 22E, Line 44*
Fred Sonaggera	*Panel 50E, Line 33*

VIETNAM VETERAN'S PARADE, CHICAGO, 1986

May 8, 1985 - This page one article caught my eye as I read the newspaper prior to leaving home for work, "New Yorkers Roar Thanks to Veterans". Reading further, the article said: "Vietnam veterans accepted New York City's thanks yesterday at a bittersweet ticker-tape parade through the canyons of lower Manhattan.

"The belated welcome home from a war that ended 10 years ago began Monday night when Mayor Koch lighted the Vietnam Veterans Memorial, adjacent to 55 Water Street. It continued yesterday when a thunderously appreciative crowd, which the police estimated at one million, lined the parade route from Cadman Plaza in Brooklyn to the Battery..."

As I finished the article, a sick, hollow feeling tore through the pit of my stomach. Pictures of the World War II homecoming parades had always been vivid in my mind. As I served my tour in Vietnam, I had often thought about a real homecoming - and a New York City ticker tape parade was right at the top of the list.

It made me even sicker knowing I could have been there that day. On Friday of the previous week, I had decided against going to an IBM meeting in New York that would have put me right on the parade route. Instead, I had sent one of the men who worked for me. If only I had known about the parade, wild horses could not have kept me from New York.

I said nothing and went on to work. For the next several weeks, I scoured the newspapers and weekly news magazines to read about the event. It had been a very emotional experience for those in attendance.

Approximately 25,000 Vietnam veterans marched in the parade, thousands more watched from the sidewalks. Men found friends they had not seen in years. The American public showed a real appreciation for the contributions the Vietnam vet had made. For the first time, the Vietnam vet seemed to be truly accepted for the sacrifices he had made for his country.

I went on about my life but, often, in moments of reflection, I felt sad I had missed that once in a lifetime experience. Like all veterans, I felt I had earned a parade. The only appreciation I had ever felt was at the Vietnam Memorial Statue dedication the previous November. That was from other vets, not from the American public.

A year later, in the spring of 1986, when I was participating in the Moving Wall ceremony in Atlanta, I heard about an upcoming Vietnam veteran's parade to be held in Chicago in June. Like in New York, it was to be a ticker tape parade. Over 50,000 veterans were expected to participate.

Immediately, my mind started debating with myself about whether or not I could go to the Chicago parade. There was no question I wanted to go, being able to afford the time and money was the question. It had never been my nature to spend money on myself, and I traveled so much in my job I felt guilty to leave my family for what, to them, would appear to be such a frivolous reason.

A few days later, I mentioned it to my wife, Jan. Much as I expected, she listened and told me to do whatever I thought was right. If anything, she encouraged me to go ahead and do it. I muddled the problem around in my mind for a few more days. I had concluded I could justify the one day away from my family to fly up there and back. I was still having a hard time justifying the $400 airplane ticket. Finally, it hit me. A few years earlier, I had spent almost $400 one night to take our family to see Michael Jackson, the famous singer, on the first night of his world tour. This had to be a more important event to me than Michael Jackson was to our kids. If they could go see Michael Jackson, I could go participate in a Vietnam veteran's parade - and not feel guilty about doing it! My mind was made up; I called Delta Airlines and made my plane reservation.

It was with mixed emotions that I boarded the first Delta flight from Atlanta to Chicago on the morning of June 13, 1986. Would I find any of the guys I had served with? How would I react to the parade? Would it be what I expected or would it be a disappointment? A flood of memories coursed through my brain on the flight to Chicago.

By 7:30 am, I was in a cab en route from O'Hare airport to the Navy pier, marshalling area for the parade. As I paid the cab driver, I saw hundreds of fatigue clad vets milling around the pier. I scanned them all, looking for a familiar face or a 4th Infantry Division patch.

For the next two hours, I roamed through the crowd, my eyes constantly scanning around me. Not since Vietnam had I been so observant of my surroundings. I found a few 4th Infantry Division patches, but no one I knew.

As the parade began to form, I moved to the group standing behind the banner with the 4th Infantry Division "Ivy Leaf" patch proudly emblazoned on it. Still, no familiar faces. Then suddenly, I saw one. General William Westmoreland, commander of all troops in Vietnam and the grand marshal of this parade, approached our group.

Not being bashful, I was the first in our group to step forward and shake his hand. It was around the time he was in the middle of a lawsuit with CBS news over their reporting of his actions during the war. Many of our emotions were mixed about the job he did in Vietnam, but he was our commander, and he deserved our respect. I was proud to have the opportunity to shake his hand.

He said one thing which still stands out in my mind. "You men in the 4th Infantry Division had one of the toughest jobs in Vietnam. No one else spent as much time in the jungle as you. You humped the hills for months on end without getting a break. And, the press seldom made it out to report on your accomplishments. You did a great job in the Central Highlands - I thank you for it."

He did not have to say that. I think he believed what he said - and I agree with him. The 4th Infantry Division was not the darlings of the press like the 1st Cavalry Division, the Marines, or the 173rd Airborne Brigade, but, by God, we did a job to be proud of.

My emotions and unit pride were starting to build. I never wanted to take anything from another unit; I just wanted our accomplishments to be recognized. I could sense this was going to be a pivotal day in my life.

Several things during the course of the parade swept me with emotion. First, the parade was led by Medal of Honor recipients from World War II, Korea, and Vietnam. There, in a group, were men who had earned the ultimate honor in defense of our country. Just like my experience in Washington the previous fall, I was in awe of Medal of Honor recipients (and still am).

Behind the Medal of Honor men were the disabled vets. My heart went out to the men who had given one, two, three, or even all four limbs and more in doing what their country had asked of them. Some pushed themselves along in wheelchairs or on four wheeled platforms; others were pushed by other vets. Some paralyzed vets were pushed on gurneys. You could see the emotion in each of these men, and feel it in yourself.

As we progressed down LaSalle street, I was overwhelmed by the reaction of the public. Men in business suits, women, children, poor people, rich people, middle class people, old men, veterans in fatigue jackets - all walks of life were represented along the parade route. The shouts of encouragement and thanks they gave us will live forever in my heart and mind. Tears streamed down my cheeks as I marched proudly along closely behind our 4th Infantry Division banner.

And, before long, I found myself walking through knee deep ticker tape. This parade was everything I had ever dreamed it would be, and more. Never have I felt as proud of my service to my country as I did that day parading through the streets of Chicago.

As our unit came to the end of the parade, I peeled off and walked back through the crowd to add to the cheers and encouragement for subsequent units coming down the street. Standing on the sideline watching the emotions in other vets passing by was as gripping as the parade had been. It struck me that men from all walks of life, many who had not had a significant break in all their life, were getting an experience they had earned and would never forget. I stood and shouted, "Welcome Home!" and "Thanks!" as each unit passed. Sheer emotion showed on each of their faces.

This was an important day to me, and I have been fortunate to receive many breaks in my life - it had to be even more overwhelming to those who had struggled all their lives, only to be snubbed for their most important accomplishment. Finally, the American public was expressing their appreciation to us.

As the parade wound down, people wandered toward Grant Park, on the shores of Lake Michigan. There, a sea of fatigue clad veterans was everywhere the eye could see. Again, my eyes swept over every person as I tried to find even one long lost friend and comrade. I walked and I wandered, I went to the amphitheater where Lee Greenwood was entertaining with his "God Bless the USA" and other songs.

I am not a fatigue wearing veteran. In fact, I wore my "IBM casual" uniform - khaki pants, blue button down shirt, and navy blue sports jacket. The only thing which designated me as a Vietnam vet was the metal 4th Infantry Division patch I wore on my jacket pocket. (Well, I did buy a "Vietnam Veteran and Proud of It" cap).

Still no old friends were to be found. But new friends were everywhere. That was the day I learned about the common bond that exists among all Vietnam vets. Never have I been hugged so genuinely, so often, and with so much emotion as by the men I ran into that day. And each hug was accompanied by what has become the slogan of the Vietnam vet, "Welcome Home, Brother". Black, white, officer, enlisted, Army, Navy, Marine, Air Force, Coast Guard, we were all the same that day - brothers.

For the rest of the day, I wandered aimlessly around Grant Park. Finally, as time approached for me to return to the airport and the flight home, I stopped by the hotel where a reception was being held for the Medal of Honor recipients. I was in the company of the largest assembly ever of recipients of our nation's highest honor. Eighty of the 247 surviving Medal of Honor men from all wars were expected to be in attendance. I wandered through the hotel lobby to pay homage to those heroes and reflect on how great it is to be an American.

Reluctantly, I hailed a cab and started my trip home. I did not want to leave but I had accomplished what I had come for. Despite not finding any old friends, I had an emotional experience of a lifetime. It was on this day I took on a new avocation - standing up for, helping, and advancing the cause of the Vietnam veteran. I forever quit trying to ignore my Vietnam experience. I started trying to understand its importance to me, and to others. What had started at the Vietnam Wall almost two years earlier was bonded into my being that one day in Chicago.

Five months later, I started writing this book. In the spring of 1988, I became almost obsessed with finding the men I had shared the Vietnam experience with. That is the subject of my next chapter.

BRINGING US BACK TOGETHER

If you are a Vietnam vet, or know a Vietnam vet, who is looking for a long lost buddy from the war, you will, hopefully, find this chapter interesting and helpful. If you are not looking for long lost friends, you may choose to skip over this chapter.

Early in 1988, I knew the whereabouts of ten people I served with, and six of them were deceased (five are discussed in the chapter, "My Speech at the Moving Wall"). Today, I know where 69 of my former comrades are, including most of my best and closest friends. My quest continues and will continue until I find everyone. It has been an interesting and rewarding challenge.

In 1984, Stanley Cameron's (my radio operator) wife called to tell me Stanley had died. She had an old address and just happened to find me even though I had moved several times since then. It was the first indication that luck and persistence plays a big part in locating people. Laura gave me the names of two of our platoon members she had been in contact with.

My next contact came in the spring of 1986 when the phone rang and a familiar voice from the past spoke to me. Bill Saling, an officer from Headquarters company, had seen my name in the Atlanta newspaper when I had spoken at the Moving Wall. Neither of us knew we lived within five miles of each other. Bill had the address of Sandy Fiacco, my company commander, and my list of "founds" slowly started to grow.

Where do you start in trying to locate people you have not seen nor heard from in over twenty years? How do you become a junior Sherlock Holmes? It can come from many sources. My first gold mine came when I found a list of my platoon's names and hometowns in one of the letters I had written my wife from Vietnam. As part of our "Pen Pals" project, I had sent her the list so her class would know a little something about the men they were writing to.

With the list firmly in hand, I eagerly started calling directory assistance to see who I could find. My results showed how mobile our society has become. From the entire list of 35 names, I found only five men. A helpful telephone operator told me one of my platoon members, Ralph Duncan, her high school classmate, had drowned in 1976. Five more names were added to my 'found' list. Sadly, I was starting a deceased list as well. Ralph Duncan's name was added to that list.

My next thought was to put a notice in the Locator section of the Vietnam Veterans Association monthly newspaper. That notice netted me three more names. But my biggest bonanza came a few months later when I read another notice in the Locator section. It leaped out at me – "Looking for men who served with B Company, 1st Battalion, 22nd Infantry, 4th Infantry Division". The contact name was John Hansen, a stranger to me. I immediately wrote John in California and started a friendship that continues today. He had a rather extensive list of names, covering all the years our unit had been in Vietnam. A few of the names were of men who had served with me. He had joined the unit a few months after I came home, in the fall of 1967, and had been successful in finding many of his friends.

The most valuable thing he gave me was information about the Army Personnel Center in St. Louis and the Freedom of Information Act. The Center maintains records on all former members of the Army. He told me the Center will not give out addresses but will forward letters to the last address they have on file. Referencing the Freedom of Information Act is what allows them to handle your request at no charge. To fill a request, they need the full name and social security or serial number.

I had a copy of my Combat Infantryman Badge orders which contained names and serial numbers of about 75 men. From that list, I selected 25 names to see what they could come up with. Several months later, I received notice they had addresses for ten of the men. Six of the addresses were still valid and my 'found' list continued to grow.

I have used the Center a few more times and each time located a few more men. (If you would like to try to locate someone through the Center, send a sealed, stamped letter with the name and Social Security or Serial number on the envelope to: Commander, U.S. Army Reserve Personnel Center, Attention: DARP-PAS-AI, 9700 Page Boulevard, St. Louis, MO 63132-5200. You can now access that information on the internet – do a Google search for Army Personnel Center).

Make reference to the Freedom of Information Act and the Privacy Act Inquiry Office in your letter of request. If they have an address, they will forward the letter for you.

What other things have worked for me? Thinking while driving to work has been one good technique. I pick a person I want to find and let my brain work on digging out, from the far reaches of my memory, what I remember. For instance, I found Ron Marksity by remembering an IBM friend had mentioned, fifteen years earlier, he knew Ron from the time they had served together in Saigon. That had been lost in my memory during the period I was trying to ignore Vietnam. With a phone call to my IBM friend, I located yet another good friend who had been lost for twenty years.

I found Buck Ator's wife by remembering the name of his home town in Washington state. A call to directory assistance put me in touch with his mother who gave me the address and phone number of his wife.

I have located other men by remembering their home town, calling multiple people with the same last name, and finally talking to a relative who put me in contact with the person I was looking for. Persistence and large phone bills are required for this technique to work. Lou Dinetz was found when I finally remembered where he had gone to college. A letter to his college's alumni office has let me renew that friendship. (Lou was as anxious to find me as I was to find him. He called me within two minutes of the time he received the letter.)

When I locate one of my friends, I ask them who they are in contact with. Some have added several names to my list; some do not have any contacts. I have tried to insure I stay in touch with each man at least once a year so I do not lose them. I have lost contact with two 'found' men by not staying in touch regularly. Andrew Hankins and John Huebner, where are you?

Two of my techniques have been clandestine in nature. A friend who works for one of the large telephone companies used his access to directory assistance records to locate Harry Troutman. All I could remember was his North Carolina twang, he found him easily by searching the telephone company records for North Carolina.

A friend with access to Army personnel records made one of my most important finds. He looked into the retiree records and found our First Sergeant, Bob MacDonald. Several years ago, I heard Bob had died so you can imagine my elation in finding him – one of the best soldiers I ever knew.

Today, with the internet and all the tools available online, finding someone is much easier than it was when I started my work back in 1988. No one should ever despair from finding an old buddy – just stay persistent and use the internet plus other techniques.

I try to never pass up a chance to find additional people, regardless of how much a long shot it seems to be. While attending the Tenth Anniversary Commemoration of the Vietnam Wall, I casually asked a lady representing the Vietnam Women's Memorial Fund if she knew Lieutenant Dexter (see chapter entitled "Lieutenant Dexter"). She did not but volunteered to check their records and send her my name if they had her address.

Six weeks later, I heard from Lieutenant Dexter. I met her and her husband in Washington, DC at the dedication of the Vietnam Women's Memorial on Veterans Day, 1993.

There are a few other random techniques I have had success with. Each month I read the Locator section of Veterans publications I subscribe to. That alone helps me find someone from my unit, or a sister unit, on the average of once every two or three months.

I have become an active member of the 4th Infantry Division Association. Through that association, I have met several old friends and made many new ones. (To find the address of the 4th Infantry Division Association or your unit's association, write Service Reunions National Registry, 3686 King Street, Suite 172, Alexandria, Virginia 22302 – or go to the 4ID web page at www.4thinfantry.org).

I frequently wear a cap with my 4th Infantry Division patch prominently displayed. Once or twice a year, someone stops me in Home Depot or at a baseball or football game and tells me about their service with the 4th Infantry Division.

All in all, I constantly let my mind think like a detective to figure a different angle to locate my comrades. It has been challenging, frustrating at times, but very rewarding. Finding people is the small reward; the big reward is when I am able to renew my friendship with them. I have had some really great experiences in reunions and phone conversations over the past few years.

Bill Saling, my first 'found', and I see or talk to each other nearly every month. For several years, we teamed twice a year to present our Vietnam experiences to an Atlanta high school class.

My business travels take me to all parts of the country. I have had several memorable reunions tied in with those travels. Ernie Redin and Mark Petrino, my two point men, spent an evening with me in Connecticut. Doug Muller met me at LaGuardia airport in New York and spent several hours updating me on his life since he was wounded and evacuated in March, 1967.

Ron Marksity drove to Atlanta to spend a weekend with me in the fall of 1990. I have since visited in his home and he and his family have spent another weekend with us. We now talk to each other on the phone regularly. Lou Dinetz and I talk frequently on the telephone and even more frequently via email and have seen each other twice.

First Sergeant Bob MacDonald, Frank Roath, and I renewed our friendships at a reunion in May, 1991 in Boise, Idaho. In addition to reliving our Vietnam experiences, I learned more from them about their Korean War exploits. I still try to stay in touch with them regularly.

Ken Cameron, Stanley's brother, and I spent an evening together in upstate New York talking about the experiences Stanley and I had together. I spent a very memorable afternoon and evening with Joanne Ator, Buck's wife, and their son, Steven.

Twice, in 1990 and again in 1992, I helped organize and encourage attendance at mini-reunions at Fort Lewis, Washington. At the most recent one, seventeen of us got together, including Sandy Fiacco and all but one of our company officers, First Sergeant MacDonald, Jim Benge, "Rawhide" Morley, and Jud Miller, our brigade commander. It was great to see friends I had not seen since 1967.

For the past fifteen years, I have attended the National 4th Infantry Division Association annual reunion (and was the national president in 1998-2000). At my first reunion, I ran into the man I had met at the Wall in 1984, the lone survivor of the ambush which had wiped out his platoon. At the second reunion, I met a section chief from the artillery battery which supported us every day and night of our year in Vietnam. I bought his drinks - I had never known who to thank for all the excellent firepower support. I also met a veteran recently returned from Desert Storm.

The following year, the artilleryman was in attendance again, as was Swede Ekstrom, the helicopter crew chief I had met in 1984 (who had participated in evacuating the wounded the day First Sergeant McNerney had earned the Medal of Honor). Several other Vietnam vets, covering all years of the War and many different units, were there to swap stories with.

At my fourth annual reunion, we had nine men from my unit in attendance. I had not seen four of them since we left Vietnam, the other five I have seen since locating them the past few years. I roomed with "Rawhide" and spent many enjoyable hours with him and Jud Miller listening to their views of the War. Battalion and brigade commanders had many interesting and valuable experiences that we lower ranking men did not know about. We visited the Wall together and looked up the names of fallen comrades. Each subsequent reunion has had similar experiences.

I have had many phone conversations. All have been interesting, some have been emotional. Most are eager to renew friendships and appear to be unaffected by the Vietnam experience. Some have spent many years questioning their actions in Vietnam. I have talked to vets from sister units who have not discussed their experiences with anyone until I called them. All seem happy to have someone to talk to. I have yet to talk to anyone who told me to leave them alone.

On occasion, I have been helpful in providing facts or memories to help them sort through memories and open questions. I always send them my list of 'founds' so they can call their old friends. I find some are as eager as I am to renew friendships; others seem satisfied with blotting that period from their memories.

I have changed portions of this book as a result of hearing another man's memories of an event. It is very interesting to hear another version of a story. Based on many factors, each person has a different perspective. I sometimes decided my memory was not the right one.

What have I learned from the experience of bringing us back together? I have learned how important the Vietnam experience is to me, and to many other veterans. I have renewed and strengthened friendships which started when I was a young man fresh out of college. They have lain dormant for too many years. I now list many of these recently found friends among my best friends.

I learned to talk to other veterans, regardless of which war they fought in. I have had in depth discussions with veterans of World War II, Korea, Vietnam, Panama, Desert Storm, Somalia, Haiti, Bosnia, Kosovo, and the Global War on Terror. I find a common bond with the experiences, no matter which conflict. I have learned that veterans can talk to each other in ways non-veterans will never understand.

And, I have not tired of the challenge of bringing us back together. Sometimes I get discouraged or disappointed when I find someone who does not appear interested in my quest. But the positive experiences have far outweighed any small disappointments. It is a good feeling to be a catalyst in bringing friends with common experiences back together.

I will continue to play junior detective. In August 1997, I found two more key men I had been looking for - Steve Angulo, our mess sergeant, and

Bill Bukovec from my third platoon. I got a copy of a morning report from the Army Personnel Center in St. Louis and found that I had been spelling their names wrong - once I knew the correct spelling of their name, I found them both the first day I started looking. Since then, Bill and I have seen each other at least once a year and become great friends.

So, if you were in my unit and read this, try to locate me - you can bet I am still looking for you. Where are you Roy Dean, Willie Cheatham, Charlie Reynolds, John Huebner, Andrew Hankins, Julian White, David Shell, Aubrey Thomas, Danny Schemp, Bob Savard, Steve Cush, David Harris, Don Gilbert, Baez, Gladney, Irizarry, Rolax, Espinoza...

A few words of wisdom to our new veterans of the Global War on Terror who might be reading this book - start now to find your friends. Although you may not realize it today, one of these days you will want to find your fellow Soldiers that you fought alongside. If you're still in the unit, get a copy of the company roster, plus rosters of the units that supported you and worked closely with you. Make sure you know full names, how they are spelled, and where their home towns are. If you can find a roster with social security numbers on it, make a copy of that for future use in finding your friends. And don't just get the names of your closest friends – the support people, commanders, key NCOs and officers, all are people that you someday will want to relive your experiences with. From all my years of experience in helping WWII and Vietnam vets find their buddies, I can guarantee you will never be sorry that you did some preliminary work now before it became important to you.

AFTER THOUGHTS

Today is August 30, 1993. Less than a month after I arrived in Vietnam, I reached the ripe old age of twenty-three. Today, I am celebrating my 50th birthday with friends and family. Little did I realize back then that twenty-seven years later, those twelve months in Vietnam would loom so large and important in my life's memories.

Lee Sherman Dreyfuss, past president of Sentry Insurance Company, former governor of Wisconsin, chancellor of the University of Wisconsin at Stevens Point, and renowned motivational speaker, described his World War II experiences far better than I could, therefore I quote: "With the Battle of Okinawa rated as a ten on my life scale, everything else I have done before or since then, is no more than a two." Vietnam had the same profound impact on my life.

As I wind down the seven year odyssey back into my Vietnam experiences and wrap up this book, a number of thoughts that have not been covered still churn through my mind. I will conclude with some random thoughts that still need to be written down.

Why did I go to Vietnam? Why didn't I turn against the war as it dragged on and on? Why would I do it again if I was called on?

I guess the answer is very simple - patriotism and love of my country.

I grew up in a protected small town environment where I learned simple values - the American flag, motherhood, and apple pie. I was young and naive. In a way I did not understand at the time, I believed in what President John F. Kennedy had said my senior year in high school, "Ask not what your country can do for you, ask what you can do for your country."

I was also influenced by World War II, the Korean War, and the Cold War. Communism was a real threat in our world in 1966 and I was going to do my part to help stop it before it hit the shores of America. Again, it may sound idealistic, trite, or naive, but I never once considered not serving my country. In fact, I would be very upset today if I had not answered my country's call to duty. I have zero regrets about serving my country in Vietnam.

It should also be noted I was in the Vietnam War during its early troop buildup stage. Grace Coggins Kidwell, a lifelong friend who lived through two tours when her first husband flew bombing missions over North Vietnam from the aircraft carrier Kitty Hawk explained it this way:

"We are the in-between generation. Even though the Vietnam war was never popular, we were in it before it became unpopular. The general public thinks of it in its later stages when it got such bad publicity and had so many protestors and dope users."

Marian Faye Novak, in her book "Lonely Girls with Burning Eyes", stated it a little differently. "We faced the future in those days of 1967 with what I think must be called courage. It's true that we were too inexperienced to feel particular fear and too unwise to be afraid of the abstract. But we knew something; I see it in the pictures of the wives. And yet we smiled and danced, and I remember laughter, too. I call that courage. And we had it."

In summary, we were a trusting, idealistic, young generation. We had not, at that time, lived through the Vietnam War, Watergate, nor experienced a press corps obsessed with sensationalism and digging up dirt on public figures. We were fresh off the assassination of JFK and still believed in Camelot. We, the young and naive, were led to war by leaders we had never had a reason to distrust. Oh, to return to such simple times.

Why was I so lucky? What made Bravo Company, 1st Battalion, 22nd Infantry Regiment, 4th Infantry Division so different from our sister units?

I have thought long and hard about this one. It always comes back to the same things - good leaders, good people, common sense, people who cared about each other, courage to do what is right, luck, and God looking over us.

I had the chance two months ago to ask "Rawhide", our battalion commander, what he thought about Bravo Company and why we were so different. His response was the same, "good leaders at all levels and the courage to do what was right".

As I have talked to veterans of Bravo Company who served later in the war, I find their luck did not hold like ours. They, however, did not have the advantage of training together as we had, served under different leaders, used different tactics, and were in different political times.

And I frequently ask myself the question, how would I have acted if I had been in a big battle? How would it have changed my life?

And the answer is – I'll never know. Would I have done a good job, would I have been a coward, would I have been killed or wounded, would it have changed the rest of my life? Like every person who has never faced the situation, I can only wonder. And I wonder frequently.

I will always hold in very high esteem those veterans of all wars who were thrown into the breech of a major battle. Over the past few years, I have talked to veterans of the D-Day invasion, the hedgerow fighting across France, the Hurtgen Forest, the Battle of the Bulge, Iwo Jima, Guadalcanal, and the Anzio beach landing in World War II.

I have talked to veterans of major battles of the Korean War and veterans of the battles of the Ia Drang Valley, Soui Tre, Dak To, Fire Base Burt, Ap Cho, Khe Sanh, the Tet Offensive, the Battle of Good Friday, and numerous other major clashes of the Vietnam war. As an Infantryman, I can identify with them. I can never, however, quit wondering how I would have reacted in those battles.

I once heard, "Any battle is a big one, if you are in it..." That statement has stuck with me. You do not think about the size of the battle when bullets and mortar fragments start flying around. You become quickly convinced each and every one is aimed directly at you. And I have experienced that.

What is it like to stay at home and wait while your son, or your husband, or your brother is in a war zone?

That question did not really enter my mind until Operation Desert Storm and I had a son approaching draft age. I looked at it from a whole different perspective when I realized some day I may be the one waiting at home thinking about my son at war.

I asked my parents, my brother, and Phyllis, my first wife to answer that question.

My parents, Hermann and Dorothy Babcock, still live in the house I was born in. When I initially asked the question, my eighty year old mother answered it very quickly, "It's hell." I asked them both to think back twenty-seven years and write down what they remembered about having a son in a combat zone.

Mother's response, "When Bob waved before boarding the plane to leave for Vietnam, that is where my worry began. Already the news in the papers was not good. You wonder why I read the news - I think it is something a Mother can not help doing. Many a night I lay awake wondering how he was faring - was he being fed right, did he have a good place to sleep, I knew he wasn't safe.

I wrote to him every day, not knowing if or when he was getting the letters. We heard from him as often as he could get a letter off.

I can not think of words to describe how I felt. I always had the feeling maybe he would not make it home again. When he did come home was one of the happiest days of my life." (My mother, Dorothy Babcock, died on February 25, 2004).

I think I understand better now why she blocked the war out of her life when I came home. It is a normal human response to try to block out and forget painful experiences.

My Dad's response, "Being the father of four young adult boys, one could naturally expect I have had many very good experiences and joys. Also one would expect there have been a few 'dark' days. The darkest day of my life was when we saw the air transport plane take-off with Bob on board, knowing full well he was going to Vietnam for full scale combat duty in a war that should never have happened.

On the bright side, I knew Bob had a strong faith in God, and never did I allow a day to pass that I did not pray for Bob's safety in Vietnam and a safe return home.

I kept in as close contact as possible with his whereabouts via radio, TV, and the newspapers. But in those days the coverage was nothing to compare with what we have today. We received a lot of letters from Bob and it was always a great lift to his Mother and me when those letters arrived.

Another thing on the plus side was the fact I knew Bob had always been a winner and he did not go to Vietnam expecting to change that image." (My father, Hermann Babcock, died on July 21, 1995. It was exactly 29 years to the day after I left for Vietnam).

My older brother, Jim, summed it up this way, "Bob is seven years my junior. I knew little of him as we grew up. He was a quiet, accommodating, non-assertive boy. I left home to join the Army while he was still in elementary school.

When Bob was in Airborne School, he visited me in Atlanta one weekend and I will never forget my thoughts. 'How was this frail (to me) young man going to survive in the real Army?' I was extremely proud of Bob for choosing the Army as I had. I was not ready for him to go 'in harm's way'. It was easier for me to put it out of my thoughts while he was in Vietnam.

To this day, I do not recall writing him. Fortunately, the year went by rapidly for me and soon Bob was on his way back. What a weight off my mind to hear he had landed in Oakland.

We have since become very close friends and rarely do more than two weeks go by without some contact." (Jim was my editor and valued critic as I wrote this book. On February 22, 1995, Jim died after almost 26 years as a quadriplegic).

Finally, my ex-wife, Phyllis, had this poignant memory when I asked her what it was like to be the one who stayed home and waited, "You mean, what was it like to wonder, every time I saw an Air Force officer walk up to the school where I was teaching, whether he was coming to pick up his children or to tell me you had been killed." (Forbes Air Force Base is located in Topeka, Kansas and many Air Force children were in her classes).

Marian Faye Novak summed it up eloquently in her book. "When the man you love is at war, life becomes a minefield, and you are forever - even in your dreams - walking point."

Why is the Vietnam experience such a powerful force in my life?

That question has gnawed at me for years, and I think I understand it much better today than I did seven years ago when I started writing this book. And the answer is complex, not simple.

Probably the most important factors are the intense individual experiences and friendships I developed. I had experiences, almost daily, which stand out above most others in my life.

No other bond measures up to those forged when operating at the most basic of levels. Mutual trust and support of the men you worked with became primary considerations over everything. All else became secondary in importance.

Again, a quote from Marian Faye Novak (I really enjoyed her book), "I watched Bob and Dave together, and I began to see the love that men can have for one another that has nothing to do with sex or romance. It is a kind of love that has to do with caring, and loyalty, and even the special sharing of knowledge about certain things." Never have I developed a bond and respect like I did with the men I served with in Vietnam.

At the age of twenty-three, I had to make more important decisions than any I have ever made in my life, before or since. Much of what we did was potentially a life or death situation. It is an awesome responsibility to be in charge of the lives of so many young American men. It is a great source of pride that I did my job, and did it well. That is not unique to Vietnam; it is true of all wars and all veterans.

It makes a lasting impression on you - and puts other decisions in your life in a different perspective. When making tough decisions even today, the question often comes to mind, "What are they going to do, send me to Vietnam?" That helps to put things into proper perspective.

There is a great deal of pride in answering the call as a soldier and living to tell about it. I have always liked the comment George C. Scott, in the title role of the movie "Patton", made as he was talking to his men prior to their going into battle. "When your grandson sits on your knee and asks, 'What did you do in the great World War II, Granddad', you won't have to say, 'Well, I shoveled sh*t in Louisiana.'"

We Vietnam vets will not have to tell our grandsons that we fled to Canada or sat the war out on a draft deferment or missed it for some other reason. We can point with pride at our service to our country. I'm sure there are other factors I have not yet found. I definitely recognize the impact Vietnam has had on me, even if I can not eloquently explain why.

How about those who did not serve? What do you think about them?

I have never had a big problem with people who did not serve in the Vietnam War. Our national leaders did not mobilize the country and I can not expect everyone to have the same streak of patriotism I have. The Vietnam period was a time in America where we lacked strong leadership and national purpose. I can not fault others of my generation for doing what their conscience dictated.

Those who flocked to the national guard and reserves took a legal and logical, for them, approach to service. I served in an Army reserve unit for several years after my return from Vietnam and worked with some outstanding individuals.

I never did agree with some of their philosophies. Neither did I ever get overly worked up with those who protested the war. What they did was detrimental to our fighting men but part of what we were fighting for was to preserve that very right to dissent. Even Jane Fonda did what she thought was right, and the Constitution I was fighting for gives every living American that right.

However, I have no respect for those who overtly and openly avoided service to their country. Those who went to Canada to avoid the draft and those who did other less than honorable things to avoid service, in my opinion, let themselves and their country down. But I can overlook that by attributing it to their youth and inexperience (or their cowardice) at the time. They are the ones who have to live with their decisions, not me.

Again, a quote from Marian Faye Novak's book sums up my feelings. "I see the lines of people when we go to the Wall; some are veterans or the friends and relatives of veterans, some are too young to remember the war. But many are not, and I wonder at all these others. Where were you, I think, when these men needed you? When we all needed you? How can you look so long and lovingly on the silent names of these dead when you were so quick to turn your backs on their living faces?"

I think many people may be silently living with the ghosts of decisions made so long ago in their late teens or early twenties.

Have I accomplished my objective of letting my children know about my Vietnam experience?

I am very pleased with how my kids have reacted to this book. When I started writing, my oldest daughter was seventeen and my youngest son was two. At that time, none of my four children had any interest in my efforts.

Over the course of the seven years I have been working on this book, they have all learned how important my Vietnam experience is to me (and, by association, to them).

Both Kristen and Rob have read various drafts of the book and regularly question me, with great interest, about my experiences. They can not wait to read the final draft. Mark, now nine years old, frequently asks me to read him a chapter or two. Stephanie has not yet shown much interest but I think, in time, she will.

Two very recent events show me the kids are in tune with what I am doing. On a family vacation to Florida a few weeks ago, we were riding on a rubber, banana shaped raft being pulled by a motor boat. When we hit an extra large wave, the raft turned over. We all found ourselves bobbing around in our life jackets waiting for the boat to circle around to load us back up.

In unison, the group asked me, with big smiles on their faces, "What you gonna do now, Lieutenant?" Their comment made me beam.

Today, for my fiftieth birthday present, the kids gave me the best present I could ever get. They had a draft copy of this book bound in a hardback green cover with the title and my name printed on the cover in gold print.

Along with the book, Kristen had needle pointed a plaque which will always hang in a place of prominence in our home. The 4th Infantry Division patch, my Combat Infantryman's Badge, my AIRBORNE Wings, my Lieutenant bar, and my Crossed Rifles of an Infantryman are prominently displayed. The plaque reads:

> For you Daddy,
> Because We thank God each
> day for the Freedom you Fought
> to give to us. We Love You, and
> are Proud that you're our Father.
> *Krissie, Rob, and Mark*

My kids know the answer to the question, "What did you do in the Vietnam War, Dad?" Do yours? So now you have heard my story. There are three million more Vietnam stories to be told. Who is going to tell the next one?

A Special Chapter for Today's Lieutenants

Since the late 1980s, I have been a regular speaker to school classes and civic groups about my experiences in Vietnam. In 1995, Pat McNabb, a good friend from IBM, asked if I would speak to his son's ROTC class at North Georgia College. I welcomed the opportunity and spoke to the Professor of Military Science to get his thoughts on what his cadets needed to hear. In a time when few cadets wanted to serve in the active Army, he wanted me to relate the value of the experiences these cadets would learn as an Army officer with success in later life - either in or out of the Army. I had long ago recognized that my two years as an Infantry lieutenant had been the most valuable leadership training experience that I had ever had. Virtually every day during my IBM career, I used skills I had learned as a lieutenant in the Army.

I developed a presentation that I titled, "The Leadership Skills You Learn in the Army Will Help You All Your Life" with the subtitle "Lieutenant Bars are Worth More Than Their Weight in Gold".

Over the years, I was asked by various active Army battalion commanders from 1-22 Infantry and 2-22 Infantry to talk to their lieutenants as part of OPD (Officers Professional Development). In the spring of 2005, I was asked by LTC John Miller III, Professor of Military Science at the University of

Georgia and CO of 2-8 Infantry of 4ID during Operation Iraqi Freedom I, to talk to his cadets who were within a few months of being commissioned. On September 30, 2005, I was further honored to be the speaker at the Dining In of the Infantry Officers Basic Class (IOBC) at Fort Benning, GA. This was especially meaningful to me since it was almost exactly forty years since I had been a young 2LT sitting in that very same officers' club, wearing my dress blue uniform for the first time, starting my journey into a lifetime of leadership.

In all the presentations I gave to young officers and ROTC cadets, I stuck with the theme I had developed in 1995 for the cadets at North Georgia College – "The Leadership Skills You Learn in the Army Will Help You All Your Life" or "Lieutenant Bars are Worth More Than Their Weight in Gold". After several young lieutenants in that IOBC presentation at Fort Benning asked me for copies of my presentation, I felt driven to include the key parts of it in this book. If some of the lessons I learned will help today's lieutenants do their job better in the current Global War on Terror and later in their lives, it is well worth the effort to make it available.

From here on in this chapter, I am talking to lieutenants, others are welcome to read it if they're interested.

My Army commission was the most valuable thing I got out of college. It set the stage for my future career as an IBM manager and leader. I made more important decisions as a twenty-three year old lieutenant than I ever did as an IBM executive. Decisions made in the heat of battle can mean life and death for you and those assigned to you. Decisions made in a business environment are never that important.

Although my war was in a different place at a different time and against a different enemy than the one you are fighting now, these thoughts are from someone who has been in your boots. As most veterans will attest, all wars are more alike than they are different. Ernie Pyle, the famous WWII correspondent said it best, "Battles differ from one another only in their physical environment – the emotions of fear and exhaustion and exaltation and hatred are about the same in all of them." Two other quotes from unknown sources say it slightly differently, "Any battle is a big one… if you are in it." and, "A battle is only as big as the few square feet of territory directly around the guy on the ground fighting it." Regardless of the historical significance, it is a life altering experience to the man (or woman) in the middle of it. If you haven't yet been in combat, your opportunity will most likely come, the date and place just haven't been determined yet. Whether you ever engage in active combat or not, the leadership skills you learn in the military will serve you well throughout your life. There is a standard of excellence and responsibility to your mission and your men/women that is far greater than what is required in civilian life.

I've categorized the key leadership traits as follows:
- Personal Courage
- Set the Example
- Look Out For Your People
- Be A Smart Risk Taker
- Be A Team Player
- Be Creative and Adaptable

Personal courage means to do what is right, even if it is unpopular. It means to have a strong standard of personal ethics. The question you should ask yourself is, "could I stand in front of (a person you highly admire and respect for their leadership skills) and explain and justify my actions?" Asking myself that question helped me many times in my IBM career. If I was comfortable with standing in front of Lew Gray, my all time favorite IBM leader, and having the courage to defend my position, I was probably on the right track. Personal courage also means to fight up and support down. If the leaders above you make decisions that you disagree with, you should do everything you can to insure they understand how those decisions will negatively impact your mission and your people. If you can't change the decision, you must just as strongly support it down through your organization (even while continuing to fight up).

You must have the courage to ask questions and to say "I don't know". Acting like you know more than you do will almost always get you into trouble. You must exemplify competence and never give in to your fears. People want to follow good leaders, and personal courage is the first step in establishing yourself as a good leader.

Good leaders **set the example**. Don't ask people to do anything you wouldn't do yourself. The stories entitled, "What Now, Lieutenant" and "Another Leadership Challenge" are examples of how I gained the confidence of my people by setting the example. Another one of my favorite quotes is, "expect and inspect – folks do well those things the boss checks". If you are consistent with what your expectations are, communicate them clearly, and inspect to insure they are met (and exceeded), you are well on your way to becoming a strong leader.

Enthusiasm is another way to set the example. Are you a person who sees things as half full or half empty? I've always had a half full outlook on life and maintained a "can do" attitude. That is the way I like to set the example – positive mental attitude and strive for excellence in all that I do.

Part of setting the example is developing your own personal style. You must be comfortable with who you are and not try to be someone else. It's good to take positive traits of others and blend those into your own style, but you should never try to be something or someone that doesn't become natural to you. People will sense if you are being yourself or acting like someone else – a good personal style that fits you is part of good leadership. And, never forget to dress for success. It does matter what you look like, especially if you are a leader. If anyone tells you otherwise, they're fooling you. Show pride in your appearance wherever you are. Appearance isn't everything, but it sure helps those casual observers, either above you or below you, who are sizing you up.

Finally, in setting the example, demonstrate a sense of urgency. Complacency is your enemy. If you don't care and act without a sense of urgency, those that you are leading will adopt your complacency. I've always thought that a good job done today is better than a great job done next week or next month. Most of what we do is not rocket science, make a decision and follow Nike's way and "just do it". Again, people like to follow leaders who show excitement and urgency in whatever it is they do.

Looking out for your people means to show that you care, that you "give a damn" about them. A good starting point is to keep your people informed. We live in an information age and people are used to understanding their environment, much more so than our predecessors in WWII who were less questioning of leaders. If they know why they are doing what you ask of them, they'll much more willingly carry out the mission in a first class manner.

Get out of your office and your comfort zone and spend time with your people. Management by wandering around, the 1980's management principle made famous by Tom Peters, was a good technique long before he popularized it and still is today. Find out what is on your people's minds, what makes them tick. Know who is having family or financial problems, who has something to brag about, find out what their hobbies are. The more your people think you "give a damn" about them, the more readily they will follow your leadership. Although your management position puts you in a position of authority, you must earn the trust and confidence of your people.

Praise in public and reprimand in private. There are exceptions but in most cases you will have time to take people aside to chew them out. Berating your people in front of others does nothing for you and sure doesn't earn you the trust and confidence of your team. When you have something positive to say, the more people you can say it in front of, the more impact it will have. Bragging about someone, by name, in front of the battalion or brigade or division commander, does great things in building respect for you, even among those that you aren't bragging on at the time. The same principle has served me well in my IBM career. It's worth saying again – praise in public and reprimand in private.

Always consider the weight of your words. The people working for you are always trying to understand the unstated meanings of your words and actions. You may mean nothing by a wisecrack or caustic remark, it may cause many sleepless nights for the person you make it to. The boss is never off duty so this applies at cocktail parties and sports events as much as on duty. People always analyze what you mean by what you say or do.

People will judge you quickly – first impressions are lasting ones. When you go into an organization, start immediately to show that you care. Little things that you do in your first days in a new job will set the stage for the future – it's never too early to show that you "give a damn" about your people.

Being a smart risk taker means to trust your skills, to know your strengths and your weaknesses. It also means you need to understand the strengths and weaknesses of others. A smart risk taker will ask for help in making decisions in the areas where they do not have strength. I've always been a strong proponent of sharing decision making with my subordinates. Your NCOs are your strongest assets, learn from them (the same hold true of key players in your civilian management career). Empower your people to make decisions, don't try to do it all yourself. Delegate down and don't let them delegate back up to you. At the end of the day, the monkeys you pass out to other should still be on their backs, not back on yours. If you have key players who can't or won't do their job, get rid of them. Weak players that you don't step up to and either train to do their job or move into something they can do will hurt you and your organization.

Consider your options, take smart risks, but avoid hip shooting. Making a few wrong decisions is okay, much better than being afraid to make a decision. Too many wrong decisions show you don't have a good grasp of your own capabilities and of those around you. Once you have made a decision, show confidence in that decision, don't second guess yourself, and move on to the next opportunity you have. Less than perfect decisions, executed with force and confidence, will solve most problems. On my desk since my first days as an IBM manager has been a desk plate which says, "Do Something - Lead, Follow, or Get Out of the Way". Good leaders know when to lead, when to follow, and when to get out of the way. They never sit around with indecision.

Good leaders know they must **be a team player**. Synergy is real, the whole is bigger than the sum of the parts. Do not worry who gets credit for a job. People know what you do and who the team players are in the organization. Think about any organization you've ever been in - you can name the best people, those who deserve credit, and those who are slackers. Always think, "We, Ours, Us – not I, Mine, Me".

A team player thinks, "Is this good for the entire organization?" They do not focus on just their piece of the total organizational goals. A team player understands the overall objectives of the organization and strives to insure his/her parts of those objectives are handled on time and with quality. Once that is done, the team player seeks out opportunities to help others. Leaders above you and subordinates below you are always looking for team players who go out of their way to help the overall organization rather than just their own personal objectives. In the end, it virtually always works out where the team player is the one who gets the great rewards. Good leaders are team players.

Leaders must **be creative and adaptable**. Good leaders show initiative and have the courage to try something different. They know how to improvise, they understand the use of field expedients. One of my best examples was when I was CO of a reserve training unit. My troops were all instructors who had no students to teach except for the two weeks each year when we were in summer camp. The topics we had to teach were not difficult, they surely didn't take a full year of training to be ready to teach to soldiers in AIT. These citizen soldiers came from all walks of life and had many diverse skills and interests. Most of them were not experienced teachers. At some risk, I improvised and let the instructors teach each other about topics they knew and liked. The one requirement I imposed on them was to create a lesson plan and teach following Army instructional methodology. John Schuerholz, then the assistant farm director of the Kansas City Royals, taught us about grading minor league baseball players (John went on to great success as general manager of the Atlanta Braves), others taught us tips to save money on our income tax, the list of topics we covered was very interesting. On occasion I had to justify to one of my superiors what I was doing, but we always did a superb job when actually teaching our military topics in our annual training – and my troops knew that I was willing to be creative, use common sense, and that I gave a damn about them.

Being adaptable means you must anticipate change. You must decide to take charge and act, or be complacent and react to what comes your way. Two more of my favorite quotes are, "The only constant is change" and "A plan never survives the first enemy contact". If a leader practices being creative and adaptable in training situations, it is second nature to act and continue being creative and adaptable under the stress of combat. A good leader "thinks outside the nine dots". A leader knows that if you do what you always did, you will get what you always got.

Finally, part of being creative and adaptable is not letting frustration or boredom set in. You must find a way to have fun and keep things interesting for yourself and your people. Much of any job, both in the Army and in civilian life, is very mundane and repetitive. Strong leaders find ways to have fun and put meaning into even the most boring situations.

In summary, I've learned that a good leader must always focus on the key leadership traits of personal courage, setting the example, looking out for your people, being a smart risk taker, a team player, and being creative and adaptable.

A few final thoughts before I wrap up this chapter...

Learn to express yourself in writing, it is a condition of success in virtually any endeavor. Less is more when writing. Learn to net your thoughts out so that busy people in important jobs can quickly understand what you are trying to tell them. When someone asks you what time it is, they don't want you to tell them how to build a clock.

Learn to express yourself verbally. Be clear, concise, and complete. Show confidence and competence. Speak up, don't mumble. Consider your audience, you don't talk to everyone exactly the same.

Don't burn bridges – the people you step over on the way up may very well be your bosses on the way down.

Keep your boss informed – no one likes surprises, either good or bad ones.

Know what is important to your boss. If you don't fully understand what makes your boss tick and what his measure of success is, you will never attain the heights you are capable of. In virtually all organizations, your boss has a very big role in determining your next job and how you are appraised. If you know what is important to your boss, then you can adapt your daily efforts to insure you make him or her happy, thus meeting your own objectives.

Don't take yourself too seriously. Have fun and enjoy what you do. If you aren't having fun and enjoying life, you're probably in the wrong line of work and should start looking for something that you enjoy. Life is too short to not have fun in it.

For many years, I have had three plaques hanging on my wall. The plaque that I received first, given to me by Gary Swanson, my favorite manager at IBM, is the famous quote from Theodore Roosevelt:

> "It is not the critic who counts, nor the man who points out where the strong man stumbles, nor where the doer of deeds could have done them better. On the contrary, the credit goes to the man who is actually in the arena – whose vision is marred by the dust and sweat and blood; who strives valiantly; who errs and comes up again and again; who knows the great devotions, the great enthusiasm; who at best knows in the end the triumph of high achievement. However, if he fails, at least he fails while daring greatly so that his place shell never be with those cold and timid souls who know neither victory nor defeat."
>
> Theodore Roosevelt

My other two plaques are at eye level, next to my desk so I can read them daily. One plaque has the IBM basic beliefs that our founder, Thomas Watson, Sr., developed as he built IBM into the powerhouse company that it is. Those basic beliefs will serve everyone well if they focus on them daily:

- **Respect for the individual** – respect for the dignity and the rights of each person in the organization;
- **Customer service** - provide the best customer service of any company in the world;
- **Excellence** – the conviction that an organization should pursue all tasks with the objective of accomplishing them in a superior way.

The other plaque is from the farewell address given by COL Glover S. Johns to the troops of the 18th Infantry Regiment serving in Berlin, Germany on 15 January 1962:

- Strive to do small things well.
- Be a doer and a self-starter – aggressiveness and initiative are two most admired qualities in a leader – but you must also put your feet up and think.
- Strive for self-improvement through constant self-evaluation.
- Never be satisfied. Ask of any project, "How can it be done better?"
- Don't over inspect or over supervise. Allow your leaders to make mistakes in training, so they can profit from the errors and not make them in combat.
- Keep the troops informed – telling them "what, how, and why" builds their confidence.
- The harder the training, the more the troops will brag.
- Enthusiasm, fairness, and moral and physical courage – four of the most important aspects of leadership.
- The ability to speak and write well – two essential tools of leadership.
- There is a salient difference between profanity and obscenity – while a leader employs profanity (tempered with discretion), he never uses obscenities.
- Have consideration for others.
- Yelling distracts from your dignity – take men aside to counsel them.
- Understand and use judgment – know when to stop fighting for something you believe is right. Discuss and argue your point of view until a decision is made, and then support the decision wholeheartedly.
- Stay ahead of your boss.

If even one of these leadership ideas helps one lieutenant, it has been worth it to include in this book. Don't forget, "The Leadership Skills You Learn in the Army Will Help You All Your Life" or "Lieutenant Bars are Worth More Than Their Weight in Gold".

EPILOGUE

This is a never ending story. My experiences in locating friends I served with, reliving old memories, helping others find information they need, preserving our Regimental and Division history, and helping family members find information about their loved ones who died without ever telling his story to them have become a major part of my life. It is my hobby, almost an obsession.

I got great joy in my job as president of the 22nd Infantry Regiment Society and trying to collect the wealth of American history that our Regiment has lived, from World War II to the present time - captured for posterity. I firmly believe that all American veterans have a debt to our nation, just as our nation owes a great debt to our veterans. The debt our veterans owe is to record their experiences for their family, for their Regimental and unit history, and for the country as a whole. If our veterans let their experiences die with them, we have lost an invaluable part of our American history - and as someone once said, "If we don't learn from history, we are destined to repeat it." Come on vets, write down your stories - it's important to your family and to America.

Since I wrote this book, I have written and published two other books about the 4th Infantry Division and their experiences. "War Stories – Utah Beach to Pleiku" is a collection of 450 personal accounts of 4th Infantry Division veterans from WWII, the Cold War, and Vietnam. "Operation Iraqi Freedom – A Year in the Sunni Triangle" was written under contract to the 4th Infantry Division and chronicles their first year in Iraq as part of the Global War on Terror, including their capture of Saddam Hussein. I also edited and published another 4ID book in 2007, the story of a mother whose Soldier son lost both legs in Iraq in June 2006 entitled, "My Son is Alive..."

The internet has become a valuable way to share stories. I suggest you check our web site at www.22ndinfantry.org to find the latest information on the 22nd Infantry Regiment, or www.1-22infantry.org to learn specifics of 1-22 Infantry, or www.4thinfantry.org to learn more about the 4th Infantry Division. New chapters are added to this proud history every year. Other military units also have web pages where you can learn how to connect with their history and veterans.

In 2002, I retired from a 34 year career at IBM. Late that year, I became an official partner of the Veterans History Project and formed a non-profit 501 (c)(3) corporation, Americans Remembered, Inc. Our sole purpose is to preserve memories of America's veterans and those who supported them in videotaped interviews. A copy of each interview is given to the veteran for preservation for their family and another copy goes to the Library of Congress where it is preserved forever in the collection of the Veterans History Project. To learn more about Americans Remembered and the Veterans History Project, go to our web site at www.americansremembered. org. Gary Swanson, my old IBM boss in Kansas City and my best volunteer, has done more interviews for the Veterans History Project than anyone in the country.

I have also become very active as an author and publisher. To find the latest on my efforts in that field, go to www.deedspublishing.com. I'm also working with my son, a very accomplished blacksmith and metal artist. You can see his work, which I have contributed a small part to, at his web site — www.babcockmetalworks.com

Who knows what the future holds for me. It is my desire to be able to continue following my passion of preserving memories of America's veterans and those who support them. With the publication of this book, I have done my part in insuring my family and America have this one veteran's perspective on his service in Vietnam. I know I will always support our Soldiers and veterans.

ABOUT THE AUTHOR

Robert O. (Bob) Babcock was born and raised in Heavener, Oklahoma. He received his ROTC commission at Kansas State College (now Pittsburg State University) in Pittsburg, Kansas in 1965. He served with Company B, 1st Battalion, 22nd Infantry Regiment, 4th Infantry Division from November 1965 through July 1967, including one year in Vietnam. From 1968 to 2002, Bob worked as a sales and marketing executive with IBM.

In 2003, Bob formed Americans Remembered, Inc., a non-profit corporation and an official partner of the Veterans History Project. He is past president and historian of the National 4th Infantry Division Association, past president of the 22nd Infantry Regiment Society, and a member of Vietnam Veterans of America, Atlanta Vietnam Veterans Business Association, Veterans of Foreign Wars, and American Legion.

Bob founded Deeds Publishing in 2005 to focus on "preserving life's experiences for future generations". In that role he has written four books and continues to serve as editor and publisher for authors with the desire to preserve their life's experiences.

He is an active supporter of 4ID Soldiers and families in the Global War on Terror and a regular volunteer with the USO. Bob and his wife, Jan, live in Marietta, Georgia.

ROBERT O. BABCOCK

Printed in the USA
CPSIA information can be obtained
at www.ICGtesting.com
LVHW041101151123
763986LV00068B/1769